T0328129

The Rise of Nonprofit Investigative Journalism in the United States

With a foreword from Michael Schudson, *The Rise of Nonprofit Investigative Journalism in the United States* examines the rapid growth, impact, and sustainability of not-for-profit investigative reporting and its impact on US democracy and mainstream journalism.

The book addresses key questions about the sustainability of foundation funding, the agendas of foundations, and the ethical issues that arise from philanthropically funded journalism. It provides a theoretical framework that enables readers to recognize connections and relationships that the nonprofit accountability journalism sector has with the economic, political, and mainstream media fields in the United States.

As battered news media struggled to survive the financial crisis of 2007–2009, dozens of investigative and public service reporting start-ups funded by foundations, billionaires, and everyday citizens were launched to scrutinize local, state, and national issues. Foundations, donors, and many journalists believed there was a crisis for investigative journalism and democracy in the United States. This book challenges this and argues that legacy editors acted to quarantine their investigative teams from newsroom cuts. It also demonstrates how nonprofit journalism transformed aspects of journalistic practice. Through detailed research including dozens of interviews, and practical discussion, it provides a comprehensive study of this increasingly important genre of journalism.

The Rise of Nonprofit Investigative Journalism in the United States is an important text for academics and students of journalism, communications theory, media- and democracy-related units, as well as journalists worldwide.

Bill Birnbauer is an award-winning journalist and academic. He is a long-standing member of the International Consortium of Investigative Journalists and is an Honorary Senior Lecturer in Journalism at Monash University, Australia. He was a metropolitan newspaper reporter and editor for three decades, has coproduced documentaries for public television, and has written academic book chapters and journal articles as well as two other books.

Routledge Research in Journalism

For more information about this series, please visit: https://www.routledge.com

The Rise of Nonprofit Investigative Journalism in the United States

Bill Birnbauer

Routledge
Taylor & Francis Group

NEW YORK AND LONDON

First published 2019
by Routledge
52 Vanderbilt Avenue, New York, NY 10017

and by Routledge
2 Park Square, Milton Park, Abingdon, Oxon, OX14 4RN

First issued in paperback 2020

Routledge is an imprint of the Taylor & Francis Group, an informa business

© 2019 Taylor & Francis

The right of Bill Birnbauer to be identified as author of this work has been asserted by him in accordance with sections 77 and 78 of the Copyright, Designs and Patents Act 1988.

Library of Congress Cataloging-in-Publication Data
Names: Birnbauer, Bill, author.
Title: The rise of nonprofit investigative journalism in the United States / Bill Birnbauer.
Description: London; New York: Routledge, 2019. |
Series: Routledge research in journalism; 25 |
Includes bibliographical references and index.
Identifiers: LCCN 2018040163 (print) | LCCN 2018051373 (ebook) | ISBN 9781351051903 (ebook) | ISBN 9781138484474 | ISBN 9781138484474_(hardback:_alk. paper) | ISBN 9781351051903_(ebk)
Subjects: LCSH: Investigative reporting—United States. | Nonprofit organizations—United States. | Press and politics—United States.
Classification: LCC PN4888.I56 (ebook) | LCC PN4888.I56 B57 2019 (print) | DDC 070.430973—dc23

ISBN 13: 978-0-367-58233-3 (pbk)
ISBN 13: 978-1-138-48447-4 (hbk)

Typeset in Sabon
by codeMantra

For Mariola, Branko and Granny

Contents

List of Figures

List of Tables

Foreword

Why did it take an Australian journalist-turned-academic to write a se-rious, readable, comprehensive, analytically expert book assessing the unprecedented expansion in recent years of a nonprofit sector of Amer-ican journalism centered on investigative reporting? That's the gift Bill Birnbauer has provided in this work, in fine style. I'm honored to write a preface for it. And I'll offer at least a bit of explanation of why no Amer-ican that I'm aware of beat him to it.

US journalism and journalism studies is drenched in a powerful story of decline, and a lot of this is oriented to the decline of the "watchdog" role of a journalism industry struggling with fewer economic resources. This decline, especially in print, of newsroom employment is real and unsettling. It is widely assumed to have reduced a once great journalis-tic capacity for investigative reporting that holds government and other centers of power accountable. The economic crisis in journalism is thus taken to be a significant threat to American democracy itself. Indeed, as Birnbauer shows, this is exactly the story that new online investigative reporting nonprofits have regularly retailed to foundations and other funders as they seek cash to start their operations and to keep them running. They play the "democracy" card; they assure foundations that supporting journalism is key to preserving democracy.

But Birnbauer notes that the major locations of investigative report-ing have specifically protected their investigative units from devastation, from the *New York Times* to the *Washington Post* to the *Boston Globe* and others. Beth Knobel, an American journalist-turned-academic, has demonstrated with new data in a recently published work that the total amount of investigative reporting in the newspaper world has not in fact declined (Knobel, 2018). Most news organizations, print and broadcast, have rarely invested very much – or anything at all – in investigative work. Indeed, Birnbauer cites a 1975 study that found that only several dozen newspapers (out of 1,750 daily newspapers), a few magazines, and no television operations did any investigative work. The severity of the current economic threat to watchdog reporting has been much overdrawn because the commitment of most US news organizations to investigation has been so meager. Ironically, the belief that a mainstay of American de-mocracy was gravely threatened by the economic downturn in newspaper advertising in the digital era helped create an impressive new phalanx of news organizations that put investigative reporting front and center.

Birnbauer has much to say about all of this. Interestingly, his focus is less on the newsrooms of the country than on the interface of nonprofit news organizations with other news organizations and with foundations. On the former, he discusses how the new nonprofit investigative units cooperate and collaborate with public broadcasting, commercial news outlets, and one another, bucking up against the traditional fierce insistence on relying exclusively on one's own reporting. On the latter, he offers a fascinating look at foundation funding for nonprofit investigative journalism. He has gone to the foundations and interviewed decision-making foundation officials. He offers a complex, fair-minded presentation of the dilemmas of journalism in seeking foundation support and of foundations in funding projects whose specific intentions ("we want to do an investigative series on topic X or on person Y") cannot normally be made known in proposals to the foundation. The primary task – journalism – could not be fully accepted as a legitimate enterprise (like, say, health-care delivery) but only as an activity that is plausibly related to strengthening "the quality of information that citizens in a democracy get to experience," in the words of one foundation officer. Moreover, foundations are not happy when they cannot know how to evaluate whether their journalism grants achieve anything. What is journalism, after all? And if your funding helped support a given story or a series of stories, how could you determine the influence of those stories in preparing citizens to do their task in a democracy? Did it matter that the story reached a lot of people? Or did it matter that it reached one person for whom it made a difference? Or one decision-maker who could act on the revelations (a prosecutor, for instance)?

Birnbauer finds that foundation support for investigative reporting favors well-established players in the field; 40 percent of the funding of 62 investigative and public service nonprofits between 2009 and 2015 went to the three most prominent and largest – Center for Public Integrity, Center for Investigative Reporting, and *ProPublica.*

Birnbauer is likewise conservative; his book offers detailed studies of the founding and work of the same three organizations – the Center for Public Integrity (Washington, DC), the Center for Investigative Reporting (Emeryville, CA), and *ProPublica* (New York City) – along with the muckraking magazine *Mother Jones.* He gives a careful and comprehensive account of them all. Of course, some of their ups and downs are clearly matters of personalities, of executive competence or incompetence, of tussles with foundations, of lawsuits – all of this important but little of it focused on what these three organizations actually do – that is, they produce news stories based on investigative reporting. How much do they produce? Which of their products have achieved the most notable consequences in advancing public integrity, in exposing corruption, in advancing worthy causes for the public good?

Like other good journalists and historians, Birnbauer focuses on what he knows – that which has already happened. He offers only a few inconclusive words about the future, that which none of us know. How sustainable will the entry of so many nonprofit organizations dedicated to accountability reporting turn out to be? We do not know. To his credit, Birnbauer usefully takes up the factors that should lead to pessimism about the nonprofits' sustainability and also those that should make us more hopeful. He himself stands on the more hopeful side, in no small part because so many of the newbies have already lasted longer than predicted and have maintained or increased their foundation support.

Investigative reporting is well known for its sobriety, its discipline, its doggedness, its earnestness, but not its sense of humor or sense of irony. Birnbauer's study is earnest, to be sure, but it is also rich in irony – the very existence of many of the nonprofits owes much to a misunderstanding. There never was a great deal of investigative reporting or accountability journalism in the United States, and its "decline" in the internet era is greatly exaggerated, notably by prospective new nonprofit operations themselves! These great advocates of factuality promoted their new enterprise based on a demonstrable error.

While the error is demonstrable, it is not easily detected amidst the rhetorical clutter of American journalists proclaiming how indispensable they are to democracy. It may be that Australian journalism, like the British journalism that influenced it, does not take itself quite so seriously as US journalism does, and I think that may be crucial. Birnbauer, after some three decades as a journalist in Melbourne, moved into an academic career and moved also – beginning in 1998 – into serving as a member of the International Consortium of Investigative Journalists, a new enterprise then whose startling premise was that journalists across many news organizations and across multiple countries could actually productively cooperative rather than compete.

Was there or is there a crisis in journalism? Birnbauer is not the first to question the notion. Jeffrey Alexander and colleagues did so in *The Crisis in Journalism Reconsidered* (2016). Neither Alexander and company nor Birnbauer denies the well-documented devastation of American newspaper newsrooms, many newspapers terminating the employment of a quarter or a third of their newsroom staff. But what has that done to US journalism as a whole? It has had various consequences and not all of them bad. And – another irony – it has emphasized, perhaps as never before, the centrality of investigative or "accountability" reporting as the heart of journalism. In that regard, the rise of investigative nonprofit journalism as a real player in the world of reporting has been a notable consequence, more fully and finely described in Birnbauer's work than any other place I know.

Michael Schudson
Professor of Journalism at the Columbia University
Graduate School of Journalism

Acknowledgments

For most of my 33 years in print journalism, I believed, like most of my colleagues, that the best investigative reporting was done by legacy newspapers. I knew little about the investigative journalism of nonprofit news organizations or the philanthropic funding of journalism. That began to change after I was awarded a John S. Knight Fellowship at Stanford University followed by an invitation to join the nonprofit International Consortium of Investigative Journalists, and finally researching the nonprofit news sector as an academic. I now believe that some of the finest watchdog reporting is done by US nonprofit news organizations. The people who helped me research the rapidly expanding though fragile nonprofit sector are listed below.

I thank especially the doyens of US nonprofit investigative journalism: Charles "Chuck" Lewis, Robert Rosenthal, Brant Houston, Bill Buzenberg, and Richard Tofel. They were generous beyond measure. Others in the sector who also gave me their precious time and insights included Bill Keller, Myron Levin, Lowell Bergman, Sue Cross, Sheila Coronel, Dan Noyes, Kevin Davis, Monika Bauerlein, Mark Schapiro, Steve Katz, Michael Stoll, Lila LaHood, Todd Reubold, Mary Hoff, Adam Hochschild, Mark Saxenmeyer, Ken Paulman, Lorie Hearn, Lee Keough, Mc Nelly Torres, A.C. Thompson, Sebastian Rotella, Louis Freedberg, Robin Heller, Cherilyn Parsons, David Weir, Evelyn Larrubia, Gerard Ryle, Drew Sullivan, and Daphne Magnawa.

The foundation program directors who patiently explained why they funded accountability journalism and without whom the sector literally would be the poorer included Elspeth Revere, Ben Shute, Kathy Im, Clark Bell, John Bracken, Amy Dominguez-Arms, Sunny Fischer, Lori McGlinchey, and the late Jack Fischer.

In the world of academia, I am most grateful to Michael Schudson, Professor of Journalism at the Columbia University Graduate School of Journalism. His deep knowledge of the history and sociology of the American news media and his accessible analysis helped me to see relationships, concepts, and frames that often were hidden in plain sight. I cannot thank him enough for his constructive feedback on my PhD and his generosity in writing the foreword to this book. I am indebted particularly for the guidance of my doctoral supervisors, Professor Julian Thomas and Associate Professor Margaret Simons, and a second assessor, Professor Ian Richards. They showed me how to think more critically and steered me through a process I knew little about. There were many academics to whom I am indebted including Professor Colleen Lewis, Professor Jenny Hocking, Professor Chris Nash, and Associate Professor Mia Lindgren at Monash university, as well as Associate Professor Colleen Murrell and friends at Swinburne and Melbourne universities. US academics Professor Jon Funabiki and Professor Robert Picard assisted my understanding of business models for journalism.

I am indebted beyond measure to Dr Gillian Dite who undertook with forensic eye and good humor the specialized work of taming the references, figures, and tables.

I am especially grateful to Routledge Editor Felisa Salvago-Keyes who commissioned this book, and more than that, remembered my initial inquiry and got back to me when the time was right, then guided my proposal through the review process and the editorial board. I also appreciate the reviewers who took the time to provide feedback on my proposal and Routledge Senior Editorial Assistant Christina Kowalski and Editorial Assistant Jennifer Vennall who both provided valuable direction in the publication process.

I would like to acknowledge the influence of the late Associate Professor Philip Chubb on both my journalistic and academic careers. We covered state politics in the early 1980s then started our academic careers at Monash University in Melbourne, Australia, on the same day in 2008. He was an inspiration and a mate, and I will always remember him and miss him.

The biggest debt I owe is to my wife, Deirdre. Working on the thesis and this book for almost 10 years interfered with an untold number of holidays and I can't thank her enough for her understanding, support, and patience. Thanks also to my daughters for their love and encouragement and my grandchildren for keeping me very grounded.

1 Introduction

The Changing Face of
Watchdog Journalism

In downtown San Francisco, *Mother Jones*'s CEO Monika Bauerlein is grappling with the final fact checking of an investigative story about the President's financial dealings.

In New York, the *Marshall Project*'s editor-in-chief Bill Keller is choreographing a partnership with the *Los Angeles Times* that will assess the impact of reduced incarceration on crime rates. At the Wall Street end of Manhattan, *ProPublica*'s president Dick Tofel is surprised and delighted at the rapid growth in the number of individual donors to his organization.

At *FairWarning*'s one-room office in Pasadena, founder and editorial director Myron Levin is figuring out his next move in a bid to extract documents relating to enforcement programs operated by the US Labor Department.

In Minneapolis, Todd Reubold, who publishes the environmental magazine, *Ensia*, is concerned that a barrage of Washington political news has upended important discussions about climate change, the state of the oceans, deforestation, and biodiversity loss.

And in New Jersey, *NJ Spotlight*'s Lee Keough is getting medical and other routine appointments out of the way in advance of the long hours she anticipates spending on a merger between her news organization and a local public television station.

These journalists are part of an expanding sector of accountability journalism in the United States that operates under a nonprofit business model. Unlike commercial media that are funded by advertising and subscriptions, nonprofit news sites depend on grants from foundations, wealthy supporters, and, to a lesser extent, individual donors and fundraising activities.

The nonprofit investigative and public service journalism sector grew rapidly after the 2007–2009 global financial crisis that devastated commercial media revenues, leading to the loss of tens of thousands of journalism jobs and concern over the future of quality journalism. Since then, the nonprofit news sector has continued expanding, matured, and contributed to democratic processes well beyond its size.

The Institute for Nonprofit News, an association whose members are nonprofit investigative and public interest news organizations, has more than 160 member organizations across the United States after being founded in 2009 with just 27 members.[1] More than 100 of the institute's nonprofit news organizations were created between 2007 and 2017. There are an additional 110 or so nonprofit accountability news organizations in the United States that are not members of the institute (S. Cross, personal communication, April 11, 2018). The United States, for all its economic, racial, political, and social issues, has at least some corrective resources when activities that support democracy are said to be at risk.

In a departure from traditional journalistic practice, many of the country's most prestigious commercial and public media organizations now partner with and publish stories written by nonprofit center reporters. This shift represents a significant change given the distrust and wariness by mainstream media toward externally produced stories and the culture of competition between newsrooms. "Collaboration is maybe the most dramatic change I have seen in newsroom culture in my lifetime," observed former *New York Times*' executive editor Bill Keller (personal communication, April 25, 2018).

New nonprofits have rapidly established themselves as vigorous players in American journalism. They have won the most prestigious awards for journalism: Pulitzer Prizes, George Polk Awards, George Foster Peabody Awards, the Edward R. Murrow Award for Investigative Reporting, and awards and honors from the American Society of News Editors, Online News Association, National Press Club, Society of Professional Journalists, and Investigative Reporters and Editors.

While not close to replacing the loss of professional journalists or the lost value of media companies since the 2007–2009 financial crisis, nonprofit journalism has invigorated a tenet of democracy by expanding the production and accessibility of civically important journalism. Nonprofit news organizations such as the Center for Public Integrity, the International Consortium of Investigative Journalists, *ProPublica*, *MinnPost*, *Texas Tribune*, *VT Digger*, and *the Marshall Project* have shown that they can produce stories, datasets, and visualizations that mainstream newspapers and broadcasters simply do not have the resources, expertise, time, or culture to create.

This book examines the creation, funding, and operation of nonprofit accountability news sites in the United States. The central question it addresses is whether philanthropically funded centers are sustainable in the longer term. This is important because these new organizations have demonstrated that they can produce serious journalism that serves or can serve democracy (Schudson, 2008, pp. 11–26). Investigative and public interest stories scrutinize and hold to account powerful corporate and government figures and institutions, expose injustice and systemic flaws, provide the public with independently validated information, and act like a sword of Damocles over the heads of politicians, government officials, and business people who might be tempted to break or bend the legal and moral standards expected of them. Communications professor James Hamilton demonstrated how investigative stories costing thousands of dollars can deliver millions of dollars of benefits to society through policy changes and social returns (Hamilton, 2016, pp. 10, 111–135).

Situating Nonprofit Investigative and Public Interest News

It is helpful to understand the interactions the nonprofit investigative and public interest news sector has with other fields of activity. Of direct relevance are the economic, political, and mainstream media sectors. For nonprofit news organizations, the biggest source of revenue derives from philanthropic grants. These funders – foundations and wealthy individuals – constitute an economic sector. The political sector consists of the Internal Revenue Service and the federal and state government agencies that establish the rules for foundations and nonprofit organizations. For example, these rules mean that foundations are required to grant a minimum 5 percent of their assets each year. The Internal Revenue Service has to approve nonprofit status before organizations can be exempted from federal and some state taxes, receive unlimited donations, and donors are able to reduce their taxable income (Digital Media Law Project, 2014; Griffith, 2013). The mainstream media sector socialized in newsroom culture key players who moved to establish or operate nonprofit news organizations, and today routinely publishes stories produced by nonprofit journalism organizations.

This is not a book of media theory. Nevertheless, the concepts of field and various forms of capital developed by French sociologist Pierre Bourdieu[2] are used to help us understand the relationships between the nonprofit sector and other sectors and why a reputable newspaper such as the *Washington Post* might be comfortable accepting a potentially controversial story from *ProPublica* or the *Marshall Project* but may reject – or write its own version of – a similar story from a citizen journalist.

My introduction to US nonprofit journalism occurred when a letter arrived from the United States in 1998 inviting me to join a new global nonprofit investigative organization based in Washington, DC. At the time, I was a reporter in a daily metropolitan newsroom in Melbourne, Australia. I had never heard of nonprofit investigative journalism and the idea of cooperating on stories and sources with unknown foreign reporters appeared unlike anything I would do. It was even bizarre. I doubted that nonmainstream media organizations were capable of undertaking serious investigative journalism. This was a time when weekend newspapers were thick with classified advertising, newsroom budgets allowed generous expense accounts, statehouse bureaus were well staffed, and few could foresee the impact that internet startups would have on traditional business models. After researching the people behind the International Consortium of Investigative Journalists, I decided to learn more and agreed to join though I remained wary. At a meeting soon after with the consortium's editors and reporter members from 60 countries, I quickly realized how similar we were in our ideas of what constituted a good story, the methodologies we used, and our ethical values. I was hooked by the vision, ambition, and impact of investigative journalism done on a global scale and soon was involved in two major consortium projects. Taking a voluntary buyout in 2008 after 33 years in print journalism, I moved to a tenured academic position and started looking more closely at the US nonprofit sector as part of my doctoral research. This book is the result of further research in the United States after I left my university appointment. No foundation or other funding was provided for the project. I had discovered that America's philanthropic foundations supported journalists and their training in the early 1990s when I was awarded a John S. Knight Journalism Fellowship at Stanford University. Until then, I knew virtually nothing about US foundations.

Differentiating between investigative and public interest news centers was not relevant to the research because I sought to examine common factors in the development of centers that practice noncommercial professional journalism. Investigative and public interest newsrooms are funded mainly by foundations, wealthy business people, and donors. Both employ professional journalists and produce nonpartisan journalism that is in the public interest. Both have faced the same ethical issues due to their funding by philanthropic organizations, and both from time to time have confronted financial, personal, and management challenges. On a practical level, some of the analysis in this book is based on the membership of the Institute for Nonprofit News, which does not distinguish between investigative and public interest organizations. Using the institute's membership as a filter offers some assurance that the nonprofit organizations cited produce nonpartisan in-depth journalism and are not fronts for advocacy organizations. Rather than indulging in an academic debate about definitions, this book simply refers to "accountability journalism" to cover investigative and public interest or public service reporting.

Nonprofit accountability journalism operates with the practices, ethics, and values of professional journalism, but its economies have elements in common with nonmarket citizen writers and bloggers. Journalists predicate their value to the community in terms of principles such as commitments to truth, accuracy, freedom of speech, unbiased reporting, the public's right to know, and independence (Webb, Schirato, & Danaher, 2002, p. 183). But these cultural values alone do not provide the income that pays journalists to do their work. The job cuts, bureau closures, and other savings measures implemented by media companies as stock markets crashed during the financial crisis are a graphic illustration of the economic sector's dominance over these cultural principles of journalism. Investigative stories, often costing hundreds of thousands of dollars to produce, have little commercial appeal, though high civic returns. That means nonprofit accountability news centers rely heavily on donor funding and therefore are vulnerable to negative impacts from the more powerful economic (foundations and wealthy funders) and political sectors, and to a lesser extent, the commercial media.

Expansion of Nonprofit Accountability Journalism

Nonprofit watchdog journalism is not new. News organizations such as *Mother Jones*, the Center for Investigative Reporting, and the Better Government Association have published deep dive journalism for decades. Well-known general media that use the nonprofit model include the *Christian Science Monitor*, *Harper's Magazine*, the *Washington Monthly*, NPR, PBS, and Associated Press.

The expansion of the nonprofit accountability reporting sector in the United States coincided with a period when commercial media were under extraordinary financial stress. The 2007–2009 financial crisis was the worst economic downturn since the Great Depression (Reuters, 2009). The financial turmoil led to a sharp decline in newspaper and broadcast advertising revenue, leading to widespread job cuts and foreboding about the future of journalism and democracy. Newspaper companies were hardest hit: the closure of newspapers, moves to digital-only publication, and bankruptcy processes in journalism powerhouses like the *Chicago Tribune*, *Los Angeles Times*, and the *Philadelphia Inquirer* sent shockwaves through the industry. Panic set in when it became known that the *New York Times* was bailed out financially by a Mexican billionaire (Lee, 2014). The industry was in difficulty even before the financial crisis due to digital startups drawing away its classified advertising, historic debt levels, and long-term declines in readership (Bagdikian, 1990; Benkler, 2006; Brock, 2013; Jones, 2009; Meyer, 2009; Nichols & McChesney, 2009; Picard, 2006).

Philanthropic foundations, journalists, academics, and civil society grew increasingly concerned that democracy would be affected by the budget cuts that swept the industry (Frank, 2009; McChesney & Nichols, 2010; Osder & Campwala, 2012; Riptide, 2013; Westphal, 2009). Investigative journalism looked particularly vulnerable: it was expensive to produce, was plagued by costly legal actions, it upset politicians and potential advertisers, and was unproductive in the number of stories it created. It was always subsidized, mostly by classified and display advertisements in commercial media; those rivers of gold as they were once called now looked like parched creek beds.

There wasn't much of it being done in any case. A content analysis of the front pages of the *New York Times*, the *Washington Post*, and the *Milwaukee Journal Sentinel* in 1955, 1967, 1979, 1991, and 2003 concluded that watchdog stories were a small fraction of overall news (Fink & Schudson, 2014, p. 13). In 2003, only 1 percent of the stories were found to be investigative, which was consistent with previous periods apart from 1991 when they constituted 3 percent of the stories. A more recent study of the front pages of nine national, metropolitan, and local newspapers in five-year intervals between 1991 and 2011 found that "deep accountability reports" as a percentage of front-page stories averaged between a high of 4.03 percent for the *Wall Street Journal* and just 0.32 percent for a small local newspaper (Knobel, 2018, p. 24).

The inevitable demise of investigative reporting became conventional wisdom among journalists, funders, and media observers. It was this "crisis" in journalism – the conventional wisdom is questioned in Chapter 4 – that led to journalists together with foundations and a handful of wealthy business people to create centers dedicated to accountability journalism.

Nonprofit news organizations in the United States differ in size, financial strength, and the stories they pursue. Some, like *ProPublica*, *Mother Jones*, the Center for Public Integrity, and the Center for Investigative Reporting, focus on national issues; others report mainly on state politics and local issues or niche topics such as the environment, criminal justice, or health. Some are destination sites for local and regional communities; others, like the International Consortium of Investigative Journalists, rely on commercial and public media to distribute their stories. Nonprofit accountability news organizations are relatively small. The biggest organization has more than 100 reporters, editors, producers, data, and information technology specialists as well as engagement and administrative staff. Smaller organizations have just one, two, or three full-time journalists. Annual incomes vary from less than $100,000 to $43 million. To put that into perspective, revenue at the New York Times Company in 2017 was $1.7 billion (Ember, 2018). In a remarkably short time, newly created nonprofit news organizations joined older nonprofits in exposing corruption, wrongdoing, systemic faults, and waste. Their stories were published in commercial and public media, and were accessed by millions of people.

Why then did the nonprofit news sector grow so quickly? Several factors contributed to a big expansion during and since the financial crisis of 2007–2009. Each factor related to the others, though the degree of influence varied. The first of the main factors was concern that the financial crisis would be a crisis also for investigative journalism and democracy due to its devastating economic impact on the businesses of mainstream media (Bergantino & Mulvihill, 2009; Lewis, 2007; Meyer, 2008; Walton, 2010).

The transfer of senior for-profit media journalists to the nonprofit sector is the second key factor. Editors who once held senior positions in legacy media transferred their skills, network links, and experience to national, state, and local nonprofit news organizations. They brought with them decades of know-how and high levels of cultural capital in the form of established journalistic reputations. These nonprofit executive editors had extensive contacts with legacy editors with whom they shared the same ethics, values, and journalistic practices. Journalists in mainstream organizations traditionally were wary about the agendas, ethics, reliability, independence, and accuracy of externally produced content, much preferring to keep their craft in-house (Kaplan, 2008). The presence of one of their own in a nonprofit news center alleviated some of those suspicions. The journalistic credentials of nonprofit editors and reporters also convinced foundations and wealthy donors that they were donating to professionally run news organizations.

The third primary factor that stimulated the growth of the sector was that individual and institutional funders donated to news organizations. Their funding, in effect, made foundations and wealthy individuals a powerful economic force, and a constant concern among nonprofits was that funding would not be renewed beyond a startup phase and that other revenue streams had to be developed. Only a handful of nonprofit centers managed to diversify their revenues away from foundations to any notable degree (Mitchell, Jurkowitz, Holcomb, Enda, & Anderson, 2013).

I also identify four secondary factors that stimulated the expansion of the nonprofit sector. They include approval by the Internal Revenue Service of media organizations as nonprofit organizations; universities accommodating and affiliating with investigative centers; creation of the Institute for Nonprofit News (formerly called the Investigative News Network), which provided nonprofits with practical assistance on technological, legal, and financial issues as well as establishing an ethical framework for the sector; and the social, political, and economic climate.

Whether these factors, or some of them, can be replicated and maintained in future or whether the period was unique and the model is unsustainable in the longer term is a question that may determine the quantity of notable journalism and ultimately the health of democracy in the United States. That makes it imperative to better understand the nonprofit business model and how it can be sustained. That is the need this book addresses.

The nonprofit accountability news sector, for all its spectacular growth, stories, and awards, is fragile due to an overreliance on foundation support and modest progress in developing alternative revenue sources. Its founders and editors struggle to stay afloat in a sea of complexity beyond their journalistic expertise: payrolls, lease agreements, syndication, fundraising, story metrics, marketing, taxation, technology, and legal issues to name a few.

The findings in the coming chapters provide new perspectives and insights on the forces that shaped nonprofit accountability journalism in the United States. This book examines why foundations donate to such journalism rather than, say, a cancer hospital. It tackles the ethical issues associated with foundation giving to journalism. What are the agendas of foundations? What do they want in return for their donations? It presents case studies of four nationally focused investigative organizations: *ProPublica,* the Center for Investigative Reporting, the Center for Public Integrity, and *Mother Jones.* It then visits several smaller state-based nonprofit news organizations that struggle to produce accountability stories. Finally, readers will see that nonprofit reporting has transformed long-held aspects of traditional journalistic practice.

Notes

1 The Institute for Nonprofit News was called the Investigative News Network when it was founded in 2009. It changed its name in 2015 when its board decided to broaden its membership base to include public service nonprofit news organizations as well as investigative reporting sites.
2 In establishing the relationships between the nonprofit sector and foundations and legacy media, I have been guided by some of the insights of French sociologist Pierre Bourdieu's field theory (Bourdieu, 1977, 1998; Bourdieu & Wacquant, 1992). Bourdieu's concepts of habitus and doxa – an intuitive disposition rather than a conscious effort and shared beliefs or conventions (Willig, 2012) – were useful in interpreting the activities of journalists and funders. Another important concept was that of various forms of capital (Benson & Neveu, 2005).

Bibliography

Bagdikian, B. H. (1990). *The media monopoly* (3rd ed.). Boston, MA: Beacon Press.

Benkler, Y. (2006). *The wealth of networks: How social production transforms markets and freedom.* New Haven, CT: Yale University Press.

Benson, R. D., & Neveu, E. (2005). *Bourdieu and the journalistic field.* Cambridge, MA: Polity.

Bergantino, J., & Mulvihill, M. (2009, Summer). Filling a local void: J-school students tackle watchdog reporting. *Nieman Reports.* Retrieved from http://www.nieman.harvard.edu/reports/article/101563/Filling-a-Local-Void-J-School-Students-Tackle-Watchdog-Reporting.aspx

Bourdieu, P. (1977). *Outline of a theory of practice.* Cambridge, England: Cambridge University Press.

Bourdieu, P. (1998). *On television.* New York, NY: New Press.

Bourdieu, P., & Wacquant, L. J. D. (1992). *An invitation to reflexive sociology.* Chicago, IL: University of Chicago Press.

Brock, G. (2013). *Out of print: Newspapers, journalism and the business of news in the digital age.* London, England: Logan Page.

Digital Media Law Project. (2014). How does the IRS interpret Section 501(c)
(3)? Retrieved from http://www.dmlp.org/irs/section-501c3

Ember, S. (2018, February 8). New York Times Co. subscription revenue sur-
passed $1 billion in 2017. *The New York Times.* Retrieved from https://www.
nytimes.com/2018/02/08/business/new-york-times-company-earnings.html

Fink, K., & Schudson, M. (2014). The rise of contextual journalism,
1950s–2000s. *Journalism, 15*(1), 3–20. doi:10.1177/1464884913479015

Frank, L. (2009, June). The withering watchdog: What really happened to investigative reporting in America. *Expose: America's Investigative Reports.*
Retrieved from http://www.pbs.org/wnet/expose/2009/06/the-withering-
watchdog.html

Griffith, T. (2013, June/July). How outdated IRS policies hurt nonprofit journalism. *American Journalism Review.* Retrieved from http://ajrarchive.org/
article.asp?id=5542

Hamilton, J. T. (2016). *Democracy's detectives: The economics of investigative
journalism.* Boston, MA: Harvard University Press.

Jones, A. S. (2009). *Losing the news: The future of the news that feeds democracy.* New York, NY: Oxford University Press.

Kaplan, A. D. (2008). *Investigating the investigators: Examining the attitudes,
perceptions, and experiences of investigative journalists in the internet age*
(Doctoral dissertation), University of Maryland, College Park, MD. Retrieved
from http://hdl.handle.net/1903/8788

Knobel, B. (2018). *The watchdog still barks: How accountability reporting
evolved for the digital age.* New York, NY: Fordham University Press.

Lee, E. (2014). Carlos Slim still reaping big rewards from NY Times loan.
Retrieved from Bloomberg website: http://www.bloomberg.com/news/2014-
01-21/carlos-slim-still-reaping-big-rewards-from-ny-times-loan.html

Lewis, C. (2007). *The growing importance of nonprofit journalism* (Working
Paper Series #2007-3). Retrieved from the Shorenstein Center on Media,
Politics and Public Policy website: http://shorensteincenter.org/wp-content/
uploads/2012/03/2007_03_lewis.pdf

McChesney, R. W., & Nichols, J. (2010). *The death and life of American journalism: The media revolution that will begin the world again.* New York, NY:
Nation Books.

Meyer, P. (2008, October/November). The elite newspaper of the future. *American
Journalism Review.* Retrieved from http://www.ajr.org/Article.asp?id=4605

Meyer, P. (2009). *The vanishing newspaper: Saving journalism in the information age* (2nd ed.). Columbia, MO: University of Missouri Press.

Mitchell, A., Jurkowitz, M., Holcomb, J., Enda, J., & Anderson, M. (2013).
Nonprofit journalism: A growing but fragile part of the US news system.
Retrieved from Pew Research Center website: http://www.journalism.org/
analysis_report/nonprofit_journalism

Nichols, J., & McChesney, R. W. (2009). The death and life of great American
newspapers. Retrieved from The Nation website: http://www.thenation.com/
article/death-and-life-great-american-newspapers/

Osder, E., & Campwala, K. (2012). Audience development and distribution strategies. Retrieved from Investigative News Network website: http://newstraining.
org/guides/whitepaper-audience-development-and-distribution-strategies/
prologue/

Picard, R. (2006). *Journalism, value creation and the future of news organisations* (Working Paper Series #2006-4). Retrieved from the Shorenstein Center on Media, Politics and Public Policy website: http://www.robertpicard.net/PDFFiles/ValueCreationandNewsOrgs.pdf

Reuters. (2009, February 27). Three top economists agree 2009 worst financial crisis since Great Depression; risks increase if right steps are not taken. *Reuters*. Retrieved from http://www.reuters.com/article/2009/02/27/idUS193520+27-Feb-2009+BW20090227

Riptide. (2013). Eric Schmidt. Retrieved from the Shorenstein Center on Media, Politics and Public Policy website: http://www.niemanlab.org/riptide/person/eric-schmidt/

Schudson, M. (2008). *Why democracies need an unlovable press*. Cambridge, MA: Polity.

Walton, M. (2010). Investigative shortfall. *American Journalism Review, 32*(3), 18–24, 26–30.

Webb, J., Schirato, T., & Danaher, G. (2002). *Understanding Bourdieu*. London, England: SAGE.

Westphal, D. (2009). *Philanthropic foundations: Growing funders of the news*. Retrieved from USC Annenberg School of Communication, Center on Communication Leadership & Policy website: https://communicationleadership.usc.edu/files/2015/07/PhilanthropicFoundations.pdf

Willig, I. (2012). Newsroom ethnography in a field perspective. *Journalism, 14*(3), 372–387.

2 New Collaborations
A Mutual Benefit

For three days from about 9.30 pm on November 26, 2008, the Indian financial center of Mumbai was rocked by a series of terrorist attacks that killed 166 people and wounded more than 300. Ten attackers, identified later as members of the Lashkar-e-Taiba organization, targeted American and British tourists (Sengupta, 2008). Using automatic weapons and grenades, they also killed Israelis, law enforcement officers, and local victims at multiple locations including the Taj Mahal Palace & Tower and Oberoi Trident hotels, a rail terminus, and a hospital (BBC, 2009). The coordinated and ongoing assault received extensive news coverage around the world including dramatic eyewitness accounts of blood-soaked victims, footage of explosions and burning buildings, as well as condemnation by world political leaders. In the following months, evidence gathered by Indian, American, and British intelligence services and admissions by top Pakistani security officials (Masood, 2009) shed new light on how the terrorists had planned the attacks. Some of the preparations had taken place in Pakistan. Pakistan's then Interior Minister Rehman Malik insisted, however, that the terrorists were "non-state actors" (IBNLive, 2009). Several Pakistanis were arrested and charged, including the leader of the anti-Indian Lashkar-e-Taiba militant group (BBC, 2010).

Almost two years after the Mumbai attack, the *Washington Post* published a two-part investigative series of more than 9,000 words that revealed in extraordinary detail the key figures, planning, and organization behind the terrorism (Rotella, 2010a, 2010d). The two articles were everything readers would expect of a major investigation by a newspaper whose Watergate revelations in the 1970s inspired enthusiasm for investigative journalism in newsrooms around the world. Quoting court documents, Interpol notices, counterterrorism investigators, high-ranking US law enforcement officials, French intelligence officials, and other sources, the articles exposed close links between the Mumbai terrorists and the Pakistani military and intelligence service. The articles also described the involvement of a Pakistani American in training with Lashkar-e-Taiba and scoping out targets in Mumbai before the attacks. The author, journalist Sebastian Rotella, revealed that the Pakistani

American was once an informant for the US Drug Enforcement Administration. US agents had passed over at least half a dozen warnings about the man's involvement in terrorism (Rotella, 2010d). For all intents and purposes, the articles continued the watchdog legacy of the Watergate revelations that ultimately saw President Richard Nixon resign in 1974. The *Washington Post*'s permanent investigative unit, established in 1982 under Watergate reporter Bob Woodward, was committed to doing "the kind of work that holds government, business and other institutions accountable for their actions" (Washington Post, 2007, para. 1). The *Washington Post*'s investigative unit website listed the names of its 14 reporters and editors – a big commitment in an era of uncertainty generally about the future of newspapers (Washington Post Staff, 2011).

The Mumbai stories, however, were not written by the *Washington Post*'s investigative journalists. Sebastian Rotella is an investigative reporter employed by *ProPublica*, a philanthropically funded nonprofit investigative journalism organization based in New York. *ProPublica* published the articles on its website at the same time as the *Washington Post* (Rotella, 2010b, 2010c). The byline credit on the *Washington Post* articles was "By Sebastian Rotella, *ProPublica*." The stories contained numerous favorable references to the nonprofit organization's journalism: "For five months, *ProPublica* has examined" and "*ProPublica* has tracked the rise of Lashkar." The stories ended with, "*ProPublica* is an independent nonprofit newsroom that produces investigative journalism" (Rotella, 2010a, paras. 9, 107; 2010d, para. 15).

That a newspaper as prestigious as the then 133-year-old *Washington Post* would publish politically sensitive stories produced by a nonprofit organization barely three and a half years old reflected a change in American journalistic culture and practice. The *Washington Post*'s cultural capital and influence are built on the foundation stones of its journalism: credibility, accuracy, independence, and impact. Mistakes or suggestions of an agenda in its stories could potentially result in political attacks, media condemnation, professional and public humiliation, public apologies, legal remedies, and reputational damage. These risks have made many legacy editors deeply skeptical about collaborating with anyone outside of their newsrooms, particularly in the field of investigative reporting (Rowe, 2011).

Marilyn Thompson was the *Washington Post*'s deputy national editor when Sebastian Rotella's Mumbai stories were published. Asked if the *Washington Post* would have taken outside stories 5 or 10 years earlier, she said the situation might have been very different then because the *Washington Post* had a large staff and a great desire to showcase its original work (personal communication, July 28, 2013).

How was it, then, that the *Washington Post* published stories from a recently formed nonprofit organization that was funded overwhelmingly by a wealthy and politically active benefactor? How is it that other mainstream media, including public broadcasters, today routinely partner with nonprofit reporting organizations? How is it possible that new nonprofit organizations, small as they are in comparison, are beating traditional media for journalism's most prestigious awards? *ProPublica* has had hundreds of publishing partners since 2008 (ProPublica, n.d.-b), including established outlets such as the *New York Times, Chicago Tribune, Los Angeles Times, Boston Globe*, and more recent online organizations *Vice, Mashable, Slate, Buzzfeed*, and Amazon (ProPublica, 2014). What has shifted in US journalism to bring this about?

The answer is complex but it is important that we better understand the factors that coalesced to support the production of serious journalism at a time when it appeared that celebrity journalism and partisan opinion would overwhelm journalism's mission of scrutinizing power and the traditional business model of journalism was collapsing. The nonprofit accountability news sector expanded at a time when politically charged attacks on commercial media prompted questions about whether democracy itself was at risk due to the declining influence and credibility of an already vastly diminished media landscape.

A Change in Traditional Journalistic Practice

Newspapers adapted slowly to the challenging environment shaped by the 2007–2009 financial crisis and the internet's disruption of the traditional business model for news. They cut reporting staff, closed bureaus, and established paywalls and other revenue streams. Many, but not all, discarded their aversion to collaborating with outside news organizations. That is not to say they embraced citizen journalism or that they began publishing news stories by bloggers and advocacy pushers. But a radical transformation was occurring to the long-standing journalistic culture of competition, exclusivity, and in-house-only investigative reporting practice.

There were good reasons for legacy editors to be unreceptive to the notion of publishing watchdog stories produced by people who were not professional journalists in their newsrooms. They worried about the accuracy of the stories, the agendas of those writing them, the professionalism and ethics of the writers, and the risk of legal action. Editors understood the reputational damage that could result from suggestions of noneditorial considerations influencing story selection and content and they steered away from trusting work produced externally. They knew also that publishing non-staff stories took away space that could have gone to one of their own reporters' stories. "You can get some grumbling from people who say, 'why are you publishing that from an outsider when my story has been held for two weeks'" (B. Keller, personal communication, April 25, 2018). Wariness about collaborating with nonprofit newsrooms was even more understandable when one looks at the often nonlinear process of checking and editing an investigative story. Agreement had to be reached on how the story would be researched, written, fact checked, and edited. Issues could arise as to whether legacy editors would be able to question and direct nonprofit reporters, or even approach their sources and access their documents. What would happen if last-minute changes were requested by one party? What if one organization wanted to delay publication for a few days?

Surveys confirmed the discomfort that for-profit investigative reporters had about working with outside groups. Half the investigative reporters who responded to one survey said they were somewhat or very uncomfortable or neutral about partnering with a nonprofit. Several expressed concerns about the quality and the funding of nonprofit stories (Kaplan, 2008). The survey of 281 investigative journalists employed at newspapers found that journalists wanted an in-depth understanding of the nonprofit's history and funding and full access to all their documents and sources before entering any partnership. "...they may have an agenda that we may not be very clear about," one reporter said (Kaplan, 2008, p. 123).

Tom Farragher, a former investigative editor with the *Boston Globe*, wanted editors to see the sausage as it was being made to ensure that corners were not cut. "You need to be careful to vet your partner. You don't want to get into bed with somebody who doesn't have the standards the *Globe* has, and I think the *Globe* has very high standards" (personal communication, February 25, 2015). Former *Wall Street Journal* managing editor Paul Steiger recalled that during his 41 years in newspaper journalism, "the idea of collaborating with another news organization was as foreign as pine trees in the Sahara. They were competitors, and you beat them or were ashamed" (Steiger, 2015, para. 53).

If we look carefully, we can find reasons why these attitudes have changed over the past decade or so. As executive editor of the *Philadelphia Inquirer* between 1998 and 2002, Robert Rosenthal opposed collaborations with other news groups because they were too difficult (Francisco, Lenhoff, & Schudson, 2012, p. 2679). Later, as executive director of the Center for Investigative Reporting, Rosenthal and his senior editors began calling their contacts in the mainstream media to see if they would run the nonprofit's stories. Personal relationships mattered above all else. "We each could get editors to respond to us nearly all of the time. As we all came from traditional news organizations we were sensitive to the needs and issues of these newsrooms whose editors we were contacting" (Rosenthal, 2011, p. 11). Rosenthal was surprised how the need for exclusivity had given way, with editors willing to share a good story rather than cede it to their competitors (Rosenthal, 2011).

Research for this book identified the transfer of senior for-profit media journalists to the nonprofit sector as one of the key reasons for both the expansion of the sector and for the growing number of collaborations between commercial and nonprofit media. The majority of successful nonprofit investigative and public interest newsrooms in the United States today were created or are edited by journalists with years of experience in commercial media. That was the case for national organizations, the Center for Public Integrity, the Center for Investigative Reporting, and *ProPublica*, as well as many of the smaller outfits. Andy Hall, the cofounder and executive director of the Wisconsin Center for Investigative Journalism, was a print journalist for 26 years at the *Wisconsin State Journal* and the *Arizona Republic*; Joel Kramer, the CEO and editor of *MinnPost*, was a publisher and president of the *Minneapolis Star Tribune*; Lorie Hearn founded *inewsource* in 2009 after 35 years reporting and editing newspapers; Lynne DeLucia, editor of the Connecticut Health Investigative Team, was a former assistant managing editor of the *Hartford Courant*; Myron Levin, founder and editor of *FairWarning*, was a long-serving writer on the *Los Angeles Times*; Samuel Fromartz, the editor and cofounder of the *Food and Environment Reporting Network*, was a reporter and editor at *Reuters*; Laura Frank, the president and general manager of content at Rocky Mountain PBS, was a senior writer and investigative journalist between 1990 and 2009 before founding the *I-News Network*; and Bill Keller was a high-profile columnist and executive editor at the *New York Times* before becoming editor-in-chief of the *Marshall Project* in 2014.

These are a limited number of examples, but similar patterns were found in a selective analysis of the websites of nonprofit accountability news organizations that were members of the Institute for Nonprofit News (Institute for Nonprofit News, n.d.). Former mainstream journalists also established nonprofit reporting centers based at or linked to universities: Charles Lewis, a former producer at *60 Minutes*, founded the Investigative Reporting Workshop at American University; Florence Graves, an investigative reporter and founder in the 1980s of *Common Cause* magazine, started the Schuster Institute for Investigative Journalism at Brandeis University; Sheila Coronel, a senior investigative reporter and editor in the Philippines, was appointed director of the Toni Stabile Center for Investigative Journalism at Columbia University in New York; and Joe Bergantino, executive director and managing editor of the Boston University-affiliated New England Center for Investigative Reporting, had been a multi-award-winning television reporter for 35 years.

These journalists brought with them decades of newsroom experience and values, strong reputations, contacts in politics, finance, and the media, and importantly, the kind of credibility that appealed to foundations and created the environment for collaborations with their commercial and public media colleagues. Their familiarity and standing dispelled many of the concerns held by legacy editors because nonprofit journalists now had the same journalistic judgment, practice, and ethics as they had. They shared dispositions and conventions based on what Bill Kovach and Tom Rosenstiel called the "elements of journalism" (Kovach & Rosenstiel, 2007, pp. 12–13). These included a discipline of verification, independence, obligations to truth, monitoring power, and so on. A former editorial director of the Institute for Nonprofit News noted: "There was a time when they [mainstream editors] would have been very reluctant to run the work of others. And there are still journalistic issues with that ... it's tricky, and it's all built on relationships" (E. Larrubia, personal communication, January 31, 2012). Bill Keller moved from the *New York Times* to the *Marshall Project* and had previously worked with editors and subeditors at the *New York Times* and the *Washington Post:* "I started with some reservoir of trust and relationships that had developed over the years" (personal communication, April 25, 2018). The *Boston Globe*'s Tom Farragher felt more comfortable dealing with a nonprofit news organization when he discovered that a former *Globe* reporter worked there. "We don't have to stare at the ceiling at night wondering if they're going to screw things up" (personal communication, February 25, 2015).

The Mumbai massacre story, written by *ProPublica*'s Sebastian Rotella and published in the *Washington Post*, well illustrates why nonprofit journalism today is generally accepted as legitimate professional journalism by the mainstream media. Rotella had what the sociologist Pierre Bourdieu called the habitus and doxa – in simplistic terms, the unconscious social dispositions or beliefs accumulated over time or a "feel for the game" and a set of professional beliefs that tend to appear as natural and self-evident – as well as a journalistic reputation that would have been known to the *Washington Post*'s senior editors (Bourdieu, 1998; Schultz, 2007).

Rotella had spent 23 years at the *Los Angeles Times* where he was a foreign correspondent and investigative reporter before moving to *ProPublica* in 2010. Good relations and common journalistic values between editors and mutual respect for each other's publications had made the process of publishing the terrorist attack revelations in the *Washington Post* very smooth.

ProPublica was a "very credible product, not like a blog or firing some screed across the bow." Publication in the *Post* had given *ProPublica* a seal of approval and had benefited the newspaper in getting the story: "It's a mutual benefit" (personal communication, March 16, 2013).

Collaborations with Nonprofits Now Are Routine

Evidence suggests that collaborations between nonprofits and commercial and public media are more common now than ever (Downie & Schudson, 2009, para. 46; Edmonds & Mitchell, 2014, para. 1; Graves &

Konieczna, 2015; O'Brien, 2016; Stearns, 2012, para. 1). The combination of journalistically sound original stories and a dearth of quality content produced by shrunken commercial newsrooms has made the offer of nonprofit stories at no or little cost irresistible.

Former *60 Minutes* producer Charles Lewis created the Center for Public Integrity in 1989 and has since established other investigative nonprofit organizations. When he opened the Investigative Reporting Workshop, a university-based reporting center in Washington in 2009, he found the established media were enthusiastic about running the Workshop's stories: "We have to tell them to go away ... we have more than we can deal with. It's slightly amusing on one level and slightly depressing on another. They are desperately seeking content because they have eviscerated their newsrooms" (Birnbauer, 2011, p. 30).

An American Press Institute survey in 2016 found 42 percent of the 146 commercial media organizations that responded had partnered with a nonprofit news center (Rosenstiel, Buzenberg, Connelly, & Loker, 2016). The survey concluded that commercial–nonprofit partnerships were growing, probably due to financial considerations. Two-thirds of the commercial organizations reported that their editorial budgets had reduced over the previous five years. Further confirmation of the trend was found in an analysis of several awards for investigative reporting that showed that the percentage of citations involving three outlets cooperating rose from 1 percent in the 1990s to 11 percent in 2010–2013, helped by nonprofits working with for-profit organizations (Hamilton, 2016, p. 47). Another study that examined 2,309 stories published in 2016 by nine national, state/local, and academic-based investigative nonprofits found that 16 percent of the stories mentioned a publishing partner (Hale, Riccardelli, & DeLuca, 2017).

Nonprofit centers were effusive about the publication of their stories in legacy outlets. Their websites and annual reports prominently listed the media organizations that had run their stories. Such partnerships were seen as a stamp of legitimacy, a means of bolstering their impact and attracting a bigger audience. As will be seen in the following chapters, publication in prestigious newspapers and broadcasters impressed the foundations and wealthy donors that had funded those stories.

Models of Collaboration

In late 2008, the *Nation* magazine and *ProPublica* published two stories by investigative reporter A. C. Thompson. One described how New Orleans police had incinerated a car that contained the body of an African-American man who had died after being shot by police. The second story recounted the shooting of an African-American in a white enclave where residents had formed an armed version of Neighborhood Watch soon after Hurricane Katrina in 2005 (Thompson, 2008a, 2008b).

Thompson started his investigation with funding from the Nation Institute and continued the project after joining *ProPublica*. He discovered more shootings had occurred immediately after the hurricane – 11 in total – and wanted to investigate them. A producer from PBS's *Frontline* program joined him with the idea of making web videos to accompany the stories, and later a television documentary. Then, the local New Orleans newspaper, the *Times-Picayune*, approached them seeking to join the project (A. C. Thompson, personal communication, November 11, 2010). Key editors met and agreement was reached for the *Times-Picayune* to provide two or three reporters to a joint project that would examine the shootings in detail.

Thompson recalled that the atmosphere among the reporters at first was "a little weird and uncomfortable." That did not last long. All were experienced reporters and shared a similar culture. "We really clicked because we were coming from the same place, we had the same bad jokes, we had the same bad attitude sometimes, and so I think that was what really made it happen" (personal communication, November 11, 2010). A challenge they encountered was that Thompson and the *Frontline* producer, Tom Jennings, worked full time on the project while the newspaper reporters had less time and other obligations. However, publication was coordinated across the *Times-Picayune*, *ProPublica*, and *Frontline*. The reporting partnership continued as police were charged, processed through the courts, appealed, civil prosecutions launched, and federal and state law probes conducted. The "Law and Disorder" series on *ProPublica*'s website carried more than 80 stories (ProPublica, n.d.-a).

Thompson said the collaboration had worked informally in that there was no contract or document setting out what everyone would contribute. In hindsight, he felt a more formal arrangement might have been better with everyone's responsibilities laid out and a designated editor appointed to run it (personal communication, November 11, 2010).

The "Law and Disorder" partnership lasted longer than most, but there is no fixed model of media collaboration. Reporters from different news organizations could collaborate from the genesis of a project or, as with the Mumbai massacre stories, there might be only basic editing of a nonprofit story by mainstream media editors.

Collaborations often involved stories that the legacy media, due to resource constraints or lack of specialist investigative reporters, could not produce or could deliver only every few years. An example was a story that won the 2010 Pulitzer Prize for investigative reporting and was researched and written by nonprofit journalist Sheri Fink. It was published in both the *New York Times Magazine* and *ProPublica*'s website (Fink, 2009). Fink spent two and a half years researching "Deadly Choices at Memorial," a harrowing narrative of mercy killings at Memorial Hospital in New Orleans in the aftermath of Hurricane Katrina

(Birnbauer, 2011). Fink interviewed 140 people. It is difficult to envisage a legacy media organization devoting such resources to a project, even in what some regard as the financially golden period between 1970 and 1990 (Picard, 2010, p. 374). A rough estimate of the cost of researching, writing, editing, and securing the legal status of the article was up to $400,000 (Jeffery, 2009).

US journalism scholars have developed a model that describes various degrees of media collaboration (Dailey, Demo, & Spillman, 2005). The model, which they called the convergence continuum, provides a conceptual framework for collaborations, ranging from cross-promotion, cloning, coopetition, content sharing, and convergence. Briefly, cross-promotion carries the least cooperation and involves referring to a partner's story on a media platform. Cloning is the republication of a partner's story with little editing; coopetition involves the organizations both competing and cooperating. For example, they may share information on stories they are working on but years of competition, cultural differences, and mutual distrust limit the degree of cooperation. Content sharing has the partners meeting and exchanging ideas, sharing costs, and independently publishing at the same time. Full convergence might involve a common assignment desk with a shared editor and cooperation in gathering and disseminating the news.

My research suggests collaborations between nonprofit and for-profit media involved primarily the cloning and content sharing categories. *ProPublica*'s Sebastian Rotella and his Mumbai terrorism series jointly published in the *Washington Post* and *ProPublica* might be described as cloning, and a content sharing example of close partnering and shared reporting could be the "Law & Disorder" series published by *ProPublica*, *Frontline*, and the *Times-Picayune* newspaper (ProPublica, n.d.-a).

Cooperation can occur at an organizational as well as a story level. The trend to media collaboration was not confined to commercial–nonprofit combinations. In Oklahoma, local rival newspapers, the *Oklahoman* and *Tulsa World*, together with the Oklahoma Press Association, a commercial television station, a public radio station, and the journalism department at the University of Oklahoma created a partnership in 2010 to launch *Oklahoma Watch*. The investigative organization was funded by a local community foundation, the Knight Foundation, and the Ethics and Excellence in Journalism Foundation. The editor, a 35-year print veteran, said, "I haven't seen anything like this since I've been in journalism" (Rowe, 2011, p. 13). It was trust and the personal relationship between the editors of the two rival newspapers that made the cooperative venture possible.

In New Jersey, *NJ News Commons*, a project of the Center for Cooperative Media, is a network of outlets, including hyperlocal digital publishers, public media, nonprofits, television, radio, and newspaper organizations, that "work together on collaborative projects, share content, network and generally support one another" (Center for Cooperative Media, n.d.). Nonprofit centers also collaborated with other nonprofit organizations: *ProPublica* and the New Orleans-based nonprofit, the *Lens*, produced an online multimedia project about Louisiana's disappearing coastline (Marshall, Jacobs, & Shaw, 2014). The *Marshall Project* and *ProPublica* won a Pulitzer Prize for their joint reporting project about a failed police investigation into a rape (The Marshall Project, 2016).

These are a small sample of the collaborative partnerships that have formed despite the traditional fierce rivalry between news organizations. Now, partnerships are common between newspapers, television stations, public broadcasters, nonprofit organizations, and web-based news. Collaborating had become an economic necessity for commercial media (Anderson, Downie, & Schudson, 2016, p. 109).

Organizational partnerships also formed between public broadcasters and nonprofit investigative centers. The New England Center for Investigative Reporting merged with public television and radio broadcaster, WGBH News, in 2013 and moved its newsroom to the broadcaster's studios (DeLench, 2013). The *St Louis Beacon* in 2014 merged with St Louis Public Radio in what was described as a logical move given their shared journalistic missions. *inewsource* in San Diego partnered with and is located at KPBS public media and the Rocky Mountain PBS merged with the *I-News Network* (Schreibstein, 2014). The Center for Investigative Reporting produced documentaries for PBS from its earliest days and the Investigative Reporting Workshop had a *Frontline* producer located in its office at American University. The Center for Investigative Reporting through its platform, *Reveal*, and in partnership with PRX, produced public radio's first program dedicated to investigative reporting (Center for Investigative Reporting, 2013). These mergers and partnerships reflected the reality of diminished newsroom resources and a realization that a noncompetitive approach could increase the reach and impact of stories and provide greater financial stability for nonprofit organizations.

The International Consortium of Investigative Journalists (ICIJ)[1] manages projects that can involve hundreds of journalists around the globe from different media organizations researching and writing local versions of a story for their publications. The journalists work with editors based in Washington, DC and other consortium reporters then publish their stories in their publications. The consortium publishes the key findings on its website. The model depends on the organization successfully managing partner relationships and a willingness by participating journalists to put aside their competitive instincts and publish at the same time as other newsrooms. It affords the opportunity of maximum, at times, global impact. "A story can be published in 35 countries in a single day," the organization's director, Gerard Ryle, said (Pitt & Green-Barber, 2017).

The consortium's reports on secretive tax havens, known as the *Panama Papers* and the *Paradise Papers* – earlier reports covered similar issues[2] – demonstrate the benefits of the collaborative model. The *Panama Papers* leak of 11.5 million documents were analyzed discreetly over a 12-month period and reported by 107 media organizations in 80 countries. The documents revealed the offshore financial dealings of the world's richest and most powerful people and those who used such entities "to facilitate bribery, arms deals, tax evasion, financial fraud and drug trafficking" (International Consortium of Investigative Journalists, 2016). The *Paradise Papers* investigation involved 380 journalists from 95 media organizations across six continents assessing more than 13.5 million leaked records that exposed the offshore accounts of political, celebrity, and corporate entities wanting to hide assets or avoid taxes (International Consortium of Investigative Journalists, 2017).

The leaks from an anonymous source or sources in both cases were to reporters at the Germany-based *Süddeutsche Zeitung* newspaper who sought to collaborate with the international consortium due to the number of documents, their global contents, and the knowledge that the consortium had access to both the technical expertise to sort and make searchable huge numbers of differently formatted documents and a network of reporters around the world.

The model challenged traditional "lone wolf" investigative practices because the consortium invited reporters to join the wolf pack, according to its deputy director, and share their stories with hundreds of other reporters (John S. Knight Journalism Fellowships at Stanford, n.d.). For news organizations, such collaborations meant giving up some control over the story. For instance, the reporters' deadlines varied across the world and media organizations had to agree to cede decisions on publication schedules to the project managers. Reporters who accessed the consortium's database of leaked documents for the *Panama Papers* did not know who the source of the leak was. It was seen as risky for some traditional newspapers to let go of normal controls. "We say it's a controlled risk, everyone working in our investigations are people that are completely trusted and people we have worked with and we know their standards are incredibly high. But for an editor of a newspaper to understand or believe that can be challenging," the consortium's deputy director Marina Walker Guevara said (John S. Knight Journalism Fellowships at Stanford, n.d., min. 44).

A different collaborative model of global investigative reporting that focuses on crime and corruption in Eastern Europe, the Caucuses, Africa, Asia, and Latin America challenges several conventions at the heart of American journalistic practice. The Organized Crime and Corruption Reporting Project (OCCRP) is the trade name of the Washington, DC, registered nonprofit, the Journalism Development Network. Its editors work from places like Sarajevo in Bosnia; Bucharest in Romania; Tbilisi in Georgia, and Kiev in Ukraine. The project boasts that it is the largest producer of investigative content in the world, having published 90 stories in 2017 (D. Sullivan, personal communication, January 24, 2018).

Unlike US commercial and nonprofit journalists who strongly oppose government support, the Project is 50 percent funded by governments, mainly by the United States Agency for International Development, and it partners with advocacy groups such as Transparency International. Its revenue in 2015 was $2.6 million. The organization has about 65 staff and 40 media partners that it assists with cross-border investigations by providing editors, programmers, researchers, and resources such as enhanced online security and searchable databases: it's a kind of Uber of journalism according to cofounder Drew Sullivan (personal communication, January 24, 2018). The organization's secondary role is to train investigative journalists and build the capacity of nonprofit centers in developing countries where corruption is endemic and intractable. In late 2016, the OCCRP and Transparency International formed the Global Anti-Corruption Consortium, a venture funded by half a dozen governments and Open Society Foundations that aimed to maximize story impact by having investigators and change agents working more closely. The partners would collaborate by exchanging information, but the Project would continue to do its own independent journalism.

Sullivan acknowledged that government funding was controversial among US journalists but argued that there would be little or no investigative journalism in many of the regions OCCRP operated without such support.

> Squeaky clean ethics are the luxury of wealthy countries. When you are working in the real world where the government is corrupt, business is corrupt, everything is political, it's much more difficult to have an independent journalism industry. In fact, it doesn't exist in corrupt countries. Basically except for us, many of our partners are the only remaining investigative reporting that is going on in these countries. It's been shut down everywhere else.
>
> (Personal communication, January 24, 2018)

Working on stories with multiple media partners remained a big challenge:

> It's brutal. We're trying to develop tools that will make this process easier but dealing with so many needs in so many different organizations which publish in so many different formats and have so many different local audiences they are serving is an intractable problem.
>
> (D. Sullivan, personal communication, January 24, 2018)

The trend for collaborative networks of journalists and media wanting to undertake cross-border investigative projects appears likely to continue with similar, though smaller, organizations such as European Investigative Collaborations (European Investigative Collaborations, n.d.), Investigate Europe (Investigate Europe, n.d.), the Balkan Investigative Reporting Network (Balkan Investigative Reporting Network, n.d.), and others forming in recent years.

Accompanying the trend to story and organizational partnerships has been a cooperative spirit aimed at improving and spreading the practice of investigative journalism around the world. This has been led by the Global Investigative Journalism Network, an association of 155 nonprofit organizations in almost 70 countries (Global Investigative Journalism Network, n.d.). Founded in 2003, the network hosts regular conferences of nonprofit investigative journalists, conducts specialized training sessions, and provides resources and consultations. The network has facilitated investigative collaborations with both the ICIJ and the OCCRP holding news meetings on their projects while attending the global conferences (B. Houston, personal communication, July 3, 2018).

Collaborations and Outsourcing

One way of seeing collaborations between commercial media and nonprofits would be to frame them as an outsourcing of investigative journalism by commercial media (Birnbauer, 2012a, 2012b). While such a categorization may not be a comfortable one for legacy players, several reports referred to the trend as such. A Federal Communications Commission study found that commercial media had outsourced civically valuable journalism to the nonprofit sector, "creating a new bundle of sorts" (Waldman, 2011, p. 272). A *Washington Post* article noted that investigative reporting was "increasingly being outsourced" (Kurtz, 2010, para. 4). In 2012, the Berkeley Graduate School of Journalism's investigative reporting program produced a report for the Knight Foundation entitled "From outsourcing to innovation." The report explored ways of strengthening the partnerships between nonprofit and commercial media (University of California, 2012). A report for the Institute for Nonprofit News noted that news executives looking to cut costs were more likely to entertain solutions such as outsourcing and collaborations (Osder & Campwala, 2012, p. 14).

ProPublica's general manager Richard Tofel disagreed that what was happening was outsourcing. "I just don't think any of the editors or publishers that I know of are thinking about this in terms of outsourcing" (personal communication, November 17, 2010). Journalist and nonprofit center founder Charles Lewis said the mainstream media had stopped doing investigative journalism due to its cost and legal issues.

Increasingly over time, the most important public service journalism would be done by nonprofits.

> You could say cynically and perhaps correctly, did some suit, some green-eyeshade turkey in some high-rise in New York decide that we don't need to do that [investigative journalism] because others will do it and we will just quote it. You could make the case that maybe that's what happened but no one actually exactly knows, and it's a little conspiratorial in the way it comes across that way, like they all planned to do this. I think that they increasingly found it to be expensive and high risk and generally from a management standpoint a difficult proposition for lots of reasons we all understand.
>
> (Personal communication, November 8, 2010)

An appealing analogy was raised by the investigations editor of the *Washington Post*. Jeff Leen compared the collaborative paradigm to that of Hollywood film studios. Like legacy newspapers, film studios once controlled everything, employing writers, actors, producers, and designers. Now, studios still made movies but there was a thriving pool of independent producers who worked with the studios (Drew, 2010). That scenario in the journalistic sector would reflect the fact that many nonprofits distribute their major investigations to broader audiences via mainstream outlets. It is not unusual that the production of high quality, niche products or content is a separate process from the distribution of that material. Leen also recognized the importance of trust and relationships when he noted that he had a personal connection with journalists employed at nonprofit investigative centers, many of whom were his friends and deeply admired journalists who had lost their mainstream jobs (Drew, 2010).

The transformation of journalistic practice toward more collaborations was just one change furthered by the expansion of the nonprofit news sector. Another was that the traditional ideal of a separation of the journalism from the business of journalism was undone due to the need for senior nonprofit staff to act both as journalists and fundraisers. Despite the founders of nonprofit news organizations having long careers in the established media and values fashioned by years of newsroom socialization, the reality they faced was that when foundations and philanthropists considered major grants, they wanted to deal with the top newsroom executives. Having to raise money was a significant change for journalists, some of whom felt tainted or even corrupt at being involved in financial decisions (Briggs, 2012, p. 73). A delicate standoff often existed between the interests of funders and nonprofit news organizations. The next two chapters explore a fundamental change to the traditional practice of journalists standing back from involvement in the business side, and the agendas and motivations of the foundations that fund accountability journalism.

Notes

1 The author has been a member of the International Consortium of Investigative Journalists since 1998. He is on the organization's Network Committee.
2 See: Secrecy for sale: https://www.icij.org/investigations/offshore/; Swiss Leaks: https://www.icij.org/investigations/swiss-leaks/; Luxembourg Leaks: https://www.icij.org/investigations/luxembourg-leaks/; China Leaks: https://www.icij.org/investigations/zhong-guo-chi-jin-rong-jie-mi/.

Bibliography

Anderson, C. W., Downie, L., Jr., & Schudson, M. (2016). *The news media: What everyone needs to know*. New York, NY: Oxford University Press.

Balkan Investigative Reporting Network. (n.d.). News from BIRN. Retrieved from http://birn.eu.com/

BBC. (2009, November 26). Mumbai attacks: Key sites. *BBC News*. Retrieved from http://news.bbc.co.uk/2/hi/south_asia/7751876.stm

BBC. (2010, May 3). Deadlock over Pakistan's Mumbai suspects. *BBC News*. Retrieved from http://news.bbc.co.uk/2/hi/south_asia/8658038.stm

Birnbauer, B. (2011). Student muckrakers: Applying lessons from non-profit investigative reporting in the US. *Pacific Journalism Review, 17*(1), 26–44. doi:10.24135/pjr.v17i1.370

Birnbauer, B. (2012a). A bumpy road ahead for non-profit investigative journalism. Retrieved from JSK: John S. Journalism Fellowships at Stanford website: http://jsk.stanford.edu/news-notes/2012/a-bumpy-road-ahead-for-non-profit-investigative-journalism/

Birnbauer, B. (2012b). Charity case: Can philanthropic journalism last? Retrieved from The Conversation website: http://theconversation.com/charity-case-can-philanthropic-journalism-last-6163

Bourdieu, P. (1998). *Practical reason: On the theory of action*. Oxford, England: Polity Press.

Briggs, M. (2012). *Entrepreneurial journalism: How to build what's next for news*. Thousand Oaks, CA: CQ Press.

Center for Cooperative Media. (n.d.). NJ News Commons membership criteria, community guidelines and FAQs. Retrieved from https://centerforcooperativemedia.org/njnewscommons/

Center for Investigative Reporting. (2013). The Center for Investigative Reporting and PRX introduce "Reveal". Retrieved from http://www.centerforinvestigativereporting.org/news/center-investigative-reporting-and-prx-introduce-reveal

Dailey, L., Demo, L., & Spillman, M. (2005). The convergence continuum: A model for studying collaboration between media newsrooms. *Atlantic Journal of Communication, 13*(3), 150–168.

DeLench, H. (2013). New England Center for Investigative Reporting, WGBH partner to support investigative and enterprise journalism. Retrieved from New England Center for Investigative Reporting website: http://necir.org/2013/09/11/wgbh-announcement/

Downie, L., Jr., & Schudson, M. (2009, November/December). The reconstruction of American journalism. *Columbia Journalism Review*. Retrieved from http://www.cjr.org/reconstruction/the_reconstruction_of_american.php?page=all

Drew, J. (2010, May/June). The new investigators. *Columbia Journalism Review*. Retrieved from http://www.cjr.org/feature/the_new_investigators.php

Edmonds, R., & Mitchell, A. (2014). Journalism partnerships: A new era of interest. Retrieved from Pew Research Center website: http://www.journalism.org/2014/12/04/journalism-partnerships/

European Investigative Collaborations. (n.d.). Home. Retrieved from https://eic.network/

Fink, S. (2009). The deadly choices at memorial. Retrieved from ProPublica website: https://www.propublica.org/article/the-deadly-choices-at-memorial-826

Francisco, T., Lenhoff, A., & Schudson, M. (2012). The classroom as a newsroom: Leveraging university resources for public affairs reporting. *International Journal of Communication, 6*, 2677–2697.

Global Investigative Journalism Network. (n.d.). About us. Retrieved from http://gijn.org/about/about-us/

Graves, L., & Konieczna, M. (2015). Sharing the news: Journalistic collaboration as field repair. *International Journal of Communication, 9*, 1966–1984.

Hale, M. L., Riccardelli, J., & DeLuca, L. (2017). *Nonprofit investigative journalism conversations about impact and reach*. Paper presented at The 11th Annual Reva & David Logan Symposium on Investigative Reporting, Seton Hall University, South Orange, NJ. Retrieved from https://works.bepress.com/njpoliticsprof/49/

Hamilton, J. T. (2016). *Democracy's detectives: The economics of investigative journalism*. Boston, MA: Harvard University Press.

IBNLive. (2009, February 12). Accept charges made by India: Pak on 26/11. *IBNLive*. Retrieved from http://ibnlive.in.com/news/2611-dossier-pakistan-accepts-indias-blame/85145-2.html

Institute for Nonprofit News. (n.d.). About INN. Retrieved June 24, 2014, from http://inn.org/about/

International Consortium of Investigative Journalists. (2016). The Panama papers: Exposing the rogue offshore finance industry. Retrieved October 10, 2017, from https://panamapapers.icij.org/

International Consortium of Investigative Journalists. (2017). Paradise papers: Secrets of the global elite. Retrieved October 10, 2017, from https://www.icij.org/investigations/paradise-papers/

Investigate Europe. (n.d.). Home. Retrieved from http://www.investigate-europe.eu/en/

Jeffery, C. (2009, August). Cost of the NYT magazine NOLA story broken down. *Mother Jones*. Retrieved from http://www.motherjones.com/mojo/2009/08/cost-nyt-magazine-nola-story-broken-down

John S. Knight Journalism Fellowships at Stanford. (n.d.). Shining a new spotlight: Innovations in investigative reporting. Retrieved from http://jsk.stanford.edu/news-notes/2016/shining-a-new-spotlight-innovations-in-investigative-reporting/

Kaplan, A. D. (2008). *Investigating the investigators: Examining the attitudes, perceptions, and experiences of investigative journalists in the internet age* (Doctoral dissertation), University of Maryland, College Park, MD. Retrieved from http://hdl.handle.net/1903/8788

Kovach, B., & Rosenstiel, T. (2007). *The elements of journalism: What newspeople should know and the public should expect*. New York, NY: Three Rivers Press.

Kurtz, H. (2010, June 21). Increasingly, nonprofits fill a need for investigative reporting. *The Washington Post*. Retrieved from http://www.washingtonpost.com/wp-dyn/content/article/2010/06/20/AR2010062003163.html

Marshall, B., Jacobs, B., & Shaw, A. (Producer). (2014). *Losing ground* [Interactive map]. Retrieved from http://projects.propublica.org/louisiana/

Masood, S. (2009, February 12). Pakistan backtracks on link to Mumbai attacks. *The New York Times*. Retrieved from http://www.nytimes.com/2009/02/13/world/asia/13pstan.html?partner=permalink&exprod=permalink

O'Brien, K. (2016). Joining forces in the name of watchdog journalism. Retrieved from Nieman Reports website: http://niemanreports.org/articles/joining-forces/

Osder, E., & Campwala, K. (2012). Audience development and distribution strategies. Retrieved from Investigative News Network website: http://newstraining.org/guides/whitepaper-audience-development-and-distribution-strategies/prologue/

Picard, R. (2010). The future of the news industry. In J. Curran (Ed.), *Media and society* (pp. 365–379). London, England: Bloomsbury Academic.

Pitt, F., & Green-Barber, L. (2017). The case for media impact: A case study of ICIJ's radical collaboration strategy. Retrieved from Columbia Journalism Review website: https://www.cjr.org/tow_center_reports/the-case-for-media-impact.php

ProPublica. (2014). *ProPublica report to stakeholders*. Retrieved from https://s3.amazonaws.com/propublica/assets/about/propublica-2014-2nd-interim-report.pdf?_ga=1.187860653.488934625.1427193785

ProPublica. (n.d.-a). Law & Disorder: After Katrina, New Orleans police under scrutiny. Retrieved from https://www.propublica.org/series/law-and-disorder

ProPublica. (n.d.-b). Partners. Retrieved from https://www.propublica.org/partners/

Rosenstiel, T., Buzenberg, B., Connelly, M., & Loker, K. (2016). Charting new ground: The ethical terrain of nonprofit journalism. Retrieved from American Press Institute website: https://www.americanpressinstitute.org/publications/reports/nonprofit-news

Rosenthal, R. (2011). *Reinventing journalism: An unexpected personal journey from journalist to publisher*. Retrieved from the Center for Investigative Reporting website: http://www.knightfoundation.org/media/uploads/publication_pdfs/CIR_IndustryReport_FINAL.pdf

Rotella, S. (2010a, November 15). An intricate plot unleashed in Mumbai, the West confronts a new threat. *The Washington Post*. Retrieved from http://www.washingtonpost.com/wp-dyn/content/article/2010/11/14/AR2010111404515.html

Rotella, S. (2010b). The man behind Mumbai. Retrieved from ProPublica website: http://www.propublica.org/article/the-man-behind-mumbai

Rotella, S. (2010c). Mumbai: The plot unfolds, Lashkar strikes and investigators scramble. Retrieved from ProPublica website: http://www.propublica.org/article/mumbai-attacks-david-coleman-headley-part-2

Rotella, S. (2010d, November 14). On the trail of Pakistani terror group's elusive mastermind behind the Mumbai siege. *The Washington Post*. Retrieved from http://www.washingtonpost.com/wp-dyn/content/article/2010/11/13/AR2010111304907.html

Rowe, S. (2011, June). *Partners of necessity: The case for collaboration in local investigative reporting* (Discussion Paper Series #D-62). Retrieved from the Shorenstein Center on Media, Politics and Public Policy website: http://shorensteincenter.org/wp-content/uploads/2012/03/d62_rowe.pdf

Schreibstein, J. (2014). Better together: Nonprofit news organisations join forces in St. Louis. Retrieved from NPR website: http://www.npr.org/blogs/thisisnpr/2014/02/05/271629479/better-together-nonprofit-news-organizations-join-forces-in-st-louis

Schultz, I. (2007). The journalistic gut feeling: Journalistic doxa, news habitus and orthodox news values. *Journalism Practice, 1*(2), 190–207. doi:10.1080/17512780701275507

Sengupta, S. (2008, November 26). At least 100 dead in India terror attacks. *The New York Times*. Retrieved from http://www.nytimes.com/2008/11/27/world/asia/27mumbai.html?pagewanted=all&_r=3&

Stearns, J. (2012). Creating a taxonomy of news partnerships. Retrieved from Mediashift website: http://mediashift.org/2012/03/creating-a-taxonomy-of-news-partnerships-089

Steiger, P. (2015). Paul Steiger: Ten guiding principles for nonprofit investigative reporting teams. Retrieved from Netzwerk Recherche website: https://netzwerkrecherche.org/blog/paul-steiger-ten-guiding-principles-for-nonprofit-investigative-reporting-teams/

The Marshall Project. (2016). The Marshall Project wins a Pulitzer Prize: "An unbelievable story of rape" honored in the Explanatory Reporting category. Retrieved from https://www.themarshallproject.org/2016/04/18/the-marshall-project-wins-a-pulitzer-prize#.3JxoMqlEO

Thompson, A. C. (2008a). Body of evidence. Retrieved from ProPublica website: https://www.propublica.org/article/body-of-evidence

Thompson, A. C. (2008b). Post-Katrina, white vigilantes shot African-Americans with impunity. Retrieved from ProPublica website: https://www.propublica.org/article/post-katrina-white-vigilantes-shot-african-americans-with-impunity

University of California, Berkeley. (2012). *From outsourcing to innovation: How nonprofit/commercial media partnerships can help fill the news gap*. Retrieved from John S. and James L. Knight Foundation website: http://www.knightfoundation.org/media/uploads/article_pdfs/From_Outsourcing_to_Innovation_by_UCB_for_KF_1.pdf

Waldman, S. (2011). *The information needs of communities: The changing media landscape in a broadband age*. Retrieved from Federal Communications Commission website: http://www.fcc.gov/infoneedsreport

Washington Post. (2007). Welcome to Washington Post Investigations. Retrieved from http://voices.washingtonpost.com/washingtonpostinvestigations/2007/11/welcome_to_washington_post_inv_2.html

Washington Post Staff. (2011, July 15). Meet the reporters. *The Washington Post*. Retrieved from http://voices.washingtonpost.com/washingtonpostinvestigations/investigative-team-meet-the-re.html

3 Crashing through the Firewall

As newsrooms cut thousands of journalists during the global financial crisis, Amy Dominguez-Arms became increasingly concerned about the diminishing capacity of commercial media to undertake serious journalism. As director of the James Irvine Foundation's California Democracy program, she viewed the media's demise in the context of her program's aim of improving political decisions by making them more open, transparent, inclusive, and accountable.

Dominguez-Arms met several senior media executives who shared her concerns but were unable to offer any solutions (A. Dominguez-Arms, personal communication, January 1, 2012). A colleague suggested she talk to Robert Rosenthal, then recently appointed as executive director of the Center for Investigative Reporting. Rosenthal's reputation as a journalist and editor drew her attention immediately. "He was very clear on what a strategy might be, and we had the sense that he had both the relationships in the fields, the credibility in the field, and the leadership skills to carry it out" (personal communication, January 1, 2012). The timing was fortuitous because Rosenthal wanted to expand the center's coverage of issues in its home state of California. Shortly after the meeting, the James Irvine Foundation donated a larger than average grant of almost $2 million to the Center for Investigative Reporting to fund the launch and operation of *California Watch*, a state-focused investigative site.

The credibility and professional reputations of nonprofit editors are significant factors when foundation program directors consider making grants. Journalistic capital in most cases was earned through years of reporting, editing, or managing in the commercial media sector.

However, the journalists who shifted to the nonprofit sector found that journalistic credibility alone was not enough to run an investigative news center.

The books on the shelves in Rosenthal's office reflect his changed responsibilities since leaving a long career in legacy newspapers. Rosenthal, a former award-winning foreign correspondent, was the executive editor of the *Philadelphia Inquirer* between 1998 and 2001 when it had 630 staff and an annual budget of $75 million. In 2002, he became the managing editor of the *San Francisco Chronicle*, a position he held for five years. As executive director of the Center for Investigative Reporting, one of his key responsibilities was raising enough money for the center to survive. His reading is testament to this: *How to Write Successful Fundraising Letters, Guide to Proposal Writing, The Non-profit Sector, and Conducting a Successful Fundraising Program.*

When Rosenthal moved to the Center for Investigative Reporting in 2008, it had seven staff and a budget of $1 million, most of which was committed to a documentary project (R. Rosenthal, personal communication, November 3, 2010). Within four years, the center had increased its budget to $11.5 million and had 70 staff. The rapid expansion followed a merger with a local nonprofit news site, the *Bay Citizen*, and the launch of *California Watch*.

Despite the extraordinary growth, financial stability remained elusive and management issues reduced Rosenthal's involvement in the center's journalism projects. He felt the pressure of having to find money to keep staff employed and the organization functioning. "I have to bring in the money, and the money in our model, 95 percent plus... comes from foundations, and the foundations want to all deal with me" (personal communication, November 3, 2012). The contrast with his former role as a newspaper editor was telling: as a newspaperman he "never had to worry about raising a dime" (Rosenthal, 2011, p. 1).

Rosenthal's frustration at having to spend much of his time fundraising and managing the organization was echoed by other nonprofit editors. As head of the Center for Public Integrity, Bill Buzenberg estimated that he pitched to almost 90 foundations annually for funding: "There is no other way to do it" (personal communication, February 8, 2012). Buzenberg had to cut staff and claw back a significant deficit in 2010. The board was not happy with him. Legacy journalists moved to the nonprofit sector wanting to do investigative stories

> and then they realize it is running a small company and is trying to raise money for a small company and many are shocked that there is an awful lot of work involved in that that is not investigative journalism.
> (B. Buzenberg, personal communication, February 8, 2012)

Bill Keller spent eight years as executive editor of the *New York Times* where it was his responsibility to obtain the resources needed for new and ongoing projects. When he moved to a nonprofit focused on criminal justice, his responsibilities were no different.

> It's less complicated getting into the elevator and going to the publisher's office and telling him, 'we need X dollars for this particular new thing we want to do', but it's the same basic principle. If you

feel it's important and you believe in it then you can't be squeamish about asking people to pay for it.

(Personal communication, April 25, 2018)

However, most journalists have not had to deal with advertisers or worry about editorial budgets. In fact, they have worked "exceptionally hard to maintain a strong boundary against commercial influence, making it a core element of their professional values" (Coddington, 2015). An uneasy relationship has existed between the news and business divisions of for-profit media companies for over a century. Journalism may be a "cultural enterprise lodged inside a business enterprise" (Daly, 2012, p. ix), but the public service values of journalists often clashed with those of publishers and media proprietors, particularly in the 1980s and 1990s when market forces rationalized newspaper ownership and the demand for greater profits became more urgent. These episodes typically manifested in conflicts over sponsored stories, advertising sections that looked like news pages, and pressure on editors to run particular stories. In response to these, journalists established independence committees, codes of ethics and charters that sought to maintain a firewall between editorial decision-making and management's business operations (Chadwick, 1991). So imperative was this boundary that a physical and symbolic separation between editorial and business historically existed with them working on different floors of the same building; the *Chicago Tribune* once had separate elevators for journalists and business staff (Coddington, 2015). This "church and state" divide has long been seen by journalists as "the cornerstone upholding American journalism's sense of autonomy" (Coddington, 2015).

Nonprofit news organizations were founded and run by journalists with many years of socialization in commercial newsroom culture. A few nonprofit journalists were in senior management positions in large media companies and had experience in negotiating with publishers and business managers. Many others, however, were investigative or beat reporters who never had to worry about business issues. As they moved to nonprofit organizations, the "wall" between journalism and business by necessity gave way. Somewhat surprisingly, it did so with barely a whimper. This represented a transformation of journalistic practice, or at least was further evidence that cultural and professional practices in journalism could be influenced and determined by external forces.

Nonprofit editors asserted that they acted like a firewall by insisting that foundations and board members would have no influence over stories, their reporters would not talk to funders, and that specific project funding would not guarantee a story outcome. At the same time, however, their roles as journalists had changed dramatically: they had partnered with wealthy benefactors and found themselves spending increasing amounts of time pitching to funders.

The pressure on nonprofits to locate new sources of revenue was evident in the findings of two surveys: an analysis in 2012 of nonprofit news publishers found that the operating budgets of 26 organizations had remained the same and had decreased in eight others over the previous two years (Lewis, Butts, & Musselwhite, 2012). More than half of the 60 nonprofit centers examined had been unable to attract additional funding. At least 10 of the organizations had annual budgets of less than $100,000 and four had just one or two employees. Another survey found that two-thirds of the 172 nonprofit news organizations that responded said they were created with a startup grant that had accounted for at least one-third of their funding. But fewer than 30 percent of those original grants were renewed to any degree. There was a "near-constant need to replenish expiring grants and drum up new sources of funding" (Mitchell, Jurkowitz, Holcomb, Enda, & Anderson, 2013, p. 11).

For the journalists, the transfer from a mainstream to a nonprofit environment was a move from a commercial pole of cultural production to what they believed would be a relatively more autonomous one in which mass markets and profit-making were less important (Bourdieu, 1983). A place where they could focus on the journalism, or so they may have believed. The editors found they were not completely autonomous in the sense of producing investigative journalism for investigative journalism's sake.[1] Apart from pitching to foundations, nonprofit editors had to create new revenue streams, locate and pay for office accommodation, find pro bono lawyers, manage salaries and staff entitlements, deal with banking, taxation, and insurance issues, and a myriad other administrative tasks. As they began to look more like publishers than reporters, those who could afford it hired editors to run journalistic projects and publishers or professional fundraisers to assist them in finding new money. Many had started trying to do both the business and editorial jobs before realizing they could not manage the two roles. Smaller nonprofit organizations could not afford to split the roles and journalists had to both raise money and do the journalism, even though they were less comfortable on the business side.

Robert Rosenthal continued to be frustrated that he still had to convince foundations to fund the Center for Investigative Reporting despite its numerous successes:

> The hardest thing for me is pulling on my boots in the morning and saying 'geez I have to go out and raise money'... don't these people know we can do it; just give us the money. Honestly, I don't have the time I'd like to be more involved in editorial.
>
> (Personal communication, November 3, 2010)

Founder of California-based *FairWarning*, Myron Levin, a former re-porter on the *Los Angeles Times* and several other newspapers, had never raised money before creating the nonprofit organization.

> It's been hard because I didn't do as good a job of it than even I could have with my lack of experience because I'm also running the edi-torial side, doing some of the reporting, almost all of the assigning, doing some of the editing ... everything got done in a mediocre way.
> (Personal communication, April 9, 2018)

The editor-in-chief of *NJ Spotlight* left most of the fundraising to the organization's CEO, but still devoted between 5 and 10 percent of her time meeting foundation directors (L. Keough, personal communica-tion, April 26, 2018). Executive director and editor of the *San Francisco Public Press* spent half his time fundraising (M. Stoll, personal commu-nication, April 16, 2018).

For nonprofit journalists, the challenge was to gain new skills that would enable them to deal with administrative and financial tasks, and conceive projects that would capture the attention of potential funders. They had to revise some of the attitudes that were ingrained during their time in newspapers and broadcast media. Business theorists describe for-mational myopia as a condition that occurs when previous knowledge, experience, and practice influence new activities in ways that limit in-novation and change (Naldi & Picard, 2012). Professor Robert Picard, a leading media economist, found that journalists who established new enterprises often were content to have little say on strategy or business matters (Picard, 2010). This attitude made it impossible to create sus-tainable news organizations.

Some journalists were frustrated by their lack of business training (Nee, 2013) and found fundraising to be distasteful and ethically ques-tionable. Former Pulitzer Prize-winning investigative reporter on the *Philadelphia Inquirer* Rick Tulsky was the managing editor of the Cen-ter for Investigative Reporting in the early 1990s. He felt uneasy about asking for money: "I couldn't get it out of my head that it felt like, at the *Philadelphia Inquirer*, going to a car dealer and saying, 'What stories would you support?' Which, we'd never do" (Enda, 2012, para. 54). Even Charles Lewis, who raised almost $40 million from foundations and had close relationships with program directors, acknowledged that pitching for funding was not a pleasant thing to do (Enda, 2012).

The challenge faced by former legacy journalists in having to raise funds was recognized by one of the biggest foundations supporting jour-nalism, the Knight Foundation. A director of its media innovation unit noted that "for better or for worse... they are journalists and that's what they do, they are not startup guys" (J. Bracken, personal communica-tion, February 17, 2012).

Journalistic Capital and Funders

Journalists may not be "startup guys," but foundation program directors turned to respected senior journalists for advice on areas of need and established trusting relationships with them.

Philanthropic foundation program directors operate in a manner that is not dissimilar to that of journalists: they develop contacts, research the field, and are drawn to those with high industry reputations. The Rockefeller Brothers Fund was founded in 1940 with a mission of advancing "social change that contributes to a more just, sustainable and peaceful world" (Rockefeller Brothers Fund, 2007). When he was exploring how accountability reporting might be strengthened, the foundation's Democratic Practice program director turned to senior nonprofit journalists Charles Lewis and Bill Buzenberg for advice rather than commissioning an outside report (B. Shute, personal communication, February 13, 2013). The director attended a symposium with Lewis and continued to build connections in an effort to gain a better understanding of how best to support investigative reporting ventures. His foundation made available its Pocantico conference venue, north of Manhattan, to a meeting of 27 nonprofit investigative groups that created the Investigative News Network (now the Institute for Nonprofit News). Soon after, the Rockefeller Brothers Fund provided general support to Lewis's Investigative Reporting Workshop, Buzenberg's Center for Public Integrity, and the Center for Investigative Reporting. "Some people say you find the stars and you back them. Well, that is some of what we do, but you also want to make sure that the stars are operating with some substance behind them" the director said (B. Shute, personal communication, February 13, 2013).

When the executive director of the Chicago-based Richard H. Driehaus Foundation sought to expand the foundation's customary funding of the arts, built environment, and open space causes to journalism, she began by talking to other funders and senior nonprofit reporters. "We asked other people in philanthropy, we ask other people in the field. It's a little bit like doing an investigative report. I talked to Bill Buzenberg ..." [then executive director of the Center for Public Integrity] (S. Fischer, personal communication, February 16, 2012).

The Chicago-based MacArthur Foundation grants millions of dollars each year to accountability news organizations. A former vice president of Media, Culture, and Special Initiatives said the foundation came to know many of the journalists who had started national nonprofit investigative reporting organizations and were enthusiastic about their vision, skills, and plans to fill gaps in the information landscape.

> We look to them as experts in the field and learn from their experience. Because we respect their judgement, we are receptive to hearing about other good work and visionary leaders from them. As long

as their organizations continued to be strong, and the foundation strategies persisted, there was a match that led to continued funding. (E. Revere, personal communication, April 24, 2018)

The nonprofit news sector is a fraction of the size of the commercial sector; yet, in a journalistic environment shaped by massive economic and technological forces, it has accelerated the trend to collaborations between the sectors and has further eroded the firewall between news and business. Nonprofit journalists maintain that they, in fact, *are* the firewall, protecting the integrity of the journalism from funder influence. That may be the case for now. A question that cannot be answered is: will future nonprofit leaders, perhaps unfamiliar with the notion of a "church-state" division, hold the line?

Note

1 See Pierre Bourdieu's "art for art's sake" comment (Bourdieu, 1983, pp. 318, 321).

Bibliography

Bourdieu, P. (1983). The field of cultural production, or: The economic world reversed. *Poetics, 12*(4–5), 311–356. doi:10.1016/0304-422X(83)90012-8

Chadwick, P. (1991). *Charters of editorial independence: An information paper.* Kensington, Australia: Communications Law Centre.

Coddington, M. (2015). The wall becomes a curtain: Revisiting journalism's news–business boundary. In M. Carlson & S. C. Lewis (Eds.), *Boundaries of journalism: Professionalism, practices, and participation* (pp. 67–82). New York, NY: Routledge.

Daly, C. (2012). *Covering America: A narrative history of a nation's journalism.* Amherst: University of Massachusetts Press.

Enda, J. (2012, August/September). Staying alive. *American Journalism Review.* Retrieved from http://www.ajr.org/article.asp?id=5389

Lewis, C., Butts, B., & Musselwhite, K. (2012). A second look: The new journalism ecosystem. Retrieved from Investigative Reporting Workshop website: http://investigativereportingworkshop.org/ilab/story/second-look/

Mitchell, A., Jurkowitz, M., Holcomb, J., Enda, J., & Anderson, M. (2013). Nonprofit journalism: A growing but fragile part of the US news system. Retrieved from Pew Research Center website: http://www.journalism.org/analysis_report/nonprofit_journalism

Naldi, L., & Picard, R. (2012). "Let's start an online news site": Opportunities, resources, strategy and formational myopia in startups. *Journal of Media Business Studies, 9*(4), 69–97. doi:10.1080/16522354.2012.11073556

Nee, R. C. (2013). Creative destruction: An exploratory study of how digitally native news nonprofits are innovating online journalism practices. *International Journal on Media Management, 15*(1), 3–22. doi:10.1080/14241277.2012.732153

Picard, R. (2010). A church-state trap. *Editor & Publisher, 143*(2), 42.
Rockefeller Brothers Fund. (2007). Program statement. Retrieved from http://www.rbf.org/programs/program-statement
Rosenthal, R. (2011). *Reinventing journalism: An unexpected personal journey from journalist to publisher.* Retrieved from the Center for Investigative Reporting website: http://www.knightfoundation.org/media/uploads/publication_pdfs/CIR_IndustryReport_FINAL.pdf

4 Saving Journalism and Democracy during the Financial Crisis

Alarm that fewer investigative journalists were employed to expose the hidden activities of governments and corporate America motivated foundations and wealthy individuals to look at alternative models for making these powerful institutions accountable. They believed there was a crisis for democracy due to the faltering state of the mainstream media and that their donations to nonprofit journalism organizations would help fill gaps in national, state, and local accountability reporting.

The 2007–2009 financial crisis had four impacts relevant to the expansion of the nonprofit sector. First, it slashed the advertising revenues of newspapers and broadcasters and resulted in their stock prices falling dramatically. Second, newspaper closures and cuts created a pool of thousands of journalists who had been laid off by print and broadcast media; some of these reporters moved to the nonprofit sector. Third, the severe economic downturn led to publicly expressed concern by nonprofit advocates, journalists, and scholars that legacy media were less able to hold power to account; and fourth, some foundations and wealthy benefactors accepted that democracy was at risk and donated to nonprofit news organizations. Figure 4.1 depicts nonprofit news organizations as a subfield of the much bigger field of journalism. Foundations and wealthy individuals, acting as an economic field, directly supported organizations within the nonprofit subfield due to alarm over the crisis.

Nonprofit centers published on their own websites and their stories often also ran in commercial, public, or niche media. Such partnerships enabled nonprofit centers, particularly those producing investigative content, to use the mainstream media as a distribution platform for their work. This increased the impact of nonprofit stories, and encouraged foundations to renew their funding. Figure 4.1 also shows that journalists who lost their jobs moved to fields outside of journalism, to nonprofit news organizations, or to other media.

Most of the alarm expressed by journalists, academics, foundations, and advocacy groups centered on what was perceived to be a reduction of investigative journalism in the print media. While there was growing concern also about local and regional news, investigative journalism's

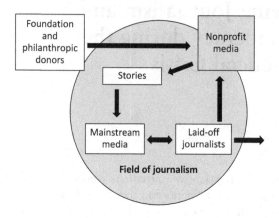

Figure 4.1 How the economic, journalism, and nonprofit fields interrelate.

status as democracy enhancing and as the pinnacle of journalistic practice made it the focus of alarm. Its inevitable demise became the conventional wisdom and that, in turn, acted as an accelerant in funding for the creation of nonprofit news organizations. Analysis of the membership of the Institute for Nonprofit News shows that 40 of its member organizations launched in 2009 and 2010 – by far the greatest period of startup activity in the sector.

Valid reasons existed for concern about the future of accountability journalism. Thousands of legacy journalists, including many older experienced reporters, lost their jobs as a direct result of the financial crisis and its impact on advertising revenues. Prominent newspapers filed for bankruptcy protection, closed or dropped their print versions in favor of online sites with fewer staff and without the cost burden of printing presses and delivery systems (Anderson, Bell, & Shirky, 2012; Downie & Schudson, 2009; Edmonds, 2009; McIntyre, 2009). The revenue problems followed a series of financial and technological assaults that had disrupted the century-old business model of journalism. The ubiquity and price advantage of the internet had opened the door to entrepreneurs who moved quickly to create popular alternative advertising sites such as Craigslist.org. Cost cutting by acquisitive media corporations chasing higher profit margins had slashed editorial budgets. Readership of newspapers was in free fall. Weekday print circulation at America's top 25 newspapers fell 41.6 percent between 2005 and 2013, a drop from 15.1 million papers on an average weekday to 8.8 million (Brock, 2013, p. 140; Newsosaur, 2013). The combined impact was less revenue for legacy media, fewer journalists, fewer stories, and uncertainty about the future (Anderson et al., 2012; Downie & Schudson, 2009; Edmonds, 2009; McIntyre, 2009). Journalists had lamented a decline in investigative journalism since the heady 1970s Watergate era, and now it seemed beyond doubt to others too.

Concern about the demise of investigative reporting was driven by nonprofit investigative journalists, nonprofit news organizations, left-leaning scholars, and articles in journalistic establishment publications such as *American Journalism Review, Columbia Journalism Review,* and *Nieman Reports* (Cullinan, 2009; Frank, 2009; Houston, 2010; McChesney & Nichols, 2010; Walton, 2010). Despite the concern and the potential ramifications of the federal republic's democracy being eroded, no authoritative survey documenting the number of investigative reporters who had lost their jobs as a result of the financial crisis could be found. To determine if there was a crisis for investigative reporting in the United States – this after all motivated foundations and wealthy people to donate hundreds of millions of dollars to the nonprofit sector – a closer examination of the contentions made at the time is required.

The Financial Crisis, 2007–2009

The roof collapsed on the US economy in the middle of 2008 with gross domestic product declining rapidly and 600,000 Americans losing their jobs each month (Bailey & Elliott, 2009, p. 7). The reasons for the worst financial crisis since the Great Depression were complex but started with falls in the value of structured securities built on unrealistically high real estate collateral, leading to a liquidity crisis and bankruptcies for a number of key financial institutions (Bailey & Elliott, 2009). Because the excesses and failures were at the core of the US banking system, the crisis was transmitted to all sectors and countries of the global economy. The International Monetary Fund reported that output per capita was projected to decline in three-quarters of the global economy (International Monetary Fund, 2009). In the United States, home construction plunged 38 percent in the first quarter of 2009 at an annualized rate and households lost $13 trillion in wealth mostly from equities and home prices (Bailey & Elliott, 2009).

The drop in economic activity led to a severe slump in media advertising, which resulted in news organizations cutting full-time daily newspaper journalists by 40 percent between 2007 and 2015 (American Society of News Editors, 2016). Those jobs were not recovered. Figure 4.2 shows that in 2015, there were fewer than 33,000 editors, reporters, writers, photographers, videographers, artists, and editorial production staff compared with 55,045 in 2007, according to the American Society of News Editors (2016).[1] That was a loss of 22,170 newsroom jobs.

The focus of this chapter is on newspapers rather than television or radio because newspapers produced most of the complex and important investigative reporting. Newspapers were hit hardest of all the media because their fixed cost structures included the essential items they

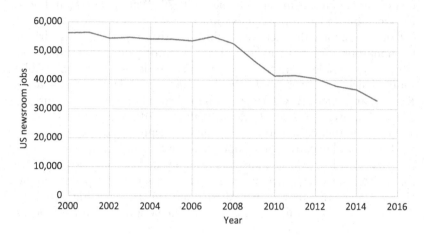

Figure 4.2 Journalism jobs did not recover after the financial crisis.
Source: American Society of News Editors. (2016). Table L – Employment of men and women by job category. Retrieved October 10, 2017, from http://asne.org/content.asp?pl=140&sl=144&contentid=144.

needed for publishing each day: printing presses, stocks of paper, and distribution networks. Journalists constituted about 50 percent of segment costs, and were one of the few areas where cuts could easily be made (Fine, 2009). Newspapers owned by media conglomerates and publicly listed companies were in a particularly precarious financial situation. Chains such as the McClatchy and Gannett companies and the New York Times Company had borrowed heavily in the 1980s and 1990s to purchase assets in the expectation that the good times would continue. In 1986, the 15 largest US newspaper groups also owned 173 non-daily newspapers, 71 television stations, 67 radio stations, more than 295 cable systems, more than 133 magazines, and 16 book companies (Lacy & Simon, 1993, p. 133). Bloated by huge growth in advertising revenues and limited competition, newspapers were extraordinarily wealthy and could add journalists, open bureaus, and make great profits (Picard, 2013). As advertisers moved to the internet and stock values plunged in the financial crisis, equity diminished increasing the costs of borrowed capital and creating severe financial problems for the companies including applications for bankruptcy protection by the Tribune and Journal Register groups (Picard, 2010). At the height of the takeover boom, the value of a share in the giant Time Warner Company hit an all-time high of $254. Ten years later in 2009, that share was worth just $25 (Daly, 2013).

One media analyst noted that the media's obsession with itself was evident from the massive coverage the layoffs and other negative news received despite the fact that such cuts had occurred in every other industry (Fine, 2009, p. 11). Adding to a sense that a low watermark had been reached in print journalism, in March 2009, *Time* magazine published a story headlined, "The 10 most endangered newspapers in America." It said that the owners of the *Philadelphia Inquirer* had filed for bankruptcy, as had the Journal Register chain; the *Rocky Mountain News* had closed and the *Seattle Post-Intelligencer* would "almost certainly close" [it closed its print version to go fully online] (McIntyre, 2009, para. 1). Leftist media critics Robert McChesney and John Nichols warned that newspapers were in crisis and "may soon become extinct" (McChesney & Nichols, 2010, p. 11). Journalism professor Philip Meyer predicted that "the endgame for newspapers is in sight" (Meyer, 2008, para. 1). *The Atlantic*'s contributing editor Michael Hirschorn said that the former *New York Times* editor Abe Rosenthal had commented that he couldn't imagine a world without the *New York Times* but "perhaps we should start" (Hirschorn, 2009, para. 5).

The prospects for newspapers looked grim: the *Chicago Tribune,* the *Los Angeles Times,* the *Minneapolis Star Tribune,* and the *Philadelphia Inquirer* had filed for bankruptcy protection; the *Rocky Mountain News* had closed; the *San Francisco Chronicle* was losing $1 million a week; and the *New York Times* was threatening to close the *Boston Globe.* The *New York Times,* facing an expiry on a $400 million line of credit, entered an arrangement with Mexican billionaire Carlos Slim, who provided the *Times* with $250 million. The deal, which proved highly profitable for Slim, enabled the newspaper to sell assets such as the *Boston Globe* and enhance its digital subscription strategy (Lee, 2014). Other newspapers faced similar fates and slashed staff, bureaus, and budgets. The *Washington Post* reduced its newsroom from 900 reporters to fewer than 550 (Lewis, 2013). The *Post*'s newspaper division recorded operating losses three years running from 2009, including a $53.7 million loss in 2012 (O'Malley, 2013).

Newspapers struggled to recover after the recession. The 2011 Pew State of the Media report found that as a result of the bankruptcies, seven out of America's top 25 newspapers fell under private equity control (Edmonds, Guskin, & Rosenstiel, 2011). The problem with such ownership was that institutional investors often had goals that were inimical to the journalistic mission. These financial rearrangements rocked a field that had become dependent on revenue from advertising and had seen little need to innovate despite long-term circulation declines and the threat to its revenue base from new digital platforms.

The Crisis Argument

That investigative reporters would be targeted in newsroom cost cutting would make sense if costs and productivity were the only criteria used by editorial managers – and if journalistic culture were pushed aside.

Investigative projects that can take months or years to research may not produce anything more than one or two stories that fail to attract reader, political, or other media attention. Even if public policy were to change as a result of an investigative story, news companies knew they could not fully monetize the positive benefits that flowed to the community (Hamilton, 2016, p. 111). Further risks for news outlets were potentially expensive and distracting litigation by people identified in the stories and complaints to media proprietors and others. Furthermore, publishers perceived that the public was tired of investigative exposés with polls showing that most readers felt newspapers carried too much bad news (Aucoin, 2005, p. 113).

These negatives suggest that powerful reasons would have to exist for investigative reporting to survive in a cost-cutting environment. The argument that mainstream media could no longer uphold a Fourth Estate role was easily made and was made consistently on the websites of newly formed nonprofit journalism centers as a raison d'être for their own existence.

For example, *ProPublica*'s website said that investigative journalism was at risk because many news organizations saw it as a luxury. Investigative reporters lacked resources and beat reporters were inhibited from doing such reporting by time and budget constraints (ProPublica, n.d.). *Investigate West*, a nonprofit site based on America's Pacific Northwest region, said that along with thousands of reporting jobs having vanished, so had in-depth, investigative reporting (Investigate West, n.d.). *Eye on Ohio* said it was well documented that investigative journalism had been under siege for many years and that competition from digital news outlets and pressure to boost profits meant reduced staff and resources for in-depth stories (Eye on Ohio, n.d.). Pennsylvania-based *PublicSource* noted that traditional news organizations provided staff little time to delve deeply into important subjects (PublicSource, 2013). The Maine Center for Public Interest Reporting's publication, *Pine Tree Watchdog*, told readers that most local newspaper and broadcast outlets had reduced their staff and that one of the first victims was in-depth journalism (Pine Tree Watchdog, n.d.). The Investigative Reporting Workshop, founded by veteran nonprofit editor Charles Lewis, said that in a drive to cut costs and maintain profits, traditional media had "slashed the capacity to do investigative journalism" (Investigative Reporting Workshop, 2013, para. 2). In Boston, the directors of the New England Center for Investigative Reporting, Joe Bergantino and Maggie Mulvihill, wrote that investigative reporting had been eviscerated and that the *Boston Globe* was "clinging to life" (Bergantino & Mulvihill, 2009, para. 1).[2]

Charles Lewis has been a high-profile advocate for nonprofit investigative journalism at conferences around the globe since the early 1990s.[3] He founded the Center for Public Integrity in 1989, and by 2004 had raised $30 million in foundation funding for the center's work. He later created the International Consortium of Investigative Journalists.[4] He was the founding executive editor of an umbrella association for non-profit organizations, the Investigative News Network [now the Institute for Nonprofit News] and was a professor of journalism at American University where he established the Investigative Reporting Workshop. He has been described as the godfather of nonprofit investigative journalism (Glaser, 2008). Lewis had the ear and trust of foundations that were the biggest supporters of journalism and his views were influential with funders. In a lengthy study for the Shorenstein Center on Media, Politics and Public Policy (previously known as the Joan Shorenstein Center on the Press, Politics and Public Policy), Lewis wrote that media managers had come to see investigative reporting as time consuming and expensive – as "vainglorious indulgences: high risk, high maintenance, high priced impracticalities" (Lewis, 2007, p. 3). Lewis told me he had no doubt that investigative journalism had been adversely affected by the financial crisis, with many of the most experienced reporters losing their jobs.

> I think that was an economic decision: 'Joe Shmoe has only done three stories last year, they happen to be gems, they happen to be on page one, but we need more than three stories from one human being – out'. It's heartbreaking, centuries and centuries of experience went right out the door.
> (C. Lewis, personal communication, November 8, 2010)

As the executive editor at the *Philadelphia Inquirer* and later the *San Francisco Chronicle* for a total of eight years until 2007, Robert Rosenthal grew increasingly disenchanted and frustrated with budget cuts and the drive for profits, which he felt conflicted with high-quality journalism. He moved to the nonprofit sector in 2008 [see previous chapter and Chapter 7]. Rosenthal believed most newsroom cutbacks were not aimed at maintaining profits but increasing them at the expense of good journalism. "Investigative reporting is something that's being shoved aside in newsrooms that really sort of have to feed the beast" (PBS Newshour, 2009, para. 8).

The proposition that investigative journalism was the first area to be cut or that it was an inevitable victim of cost cutting was maintained by former senior journalists, information technology leaders, and scholars (Frank, 2009; Nichols & McChesney, 2009; Osder & Campwala, 2012; Riptide, 2013; Westphal, 2009). Philanthropic foundation directors – particularly those with responsibility for media or democracy programs – also believed it [see next chapter]. In a 2011 article that was a finalist in awards for media industry reporting judged by journalists and journalism educators (Mirror Awards, 2011), veteran reporter and author Mary Walton wrote:

> Kicked out, bought out or barely hanging on, investigative reporters are a vanishing species in the forests of dead tree media and missing in action on Action News. I-Teams are shrinking or, more often, disappearing altogether. Assigned to cover multiple beats, multitasking backpacking reporters no longer have time to sniff out hidden stories, much less write them.
>
> (Walton, 2010, para. 6)

Walton quoted the then executive director of Investigative Reporters and Editors, a membership organization for investigative reporters, as saying there was no question that there were fewer investigative reporters than a few years earlier. Membership of Investigative Reporters and Editors in 2009 was at a 10-year low of 3,695,[5] 30 percent fewer members than in 2003. Walton conceded, however, that membership grew to more than 4,000 in 2010 due to what she said was a "vigorous membership drive" (Walton, 2010).

As evidence of newspapers abandoning the genre, Walton noted a drop in the number of entries for investigative categories of the Pulitzer Prize: between 1985 and 2010, entries in the Investigative Reporting category had declined by 21 percent, from 103 to 81; in the Public Service category, the drop was even greater: 43 percent, from 122 to 70.

Other commentators observed that investigative reporters who had survived the cutbacks worked in newsrooms with fewer resources and were often pressed to fill the gaps in daily reporting (B. Houston, personal communication, November 19, 2010). Surviving newsroom reporters operated like wire service reporters of the 1930s, "scurrying on what the *Columbia Journalism Review* calls 'the hamster wheel' to produce each day's quota of increasingly superficial stories. They can describe the landscape, but they have less time to turn over rocks" (Waldman, 2011, p. 13). Media commentators worried about the survival of serious journalism in the United States (Frank, 2009). One found there was a "striking decline in costly (though essential) journalistic practices such as investigative reporting" (Scott, 2005, p. 90). Investigative reporting was "singularly threatened" (Westphal, 2009, p. 2).

Many years after the recession, the general belief that investigative reporting had waned and that there were fewer investigative journalists remained unchanged. *ProPublica*'s president Richard Tofel is in regular contact with editors across the United States. "Everybody says, 'I have cut it back. We used to have X and we now have Y'" (personal communication, April 24, 2018). Monika Bauerlein, CEO of *Mother Jones*: "The capacity of local news organizations to do serious investigative reporting has declined dramatically. There's absolutely no question about that" (personal communication, April 12, 2018). Sue Cross from the Institute for Nonprofit News said as a compulsive news consumer she knew that there had been a drastic reduction of accountability reporting at state level and that investigative reporter numbers had been cut (personal communication, April 11, 2018).

The State of Investigative Reporting

Quantifying the number of investigative reporters in the United States in any given period is complicated by definitional issues. General and beat reporters sometimes do investigative stories. There are reports produced by journalists and researchers at NGOs such as Human Rights Watch, Global Witness, and Greenpeace that are deeply researched, read like investigations and could be said to be in the public interest. There are expert individuals who produce similar material. Then, there is the question of whether investigative journalism is a distinct genre or whether all journalism should be investigative in character (Aucoin, 2005, p. 85; Bennett & Serrin, 2005; Lanosga, Willnat, Weaver, & Houston, 2015; MacDougall & Reid, 1987; Protess et al., 1991, p. 4). My opinion based on decades of experience as a journalist and academic is that investigative reporting is a distinct genre and it is treated as such in this chapter. It is more complex and original than breaking news or beat journalism, it takes longer, it upsets people, it questions official versions and assertions, it has greater impact, and it is more demanding of official responses. It has an energy, urgency, and force that daily journalism lacks.

When I refer to investigative journalists in this chapter, I mean those employed as such by media organizations, mainly newspapers. That is the group that the nonprofit websites, journalists, and academics referred to when commenting on what they perceived as a crisis for investigative journalism. I recognize that beat reporters do step away from daily reporting to work on original investigative stories. The cuts to beat and general reporting staff reduced the investigative reporting capability available in newsrooms. I acknowledge that other individuals and groups – seldom mentioned by those expressing concern about the state of investigative reporting – also produce investigative stories, and increasingly so. They are part of a movement, a "mass amateurization of publishing," that includes expert bloggers, NGOs, citizens, nonprofit centers, and the public interest journalism of decentralized nonmarket players (Benkler, 2006; Shirky, 2008, p. 65). Those expressing concern at conferences, on websites, and in journalism publications about the plight of investigative reporting focused their concerns on the mainstream field, and largely ignored these groups.

Entries to the Pulitzer Prize

As evidence that investigative reporting was in crisis, commentators referred to a reduction in the number of entries to the Public Service and Investigative Reporting categories of the Pulitzer Prize compared with the mid-1980s (Waldman, 2011; Walton, 2010). Data supplied by the Pulitzer Prize organization confirmed that entries in both categories during the financial crisis years of 2007–2009 were substantially fewer than in 1986 and also 1996. But the evidence was not as clear cut as some commentators maintained.

I obtained from the Pulitzer Prize organization annual entry numbers between 2005 and 2014. The financial crisis occurred between 2007 and 2009, so the impact, if there were one, would be noticeable in the entries for 2008, 2009, and 2010 because entries represent work published in the previous calendar year. I also obtained data for 1986 because commentators had used a mid-1980s figure as a baseline for comparison, and I asked for the 1996 figure to assist the analysis.

Table 4.1 shows that in 2006 there were 99 entries in the Investigative Reporting category. In 2007, the category had 67 entries. That was one of the biggest year-on-year declines detected but did not appear to be linked to the financial crisis because the entries for the 2007 prize represented stories written in 2006. In 2008, there were 75 entries, an increase that was surprising given that the stories were published in the first year of the financial crisis (2007). By 2009, the number of entries had dropped to 60. But the following year, 2010, they jumped to 81, despite those entries being for stories that were written in the last year of the financial crisis. In the earlier decades, the number of entries

Table 4.1 Pulitzer entries in Investigative Reporting and Public Service categories

Year	Public Service	Investigative	Total Pulitzer Entries[a]
1986	131	119	1,634
1996	104	112	1,484
2006	72	99	1,324
2007	55	67	1,225
2008 (FC)	58	75	1,167
2009 (FC)	60	60	1,028
2010 (FC)	70	81	1,103
2011	68	65	1,097
2012	71	72	1,113
2013	67	65	1,081
2014	69	75	1,132

Note: FC = impacted by financial crisis; [a]All categories.
Source: Data obtained from Pulitzer Prizes (personal communication, October 2, 3, & 5, 2013 and November 25, 2014).

was significantly higher for both categories. Investigative Reporting attracted 119 entries in 1986 and 112 in 1996. In the Public Service category, there were 72 entries in 2006; a drop to 55 entries in 2007; 58 in 2008; 60 in 2009; and 70 in the following year. These compared with 131 entries in 1986 and 104 in 1996.

The trend line in Figure 4.3 shows that the most significant trend has been a reduction in the number of entries in both categories since the mid-1980s. The chart also suggests a negative impact in the years 2007, 2008, and 2009 and then relative stability after 2010.

The most discernible impact that could be linked to the financial crisis occurred in 2009. There were only 60 entries in each of the two categories. However, there was a jump from 120 combined category entries in 2009 to 151 for the two categories in 2010. There was also a significant drop in the number of entries in 2007 from the previous year, from 171 entries to 122. These were for stories published in 2006, before the financial crisis, for which I have no explanation other than there being a high number (99) entries in the Investigative Reporting category in 2006 and 72 entries in the Public Service competition.

The total number of entries to all the 14 categories of Pulitzer Prize has also declined since the mid-1980s. In 1986, a total of 1,634 entries were received; in 1996, there were 1,484, but by 2007, the total had dropped to 1,225; then 1,167 in 2008, 1,028 in 2009, and a slight rise in 2014 to 1,132. Table 4.2 shows that the percentage decline in the Public

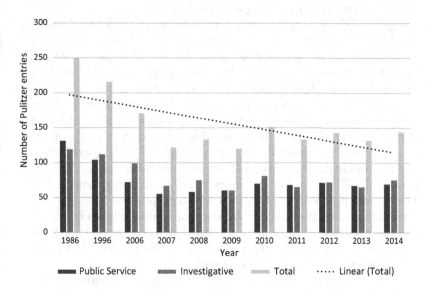

Figure 4.3 Long-term decline in entries to investigative Pulitzer categories.
Source: The Pulitzer Prizes (personal communication, October 2, 3, & 5, 2013 and November 25, 2014).

Table 4.2 Comparison of Pulitzer entries with entries in 1986

Year	Public Service		Investigative		Total Pulitzer Entries	
	N	Change	N	Change	N	Change
1986	131		119		1,634	
2005	89	–32%	79	–34%	1,326	–19%
2006	72	–45%	99	–17%	1,324	–19%
2007	55	–58%	67	–43%	1,225	–25%
2008	58	–56%	75	–37%	1,167	–29%
2009	60	–54%	60	–50%	1,028	–37%
2013	67	–49%	65	–45%	1,081	–34%
2014	69	–47%	75	–37%	1,132	–31%

Source: Compiled by the author from data obtained from Pulitzer Prizes (personal communication, October 2, 3, & 5, 2013 and November 25, 2014).

Service and Investigative Reporting categories using 1986 as the base year was consistently greater each year than the percentage drop for the total of all the categories. The reasons for the greater percentage decline were unclear.

Looking at Public Service and Investigative Reporting entries as a percentage of entries to all the Pulitzer Prize categories confirms that 2007 was a lean year for the journalism categories. The average percentage between 2005 and 2014 for Public Service was 5.8 percent of total entries, and for Investigative Reporting it was 6.3 percent.

Figure 4.4 shows that the Public Service entries constituted 4.4 percent, and Investigative Reporting, 5.4 percent of the total entries in 2007. By 2008, Public Service was still below the average, while the Investigative Reporting category was slightly above its average. Since 2010, both categories have been slightly above or around the average mark.

This analysis demonstrates that the overall context must be taken into account when using Pulitzer Prize entries in arguments about the health of investigative reporting. In raw numbers, the variation in the number of entries was not great: in 2008 [first impacted year], there were 11 fewer entries in the Investigative Reporting and Public Service categories than in 2007, and in 2009, there were only two fewer than in 2007. There could be a variety of reasons why reporters and news organizations did not enter the Pulitzer Prizes and care must be taken in reaching conclusions based on these figures, other than to say they do not constitute evidence that investigative reporters en masse had lost their jobs or that fewer investigative stories were written.

Other data used in support of concern about the quantity of investigative journalism in the United States included membership of the Investigative Reporters and Editors (n.d.) organization. Investigative

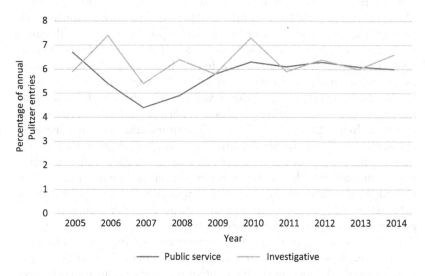

Figure 4.4 Investigative stories as a percentage of annual Pulitzer entries.
Source: Compiled by the author from data obtained from Pulitzer Prizes (personal communication, October 2, 3, & 5, 2013 and November 25, 2014).

Reporters and Editors was created in 1975 and conducts annual conferences where issues confronting watchdog reporting are discussed and reporters' panels highlight the lessons they learned from their projects. Investigative Reporters and Editors also runs boot camps and workshops on investigative techniques and has an extensive library of investigative stories. The organization's executive director said membership had dropped by about 30 percent between 2003 and 2009 and that there was less investigative reporting being done in the United States than a few years earlier (Waldman, 2011, p. 52; Walton, 2010). More recent figures supplied by the current executive director show that the organization had an average of 5,389 members in 2017, a 36 percent increase from 2012.[6] Despite this significant rise in membership, articles suggesting that more investigative reporting was now being produced could not be found. If a fall in membership was evidence of watchdog reporting's demise, shouldn't by that logic an increase signal the opposite? Another critical fact is that members of Investigative Reporters and Editors include educators, staff and beat reporters, editors, producers, and bloggers, which make membership a misleading measure of investigative journalism. A survey of 861 Investigative Editors and Reporters members found that 38.8 percent were investigative reporters or producers and that only 28.8 percent worked fulltime on a projects team (Lanosga & Houston, 2017).

More than 23,300 newsroom jobs were lost between 2007 and 2015 (American Society of News Editors, 2016). Artists, photographers, videographers, copy and layout editors, online producers, editorial supervisors, as well as reporters were casualties of the cuts. Editors tried to preserve local accountability reporting by beat reporters in areas such as councils, police, and courts, suburban developments, urban neighborhoods, and statehouses. Editors wanted to tighten budgets without hurting core news operations, and beat reporters were seen as indispensable (Waldman, 2011, p. 43). Despite the editors' efforts to limit the cuts, accountability beats suffered cutbacks of varying degrees (Waldman, 2011). There is no doubt that cuts of that magnitude had a negative impact on the breadth and depth of news coverage in many parts of the United States, particularly at local and regional dailies. The decline in local reporting was severe enough to shift power away from citizens to government and powerful institutions despite digital technology empowering the public, according to one commentator (Waldman, 2011, p. 6).

However, it is possible to argue that only a small fraction of the job losses would have involved investigative reporters because many news organizations employed just one or two journalists dedicated to investigations or did not have an investigative team.[7] The ability of local beat and general reporters to undertake longer investigations – difficult at the best of times due to the pressure of daily breaking news and the reluctance of editors to approve time-consuming projects – may have been made even more difficult. There was evidence that newsrooms retained or even increased their watchdog teams. Eminent journalists and scholars agreed that local news reporting at metropolitan daily newspapers was more endangered than investigative reporting that "might be provided by other sources" (Downie & Schudson, 2009, p. 12).

Other Perspectives on the State of Investigative Reporting

While some people were warning of a crisis for investigative journalism, senior mainstream news executives were bullish about the numbers doing such work (Weinberg, 2009) and larger newspapers retained their investigative approach (Walton, 2010). Mary Walton's article, "Investigative Shortfall," in *American Journalism Review* (Walton, 2010) quoted editors restating their commitment to investigative reporting at the *Los Angeles Times*, the *New York Times*, the *Washington Post*, the *Philadelphia Inquirer*, the *Wall Street Journal*, the *Dallas Morning News*, the Gannett company, and National Public Radio. "There are others where the accountability torch still burns, notably the *Milwaukee Journal Sentinel*, the *Oregonian*, and the *Seattle Times*" (Walton, 2010, para. 35). The *Milwaukee Journal Sentinel* "through all the financial stress... has maintained – even extended – its commitment to watchdog, investigative reporting" (LaFrance, 2013, para. 5).

Anticipating losses of $85 million in 2009, the *Boston Globe* closed foreign bureaus in London, Jerusalem, Tokyo, and South America and eliminated the jobs of national correspondents and other staff. Its then owner, the New York Times Company threatened to shut the newspaper, one of the United States' oldest and best, unless unions agreed to pay cuts and concessions totaling $20 million (Gavin & O'Brien, 2009). Tom Farragher was the *Boston Globe*'s investigations editor at the time and thought at first that he would lose his job. He recalled his daughter in tears at the prospect of the family not being able to afford university fees (personal communication, February 25, 2014). However, the *Boston Globe*'s then editor Martin Baron made no cuts to the investigative team as he reduced the size of the newsroom.

> Even when things were shutting down and people were fearful about their jobs ... I like to say Baron protected the nuclear core and never wavered in his support for investigative journalism. We continued to do very vibrant, vigorous and ambitious investigative reporting even in the darkest financial times of the newspaper.
>
> (Personal communication, February 25, 2014)

Other editors reported that staff cuts had resulted in less focus on some forms of news to the advantage of original investigative stories. An editor at the *Milwaukee Journal Sentinel* explained that the paper had expanded its local investigative efforts figuring that high-impact projects were part of what readers most wanted; the *News Tribune* in Washington state stopped covering smaller communities and refocused on local enterprise and investigative reporting (Pew Project for Excellence in Journalism, 2010). Editors and publishers recognized that investigative reporting was their franchise. Martin Baron, who moved from the *Boston Globe* to the *Washington Post* in 2012, expanded on the watchdog mission in a speech:

> If we as journalists abandon that mission – because we say we can't afford it, because we claim it's not cost effective, or because the risks seem too great – we will betray the foundational principle of a free press. It would be the most irresponsible thing we do.
>
> (Baron, 2015, para. 110)

A study of newsroom resources in 2007–2008 concluded that while the crossword, TV listings, and stock tables had disappeared, local coverage had increased and investigative reporting remained highly valued (Pew Project for Excellence in Journalism, 2008, para. 1). The study by journalist Tyler Marshall and the Pew Research Center's Project for Excellence in Journalism was based on responses from 259 senior newspaper executives to a survey administered by Princeton Survey Research

Associates International. It was conducted in the midst of the financial crisis in January and February 2008. Marshall also interviewed senior editors at 15 daily newspapers between November 2007 and January 2008 (Pew Project for Excellence in Journalism, 2008). The majority of newspapers had cut staff and the amount of space they devoted to news. Two-thirds had cut back on foreign news, over half had cut national news, and more than a third had reduced business coverage. The editors' greatest concern was the loss of talent and experienced reporters – often targeted for buyouts because of their higher salaries – followed by the loss of other staff. Despite such concerns, a majority of editors (56 percent) felt their newspapers were better than three years earlier. One editor, whose newsroom had lost 70 staff, commented: "There's an improvement in enterprise, in investigations and in the coverage of several core beats" (Pew Project for Excellence in Journalism, 2008, p. 3). Most editors believed the stories in their publications were better written, more in-depth, and more comprehensive than three years earlier. Given that the editors appeared to be commenting mainly on their own competence and performance and the strong loyalty that journalists generally have to their publications, these results may not be surprising.

One-third of the editors answered that the comprehensiveness of their newspapers' coverage had worsened, a response that likely related to job losses. But more editors believed that investigative reporting resources had increased than those who believed that resources were reduced when compared with three years earlier. The responses in this study are telling because they reflect the views of 259 mainstream newspaper editors and executives at a time when alarm was being expressed about the future of serious journalism. Despite severe cutbacks, the editors were not despairing about the future. They had cut soft news coverage and focused on core journalistic areas that most affected their readers. They had a strong commitment to local hard news stories in beats like education, crime, local politics, investigative reporting, sport, and the environment. In each area, editors said more resources had been devoted than three years earlier. Thirty percent said investigative reporting was better resourced at their newspapers than in the earlier period, while 24 percent disagreed (Pew Project for Excellence in Journalism, 2008).

The culture and values of professional journalism help us to understand the reasons why newsrooms preserved investigative teams despite their cost, relatively few stories, and legal and other complications. Rather than being the first area to be cut, the Pew survey found that most executives insisted that investigative reporting would be the last to be hit by downsizing. "Those who manage papers both small and large seem to believe this is an essential part of a paper's role, and one that fits with whatever their future business model will be" (Pew Project for Excellence in Journalism, 2008, Investigative Teams – and Their Stories – Survive, para. 1). Ninety-one percent of all newsroom executives considered investigative or enterprise reporting to be either very essential or somewhat essential to the quality of their news product. Editors said financial pressures had forced them to be more selective when deciding which labor-intensive stories to pursue. Investigative stories were shorter than previously and cost more to produce due to the extra editing time needed for print and digital display.

Who were the newsroom staff that lost their jobs? Forty-two percent of the 259 editors and news executives surveyed said they had reduced the number of copy editors over the previous three years (Pew Project for Excellence in Journalism, 2008). Of the bigger newspapers surveyed, 67 percent had cut back on copy editors. Other big cuts were made to the number of general editors, specialized editors, and graphic artists. One-third of the newspapers had reduced photographer numbers with half of the bigger newspapers cutting photographers. This finding was confirmed in later figures compiled by the American Society of News Editors (2016). Table 4.3 shows the biggest staff decline of 51 percent was among photographers, videographers, and artists. The second biggest cut was among supervisors; these were journalists employed as general editors, assistant metro editors, features editors, and section editors. Reporter and subediting numbers – the core of any newsroom – reduced by 37 percent, less than the percentage reduction in total jobs.

Despite their jobs apparently being preserved and despite being satisfied with their own media organizations, investigative reporters were glum about the general state of investigative journalism. This may be another characteristic of journalistic culture. Andrew Kaplan conducted a survey of 281 print investigative journalists as part of his PhD research at the University of Maryland. Like the Pew survey, Kaplan found that newsrooms placed high value on investigative reporting: 81 percent of respondents said their newspapers were somewhat or very supportive of their work. Forty-five percent said that the number of editors and reporters assigned to investigative projects compared with five years earlier had decreased, but a majority believed the number had either risen or remained the same, "surprising given the considerable layoff and buyouts that have occurred during the five years" (Kaplan, 2008, p. 85).

Table 4.3 Job losses by category

	2007	2015	Change
Supervisors	13,841	7,947	–42%
Copy/layout/online	11,159	6,967	–37%
Reporters/writers	24,286	15,155	–37%
Photographers/artists	5,759	2,806	–51%
Total	55,045	32,875	–40%

Source: Compiled by the author from data obtained from American Society of News Editors (2016).

Kaplan found a dichotomy between what investigative reporters thought of the news industry or the state of investigative journalism in an abstract sense and what they felt about their own newsrooms. A majority of the 281 investigative reporters said investigative journalism was worse off than 10 years earlier, despite believing that their own newsrooms supported them. Kaplan speculated that a reason for this belief could be that everything written about investigative reporting in books, magazines, newspapers, websites, blogs, and on television was downbeat. Another explanation could be the third-person effect proposed by sociologist W. Phillips Davison, in which people generally did not recognize media effects on themselves but acknowledged them in others. Other explanations might be found in cognitive dissonance theory, or that the reporters who perceived low newsroom support had already left. While gloomy about investigative reporting elsewhere, investigative reporters said that compared with five years earlier, they were spending more time on investigative reporting, with one-quarter responding the time had increased significantly. The journalists split evenly on the question of whether reports taking longer than three months had increased, dropped, or stayed the same over the previous five years: "given the budget and staff cutbacks over the past five years, one would have expected a noticeable decrease in the amount of longer investigations" (Kaplan, 2008, p. 84).

The same phenomenon of personal satisfaction but industry gloom was evident in a 2013 email survey of 861 members of the Investigative Reporters and Editors organization. The survey found that almost 70 percent of the respondents agreed or somewhat agreed that the commitment to investigative reporting in their own newsrooms was as strong as it was a year or two earlier (Lanosga & Houston, 2017). Four out of five said they were fairly or very satisfied in their jobs. Three out of five responded that the number of projects they worked on that took more than three months had increased or remained the same.

> They were much more likely to agree that their newsrooms are more committed to investigative work than a year or two ago. They also reported, in significantly higher proportions, that the number of investigative reporting staff as well as the number of longer-term projects have increased.
>
> (Lanosga & Houston, 2017, p. 1111)

Despite these findings, the authors found that investigative journalists held "somewhat incongruous views" about the state of their craft. Almost 45 percent said journalism generally was headed in the wrong direction and about half thought it was becoming more difficult to get the time and resources to do investigative work. "Despite those negative impressions, however, more than two-thirds of respondents actually said they are optimistic or very optimistic about future prospects for investigative reporting" (p. 1110). The authors suggested such optimism likely stemmed from the positive views they had about their own newsrooms. Overall, the authors concluded that it was "clear that practitioners as a whole view the practice of investigative reporting as persevering, if not flourishing" (Lanosga & Houston, 2017, p. 1115).

Retention of Investigative Reporting

The most persuasive scholarly work on the state of US accountability journalism – a field that is surprisingly bereft of contemporary research given the gravity of the concerns expressed – was conducted by Beth Knobel, associate professor of communications and media studies at Fordham University. Her findings are reflected in the title of her book, "The watchdog still barks" (Knobel, 2018). Knobel analyzed the front pages of nine newspapers – three national, four metropolitan dailies, and two local papers – for the month of April in 1991, 1996, 2001, 2006, and 2011. She eliminated breaking news stories and focused on accountability journalism, which she defined as "original nonbreaking news reporting about the work of government and of public policy issues" (Knobel, 2018, p. 7). In particular, she focused on watchdog reporting where journalists searched for malfeasance by government, and through deep and sustained reporting, held public officials accountable (Knobel, 2018, p. 8).

A total of 1,491 stories were selected for analysis. They were categorized as "simple enterprise" or "deep accountability" stories. The study found that contrary to the conventional wisdom, watchdog reporting was "far from dead" and that the data showed a steady growth in deep accountability reporting. Despite the financial challenges of the recession, "newspapers have not abandoned their watchdog role" (Knobel, 2018, p. 24). The national newspapers studied, the *New York Times*, the *Washington Post*, and the *Wall Street Journal*, not surprisingly produced more front-page deep accountability stories than the other papers. But the metropolitan dailies, the *Atlanta Journal-Constitution (AJC)*, *Minneapolis Star Tribune*, the *Denver Post*, and the *Albany Times Union*, which had all cut staff, produced only 15 percent fewer deep accountability reports than the nationals. Despite declining resources, these newspapers "somehow did *more* digging over time – not less and they did so because editors deemed deep accountability reporting as crucial to their missions" (Knobel, 2018, p. 56). Of the two local newspapers studied, the *Bradenton Herald* and the *Lewiston Tribune*, the McClatchy-owned *Herald* had managed to produce a steady stream of "deep watchdog" stories over time despite its small staff (Knobel, 2018, p. 94). The *Tribune* produced "simple enterprise" stories but hardly any deep accountability reporting due to its small size and limited resources (Knobel, 2018, pp. 91–92).

The study concluded that the findings refute the fear of some editors and scholars that newspapers had been so adversely affected by financial issues to be unable to perform a watchdog function. Knobel also interviewed editors who said they directed their limited resources to public affairs journalism because it served their newspaper's core mission: this cultural factor was the single most important reason why they dedicated so many resources to accountability journalism (Knobel, 2018, p. 9). However, Knobel also found that watchdog reporting was at risk in the local newspapers examined. There was less original public service journalism on their front pages after 1996 (Knobel, 2018, p. 84). They produced 80 percent fewer deep dive stories than the large papers, and three of the smallest newspapers studied lacked any deep investigations of nongovernmental entities such as businesses, NGOs, and other public policy players (Knobel, 2018, pp. 26, 99).

The study's findings replicate those of former journalist and political science academic Andrea Carson who conducted a newspaper content analysis in Australia where the two main newspaper organizations, Fairfax Media and News Corp, also had shed hundreds of journalists' jobs but where there were no newspaper closures. Carson's content analysis examined the amount of investigative journalism published in the nation's four main broadsheet newspapers over five decades in the month of April for each of 1971, 1981, 1991, 2001, and 2011. The newspapers selected were the *Age*, the *Sydney Morning Herald*, the *Australian*, and the *National Times*. Her thesis noted that, as in the United States, a perception existed among journalists and academics that there were fewer investigative stories today than previously. However, her content analysis and a review of stories that had won Australia's national journalism awards, the Walkleys, contradicted this widely held view. Carson found that more stories meeting the definition of investigative reporting were being done than ever before. As circulations and revenues of newspapers fell, the amount of investigative reporting did not decline (Carson, 2013).

The internet disrupted the business model of newspapers and the financial crisis devastated the advertising revenues of print media. These shocks forced editors to adjust their products to new platforms and work with fewer resources. But the culture and values of professionally employed editors and reporters did not change (Willig, 2012, p. 374). Journalists continued to believe in the watchdog role of the media. Media scholars, economists, and non-journalist commentators tend to underestimate just how deeply ingrained is this culture. A managing editor of the *San Jose Mercury News* summarized the investigative ethos like this: "It's part of the heart and soul of journalism" (Abbott, 1988, p. 3)

The survival of investigative reporting in established media could be attributed to four factors. First, some slack existed between the interests of journalists, managers, and owners. Managers did not have perfect oversight over the work of journalists, allowing them to pursue stories that had broad social returns but were not profit maximizing. "This is because it is costly for owners and managers to monitor constantly whether reporters are paying sufficient attention to reader interests and production costs" (Hamilton, 2004, p. 261). As long as journalists were needed to report the news, they would have some power within media organizations. "The desire of journalists to produce news according to their own best judgment can be a significant constraint on commercial motives" (Schudson, 2003, p. 115). Journalists had the power to stand up to corporate executives by evoking the traditions of independence and free inquiry.

Second, the media's watchdog role was commonly described by scholars, politicians, and journalists as integral, or indeed the same, as democracy: "journalism is usefully understood as another name for democracy" (Carey, 1997, p. 332). Others argued they were not the same thing (Schudson, 2008, p. 11). Nevertheless, journalists pursued investigations because they believed they were of broad societal benefit. Economists define positive externalities as actions by individuals or firms that benefit society more than individuals or firms. Investigative stories that might attract the attention of a minority of engaged citizens, politicians, or government agencies nevertheless created positive externalities since "other consumers may benefit from the coverage even if they were not the targets of advertisers and did not pay for the creation of the information" (Hamilton, 2004, p. 19).

The third factor was the heart and soul argument that within the field of journalism, investigative reporters had high levels of symbolic capital and that this was true also for news organizations that consistently published high-quality investigative stories. Such stories received prominent display and initiated reaction and reform. They created a brand for news outlets that differentiated them from organizations that produced soft news or daily coverage. A reputation for reliable, high-quality information could lead to public trust, higher circulation, and societal influence that readers and advertisers might want to be associated with (Meyer, 2009, p. 20). Editors recognized that the internet gave people the ability to find all manner of information and news sources and that their product could differentiate if they made investigative reporting a franchise element that gave people a reason to read their publications (Pew Project for Excellence in Journalism, 2008).

Finally, editors believed that a significant minority of people demanded quality journalism and would pay for it. This audience could be classified broadly as engaged citizens rather than general readers due to their interest in politics and public issues. Socially, politically, or economically active heavy news users tended to represent 15–20 percent of the population (Picard, 2010, p. 372). Recent spectacular rises in the digital subscriptions of the *Washington Post*, and the *New York Times* following the election of Donald Trump as President, confirmed that the appetite for quality independent journalism remained strong in American society despite being labeled fake news by Trump.

In summary, those arguing that investigative reporting was at risk could attest to little or no evidence in support of their assertions other than the general contraction of the industry. While editors and reporters in public forums often boast about their investigative teams and stories, the reality was that even in the national newspapers, "deep accountability" stories averaged only between 4.03 percent and 2.46 percent of their front-page stories (Knobel, 2018, p. 24). While strong in the more romanticized ideals of journalistic practice, investigative reporting in fact has been "weakly institutionalized in the daily routines and responsibilities of the press" (Bennett & Serrin, 2005, p. 170).

A major impact of the concerns expressed about investigative journalism and the reason why it is explored at length in this chapter is that it opened streams of funding to new and established nonprofit news ventures, expanding the sector dramatically. Nonprofit organizations may not have set out to exploit the mainstream media's financial problems to attract more philanthropic funding for themselves. But the conventional wisdom that investigative journalism was in trouble and that US democracy was somehow at risk did generate hundreds of millions of dollars for the nonprofit investigative and public interest news sector, as will be seen in the next chapter.

Notes

1 2015 was the last year in which the American Society of News Editors categorized newsroom jobs as "reporters, copy editors, photojournalists", etc. In subsequent years, the survey results categorized journalists into "newsroom leader" or "all other journalists" because it felt the survey missed journalists who were not in traditional positions. See http://asne.org//Files/census/2017%20ASNE%20diversity%20survey%20tables.pdf for the American Society of News Editors's methodology and detailed tables.

2 The *Boston Globe*'s Spotlight team started investigating sexual abuse by Catholic clergy in July 2001. Its first major report was published in January 2002. All told, the team published more than 600 stories with eight reporters playing key roles (Rezendes, 2015). The *Globe* was awarded the 2003 Pulitzer Prize for Public Service and in 2015, a movie, Spotlight, was released, highlighting the team's investigations.

3 Charles Lewis, as executive director of the Center for Public Integrity, was one of two people who invited me to join the International Consortium of Investigative Journalists in February 1998. The other was the consortium's then director, Maud Beelman.

4 I am still a member of the International Consortium of Investigative Journalists and a member of its Network Committee.

5 Later figures supplied by the Investigative Reporters and Editors' Doug Haddix showed membership in 2009 was 3,430, email communication on January 26, 2018.

6 Email communication from Investigative Reporters and Editors executive director Doug Haddix on January 26, 2018.
7 Few scholarly efforts have been made to quantify the number of investigative journalists working in the United States (Lanosga et al., 2015). A 1977 study of 174 newspapers found that 32 had at least one person with the title of investigative reporter (Harmening, 1977, as cited in Lanosga et al., 2015). A survey by university students of 100 of the United States' biggest newspapers in 2006 found 39 percent had investigative teams and 37 percent had no full-time investigative reporters (Walton, 2010).

Bibliography

Abbott, S. (1988, Winter). Critics question "staying power" of investigative journalism. *IRE Journal*, 15–16.

American Society of News Editors. (2016). Table L – Employment of men and women by job category. Retrieved October 10, 2017, from http://asne.org/content.asp?pl=140&sl=144&contentid=144

Anderson, C., Bell, E., & Shirky, C. (2012). *Post-industrial journalism: Adapting to the present*. Retrieved from the Tow Center for Digital Journalism website: http://towcenter.org/research/post-industrial-journalism/

Aucoin, J. (2005). *The evolution of American investigative journalism*. Columbia: University of Missouri Press.

Bailey, M. N., & Elliott, D. J. (2009). The US financial and economic crisis: Where does it stand and where do we go from here? Retrieved from The Brookings Institution website: http://www.brookings.edu/research/papers/2009/06/15-economic-crisis-baily-elliott

Baron, M. (2015, April 8). Washington Post Executive Editor Martin Baron on journalism's transformation from print to digital. *The Washington Post*. Retrieved from https://www.washingtonpost.com/pr/wp/2015/04/08/washington-post-executive-editor-martin-baron-on-journalisms-transition-from-print-to-digital/

Benkler, Y. (2006). *The wealth of networks: How social production transforms markets and freedom*. New Haven, CT: Yale University Press.

Bennett, W. L., & Serrin, W. (2005). The watchdog role. In G. Overholser & K. H. Jamieson (Eds.), *The press* (pp. 169–188). New York, NY: Oxford University Press.

Bergantino, J., & Mulvihill, M. (2009, Summer). Filling a local void: J-school students tackle watchdog reporting. *Nieman Reports*. Retrieved from http://www.nieman.harvard.edu/reports/article/101563/Filling-a-Local-Void-J-School-Students-Tackle-Watchdog-Reporting.aspx

Brock, G. (2013). *Out of print: Newspapers, journalism and the business of news in the digital age*. London, England: Logan Page.

Carey, J. (1997). Afterward: The culture in question. In E. S. Munson & C. Warren (Eds.), *James Carey: A critical Reader* (pp. 308–399). Minneapolis: University of Minnesota Press.

Carson, A. L. (2013). *Investigative journalism, the public sphere and democracy: The watchdog role of Australian broadsheets in the digital age* (PhD thesis), University of Melbourne, Australia. Retrieved from http://hdl.handle.net/11343/38200

Cullinan, K. (2009). Watchdogs don't come cheap: Newsroom budget woes and the evolving landscape of journalism take their toll on reporting. *The News Media and the Law, 33*(1), 16–17.

Daly, C. (2013). The decline of Big Media, 1980s–2000s: Key history lessons and a brief survey of trends. Retrieved from Journalist's Resource website: http://journalistsresource.org/studies/society/news-media/covering-america-journalism-professor-christopher-daly

Downie, L., Jr., & Schudson, M. (2009, November/December). The reconstruction of American journalism. *Columbia Journalism Review.* Retrieved from http://www.cjr.org/reconstruction/the_reconstruction_of_american.php?page=all

Edmonds, R. (2009). Shrinking newspapers have created $1.6 billion news deficit. Retrieved from Poynter website: http://www.poynter.org/latest-news/business-news/the-biz-blog/98784/shrinking-newspapers-have-created-1-6-billion-news-deficit/

Edmonds, R., Guskin, E., & Rosenstiel, T. (2011). *Newspapers: Missed the 2010 media rally* (The State of the News Media 2011). Retrieved from Pew Research Center's State of the News Media website: http://assets.pewresearch.org/wp-content/uploads/sites/13/2017/05/24141615/State-of-the-News-Media-Report-2011-FINAL.pdf

Eye on Ohio. (n.d.). About Eye on Ohio. Retrieved from http://eyeonohio.org/about/

Fine, L. R. (2009). *Bad public relations or is this a real crisis? YES.* Paper presented at the Duke Conference on Nonprofit Media, Duke Sanford School of Public Policy, Duke University, Durham, NC. Retrieved from http://www2.sanford.duke.edu/nonprofitmedia/documents/dwcrichfinefinal.pdf

Frank, L. (2009, June). The withering watchdog: What really happened to investigative reporting in America. *Expose: America's Investigative Reports.* Retrieved from http://www.pbs.org/wnet/expose/2009/06/the-withering-watchdog.html

Gavin, R., & O'Brien, K. (2009, May 6). Globe, guild reach deal: Details of pact to be released. *The Boston Globe.* Retrieved from http://www.boston.com/business/articles/2009/05/06/globe_and_guild_talk_into_the_night/

Glaser, M. (2008). Charles Lewis tries to solve – not bemoan – state of investigative journalism. Retrieved from MediaShift website: http://www.pbs.org/mediashift/2008/06/charles-lewis-tries-to-solve-not-bemoan-state-of-investigative-journalism170/

Hamilton, J. T. (2004). *All the news that's fit to sell: How the market transforms information into news.* Princeton, NJ: Princeton University Press.

Hamilton, J. T. (2016). *Democracy's detectives: The economics of investigative journalism.* Boston, MA: Harvard University Press.

Hirschorn, M. (2009, January/February). End times. *The Atlantic.* Retrieved from http://www.theatlantic.com/magazine/archive/2009/01/end-times/307220/

Houston, B. (2010). The future of investigative reporting. *Daedalus, 139*(2), 45–56. doi:10.1162/daed.2010.139.2.45

International Monetary Fund. (2009). World economic outlook: Crisis and recovery. Retrieved from http://www.imf.org/external/pubs/ft/weo/2009/01/pdf/text.pdf

Investigate West. (n.d.). About us. Retrieved from http://www.invw.org/about

Investigative Reporters and Editors. (n.d.). About IRE. Retrieved from http://ire.org/about/

Investigative Reporting Workshop. (2013). About the Investigative Reporting Workshop. Retrieved from http://investigativereportingworkshop.org/about/

Kaplan, A. D. (2008). *Investigating the investigators: Examining the attitudes, perceptions, and experiences of investigative journalists in the internet age* (Doctoral dissertation), University of Maryland, College Park, MD. Retrieved from http://hdl.handle.net/1903/8788

Knobel, B. (2018). *The watchdog still barks: How accountability reporting evolved for the digital age.* New York, NY: Fordham University Press.

Lacy, S., & Simon, T. F. (1993). *The economics and regulation of United States newspapers.* Norwood, NJ: Ablex Publishing Corporation.

LaFrance, A. (2013). What does the Milwaukee Journal Sentinel know that your newsroom doesn't? Retrieved from Nieman Lab website: http://www.niemanlab.org/2013/09/what-does-the-milwaukee-journal-sentinel-know-that-your-newsroom-doesnt/

Lanosga, G., & Houston, B. (2017). Journalists assess investigative reporting and its status in society. *Journalism Practice, 11*(9), 1101–1120. doi:10.1080/17512786.2016.1228472

Lanosga, G., Willnat, L., Weaver, D. H., & Houston, B. (2015). A breed apart? A comparative study of investigative and US journalists. *Journalism Studies, 18*(3), 265–287. doi:10.1080/1461670X.2015.1051570

Lee, E. (2014). Carlos Slim still reaping big rewards from NY Times loan. Retrieved from Bloomberg website: http://www.bloomberg.com/news/2014-01-21/carlos-slim-still-reaping-big-rewards-from-ny-times-loan.html

Lewis, C. (2007). *The growing importance of nonprofit journalism* (Working Paper Series #2007-3). Retrieved from the Shorenstein Center on Media, Politics and Public Policy website: http://shorensteincenter.org/wp-content/uploads/2012/03/2007_03_lewis.pdf

Lewis, C. (2013, March/April). How we hired that reporter. *Columbia Journalism Review.* Retrieved from http://www.cjr.org/behind_the_news/how_we_hired_that_reporter_1.php

MacDougall, C. D., & Reid, R. D. (1987). *Interpretive reporting.* New York, NY: Macmillan.

McChesney, R. W., & Nichols, J. (2010). *The death and life of American journalism: The media revolution that will begin the world again.* New York, NY: Nation Books.

McIntyre, D. A. (2009, March 9). The 10 most endangered newspapers in America. *Time.* Retrieved from http://www.time.com/time/business/article/0,8599,1883785,00.html

Meyer, P. (2008, October/November). The elite newspaper of the future. *American Journalism Review.* Retrieved from http://www.ajr.org/Article.asp?id=4605

Meyer, P. (2009). *The vanishing newspaper: Saving journalism in the information age* (2nd ed.). Columbia: University of Missouri Press.

Mirror Awards. (2011). Finalists announced. Retrieved October 23, 2013, from http://mirrorawards.syr.edu/2011/04/18/finalists-announced-2/

Newsosaur. (2013). Print circ fell 42% at top papers since 2005. Retrieved from Reflections of a Newsosaur website: http://newsosaur.blogspot.de/2013/05/print-circ-fell-42-at-top-papers-since.html

Nichols, J., & McChesney, R. W. (2009). The death and life of great American newspapers. Retrieved from The Nation website: http://www.thenation.com/article/death-and-life-great-american-newspapers/

O'Malley, N. (2013, August 10). Billionaires swoop in to buy US newspapers. *The Age*. Retrieved from http://newsstore.theage.com.au/apps/viewDocument.ac?page=1&sy=age&kw=Billionaires+swoop+in+to+buy+us+newspapers&pb=all_ffx&dt=selectRange&dr=6months&so=relevance&sf=text&sf=headline&rc=10&rm=200&sp=nrm&clsPage=1&docID=AGE130810VO399F1TG2V

Osder, E., & Campwala, K. (2012). Audience development and distribution strategies. Retrieved from Investigative News Network website: http://newstraining.org/guides/whitepaper-audience-development-and-distribution-strategies/prologue/

PBS Newshour. (2009). Investigative reporting hard hit by media cutbacks. Retrieved from PBS website: http://www.pbs.org/newshour/bb/media-jan-june09-reporting_04-20/

Pew Project for Excellence in Journalism. (2008). The changing newsroom: What is being gained and what is being lost in America's daily newspapers? Retrieved from The State of the News Media website: http://assets.pewresearch.org/wp-content/uploads/sites/13/legacy/PEJ-The%20Changing%20Newspaper%20Newsroom%20FINAL%20DRAFT-NOEMBARGO-PDF.pdf

Pew Project for Excellence in Journalism. (2010). News investment. Retrieved from The State of the News Media website: http://assets.pewresearch.org.s3.amazonaws.com/files/journalism/State-of-the-News-Media-Report-2010-FINAL.pdf

Picard, R. (2010). The future of the news industry. In J. Curran (Ed.), *Media and society* (pp. 365–379). London, England: Bloomsbury Academic.

Picard, R. (2013). Killing journalism? In H.-W. Nienstedt, S. Russ-Mohl, & B. Wilczek (Eds.), *Journalism and media convergence* (pp. 1–28). Berlin, Germany: De Gruyter.

Pine Tree Watchdog. (n.d.). About us. Retrieved from http://pinetreewatchdog.org/about/

ProPublica. (n.d.). About us. Retrieved from http://www.propublica.org/about/

Protess, D., Cook, F. L., Doppelt, J. C., Ettema, J. S., Gordon, M. T., Leff, D. R., & Miller, P. (1991). *The Journalism of outrage: Investigative reporting and agenda building in America*. New York, NY: Guilford Press.

PublicSource. (2013). About PublicSource. Retrieved from http://publicsource.org/about-publicsource

Rezendes, M. (2015, November 20). 'Spotlight' journalists didn't foresee impact of church abuse investigation. *The Boston Globe*. Retrieved from http://www.bostonglobe.com/metro/2015/11/20/journalists-who-broke-church-sex-abuse-scandal-could-not-have-foreseen-impact/iIMZJD8RfLZXxKBVqh8h4K/story.html

Riptide. (2013). Eric Schmidt. Retrieved from the Shorenstein Center on Media, Politics and Public Policy website: http://www.niemanlab.org/riptide/person/eric-schmidt/

Schudson, M. (2003). *The sociology of news*. New York, NY: Norton.

Schudson, M. (2008). *Why democracies need an unlovable press*. Cambridge, MA: Polity.

Scott, B. (2005). A contemporary history of digital journalism. *Television & News Media,* 6(1), 89–126. doi:10.1177/1527476403255824

Shirky, C. (2008). *Here comes everybody: The power of organizing without organizations.* New York, NY: Penguin Press.

Waldman, S. (2011). *The information needs of communities: The changing media landscape in a broadband age.* Retrieved from Federal Communications Commission website: http://www.fcc.gov/infoneedsreport

Walton, M. (2010). Investigative shortfall. *American Journalism Review, 32*(3), 18–24, 26–30.

Weinberg, S. (2009). Showcase: Finding positives, despite dark moments. Retrieved from Investigative Reporters and Editors website: http://www.ire.org/blog/ire-news/2009/06/14/showcase-finding-positives-despite-dark-moment/

Westphal, D. (2009). *Philanthropic foundations: Growing funders of the news.* Retrieved from USC Annenberg School of Communication, Center on Communication Leadership & Policy website: https://communicationleadership.usc.edu/files/2015/07/PhilanthropicFoundations.pdf

Willig, I. (2012). Newsroom ethnography in a field perspective. *Journalism, 14*(3), 372–387. doi:10.1177/1464884912442638

5 Funding Nonprofit Accountability Journalism

The expansion of the US nonprofit news sector since 2007 would not have occurred without funding from foundations and wealthy donors. In a sense, multibillion-dollar foundations and very wealthy donors might seem odd bedfellows for investigative journalists. Foundations have been characterized by critics as unaccountable conservative elites that operate behind the scenes to implement hidden subversive agendas (Barkan, 2013; Roelofs, 2007). The activities of some corporate titans have been found to be illegal, immoral, and secretive. Investigative journalists work to expose information that someone is trying to hide suggesting that foundations and the activities of some wealthy individuals would be an obvious target for muckraking journalists. Academics have accused funders of interfering with normal editorial judgments: "By and large, it is the funders who are calling the tune" (Roelofs, 2007, p. 502). My research suggests that the relationship between funders and nonprofit accountability news organizations is more complex and nuanced. The ethical issues that might arise from philanthropic funding of journalism are discussed in Chapter 9.

Philanthropic funding was the most important of the primary factors identified in the introduction of this book as driving the growth of nonprofit reporting. The other two were the financial crisis and the transfer of mainstream news executives to the nonprofit field, both examined in previous chapters. Large donations by wealthy individuals in some cases provided the startup capital to create new nonprofit journalism ventures and institutional foundations, which are more risk averse, then came on board with additional funding.

Foundations and wealthy donors granted hundreds of millions of dollars to nonprofit journalism; yet, the long-term sustainability of many nonprofits remains an open question for those in the sector. That foundations fund startups for several years then leave was a common view in the sector in 2009. Ten years later, it is clear that some foundations have been willing to renew their grants year in year out.

Nevertheless, the risk of foundations not renewing grants presented an existential threat, leading to near constant pressure to replenish expiring grants and find new funding sources (Mitchell, Jurkowitz,

Holcomb, Enda, & Anderson, 2013). In fact, the nonrenewal of grants had forced several nonprofit organizations to shut down. Nonprofit news organizations were "just as beholden to economic imperatives as commercial news organizations" (Picard, 2014, p. 502). More recently, some nonprofit news organizations have increased their efforts to attract smaller donations from individuals. Recognition of the potential of this source of revenue followed the election of Donald Trump as President and saw smaller donations surging to nonprofits such as *ProPublica* and *Mother Jones*. *ProPublica*'s editor-in-chief in 2012 declared, "We're not like [National Public Radio]" and expressed little interest in harnessing smaller donations (Harris, 2012, para. 3). But that changed after Trump was elected and the number of donors to *ProPublica* jumped from 3,400 to about 34,000 in just two years (R. Tofel, personal communication, April 25, 2018).

Foundations in the United States

Massive trusts with billions of dollars in holdings are a distinctively US institution. No other civilization has been "designed by the imagination of its organized philanthropists to quite the same degree" (Dowie, 2001, p. xxii). US foundations helped shape medical research, health, university and other education, the arts and culture, religion, science, public affairs, the environment, and a multitude of areas that impact the lives of ordinary Americans. Foundations operated as private institutions that played an increasingly public role in US society (Dowie, 2001, p. 20) because many of the traditional roles of government in other democracies, such as welfare, health, and education, had been privatized in the United States.

Some of today's biggest philanthropic foundations were created in the late nineteenth and early twentieth centuries by industrialists looking to minimize tax and put their wealth to use in new ways. In recent years, big philanthropy in the United States expanded enormously, due in part to the massive wealth generated by high-tech industries and a growing global market. But it was not just big foundations like the Rockefeller, Ford, Carnegie, and more recently the Bill & Melinda Gates Foundation that made American philanthropy distinct from that in other Western democracies. US giving patterns reflected the nation's attitude to government and the characteristics of its people (Wright, 2002). Philanthropy was not considered to be charity associated with a redistribution of wealth, but rather about investing to create opportunity and more widespread economic prosperity (Acs & Phillips, 2002). US foundations, required by law to donate a minimum 5 percent of their investment assets each year to charitable causes, gave $60.2 billion in 2014. These grants were made by 86,726 foundations with assets of $865.2 billion (Foundation Center, 2014).

Despite creating great universities such as Stanford, Massachusetts Institute of Technology, Johns Hopkins, Carnegie-Mellon, Duke, Chicago, and funding global medical research into vaccines and cures for malaria, yellow fever, and hook worm, the biggest foundations encountered hostility from the start, much of which came from scholars and politically motivated individuals. The criticism focused on the foundations' influence and lack of accountability: they were seen as constructors of hegemony by discouraging dissent against capitalistic democracy; they could shape public policy but had no accountability to the public or those affected by their programs (Barkan, 2013; Roelofs, 2007, p. 480).

The financial reliance of nonprofit news organizations on foundations, both for their formation and operation, handed funders a potentially powerful voice in the production of quality journalism in the United States. By funding the coverage of topics like education, health, the environment, and criminal justice, foundations – without directly interfering in stories – could skew editorial decisions by influencing the topics covered in thousands of investigative and public interest news projects.

Despite this, there has been little scholarly research on the relationship between foundations and nonprofit journalism. The reliance on foundation support was a consistent concern expressed by nonprofit editors. Only 28 percent of the 172 nonprofit organizations surveyed reported that their grants had been renewed by their original funders (Mitchell et al., 2013). Nonprofit organizations attempted to diversify their revenues through a combination of earned revenues that included event hosting, syndication and sale of stories, training, partnering with organizations, advertising,[1] and smaller donations. Some succeeded. However, a Knight Foundation survey of 20 local, state, and regional nonprofit news organizations found that while revenue from individual donors was rising, nonprofits remained very reliant on foundations with almost 60 percent of the total revenues coming from foundation funding (Knight Foundation, 2015).

A selective analysis of the Internal Revenue Service returns of nonprofit organizations demonstrates the extent of the reliance on contributions and grants from foundations and wealthy individuals compared with earned revenue. It shows that award-winning journalism does not translate into earned revenue. For example, the 2014 Form 990 return by the Wisconsin Center for Investigative Reporting records that it received $609,407 in contributions and gifts. Its only other revenue was $20,000 from program services, $9,017 from subscriptions to the *Wisconsin Watchdog*, $4,755 from journalism reports, $301 from investments, and $895 from miscellaneous revenue (Wisconsin990, 2014). In its return, the organization says that since being launched in 2009, it had produced more than 250 major reports and 200 money and politics columns that were published or cited by nearly 350 news organizations. Its coverage had reached an estimated audience of 46 million (Wisconsin990, 2014).

The Wisconsin Center for Investigative Reporting's earlier Internal Revenue Service return noted a remarkable year of journalistic achievement through high-impact stories and winning eight Milwaukee Press Club awards (Wisconsin990, 2013). Despite these successes, less than 5.5 percent of its total revenue in 2014 derived from earned revenue.

The *Voice of Orange County* received $543,345 in contributions, and grants and made no income other than $9 from an investment in 2012 (Voice of OC, 2012). In 2015, the only other income was $64 (Voice of OC, 2015). The *Austin Bulldog* in 2011 recorded $45,045 in donation funding and no other revenue (Austin Investigative Reporting Project, 2011). The Southern Investigative Reporting Foundation was granted $163,628 in 2013 and recorded no other income in its return (Southern Investigative Reporting Foundation, 2013). The *Voice of San Diego* did better. It generated $47,935 in syndication income and $2,842 in advertising in 2013, but the bulk of its support, almost $1.3 million, was from gifts, grants, and contributions from foundations and other major donors (Voice of San Diego, 2013). Two years later, it received $1.8 million in donations but managed to raise only $46, 945, nearly all of which was from story syndication (Voice of San Diego, 2015).

Billionaire Philanthropists

The most successful nonprofit organizations created after 2007 involved partnerships between journalists and wealthy individual philanthropists who donated large sums of startup capital. These funders, many of whom were self-made millionaires and billionaires, possessed an entrepreneurial spirit and an understanding of how to grow and operate enterprises – key skills that were lacking in journalists. Early financial security from large upfront donations provided a platform for the production of investigative journalism and breathing space for proof of concept. Centers were able to hire top journalists leading to great stories and recognition through awards and collaborations with quality legacy publishers. These, in turn, helped to attract foundation and other funding. Many of the organizations rapidly diversified their revenue sources due to the greater emphasis experienced business people placed on building a sustainable model. In 2017, "major gifts" constituted 20 percent of the revenue of the 91 nonprofits that responded to a survey (Institute for Nonprofit News, 2018).[2]

The mindsets of these philanthropists differed from those of institutional foundation program directors. First, it was their own money. Second, wealthy donors sometimes acted more like venture capitalists, wanting to create new organizations, whereas foundations tended to act more conservatively, often making or renewing grants to well-established nonprofit organizations. Third, foundations had to give a minimum – many took it as a maximum – of 5 percent of their assets each year.

Individuals could time their contributions almost any way they wished by using donor-advised funds or their private foundations.

One of the first major donations to attract wider interest was made by billionaire former banker Herbert Sandler and his wife Marion in 2008. They promised to provide $10 million a year in funding to a new national nonprofit called *ProPublica* (Nocera, 2008).[3] The size and scope of the donation sent clear signals to the broader journalistic community. First, some wealthy businessmen were prepared to support nonprofit investigative journalism. Second, their funding could entice top editors and reporters from the legacy press to transfer to the nonprofit sector. Third, nonprofit stories were readily copublished in quality mainstream outlets. Fourth, the initial contributions and the success of the journalism attracted other funders. Fifth, business people like the Sandlers knew other wealthy people they could approach for contributions. And finally, some philanthropic businessmen were prepared to repeat their donations year after year, a key issue for long-term sustainability. The Sandler Foundation contributed almost $40 million to *ProPublica* between 2007 and 2015.

Venture capitalist John Thornton cofounded the *Texas Tribune* in 2009, teaming up with the editor of the *Texas Monthly* to build the organization. Thornton had a business mindset: he had been a consultant at McKinsey & Co. with clients in the United States and Europe. He was a founding board member of the Entrepreneurs Foundation. He had an MBA from Stanford Graduate Business School and a BA summa cum laude from Trinity University (Texas Tribune, 2009). Thornton initially invested $1 million and helped raise a further $3 million from individual donors and charitable foundations (Knight Foundation, 2009; McGeveran, 2011; Phelps, 2011). He likened the nonprofit to any commercial startup that he would invest in (Barnett, 2010). The organization would be run like a business even though the goal was "public service rather than profitability" (Thornton, 2010, paras. 8, 9).

Wealthy businessmen and their contacts supported new nonprofit startups elsewhere in the United States. Neil Barsky, a former journalist and hedge fund manager, provided the upfront funding for the creation of the *Marshall Project*, a site that focuses on criminal justice issues. Buzz Woolley invested hundreds of thousands of dollars in the *Voice of San Diego*. Warren Hellman, a former Lehman Brothers Holdings, Inc. president and the founder of the private equity firm, Hellman and Friedman in 2010 provided $5 million from his family foundation to launch the *Bay Citizen*, an online news site in the San Francisco area. His business network helped the startup raise a further $3.7 million, including three separate million dollar gifts and $250,000 from the Knight Foundation (Rauber, 2010). *MinnPost* was created in 2007 by Joel Kramer, a former editor and publisher of the *Minneapolis Star Tribune* in Minneapolis with other investors. Kramer, with his partners and a foundation grant, launched the nonprofit with $1.1 million (Edmonds, 2007). In 2013, eBay founder Pierre Omidyar committed to provide $250 million to a new media venture based on news and investigative reporting and established First Look Media as a multiplatform media company. First Look Media funded an online investigative organization, the *Intercept,* founded by lawyer and journalist Glenn Greenwald with documentary director and producer, Laura Poitras, and the *Nation*'s Jeremy Scahill. The *Intercept* received $26 million from First Look Media between 2013 and 2016 (First Look Media, 2013, 2014, 2015, 2016).

These examples suggest that it was individual donors rather than institutional foundations that provided the venture-like capital to create successful nonprofit news organizations.

> There is not a single successful nonprofit in America that I know of whose dominant initial investors were an institutional foundation. Not one. *Mother Jones, Texas Tribune, ProPublica,* the *Marshall Project, Chalkbeat, Inside Climate News* … on and on and on. There's not one where the venture money actually came from institutional foundations.
>
> (R. Tofel, personal communication, April 24, 2018)

Individual Donors

Small to medium donations by readers and supporters of nonprofit news organizations had the potential to provide a substantial percentage of a site's revenue. Some nonprofit fundraisers believed that it may be better to have 100 donors giving $1,000 than one donation of $100,000. "Grant that you have to work harder but you can afford to lose a few donors when you have a hundred. You have to have diversity so that you don't have all your eggs in one basket" (L. Kaplan, personal communication, April 10, 2018). Other fundraisers saw strong public support as a path to sustainability and as an indicator of their relevance to the local community (L. LaHood, personal communication, April 16, 2018). The challenge for nonprofits was how to monetize the goodwill that exists among readers and find ways to reach out to them. In 2017, "small donations" accounted for 8 percent of the revenue of 91 nonprofit organizations surveyed by the Institute for Nonprofit News (Institute for Nonprofit News, 2018).

Asking readers to donate or contribute through a membership scheme might seem counterproductive in an era in which consumers can access any number of news and magazine sites free of charge. But nonprofits had evidence that it could be done. Public media – well known in the United States for their on-air funding drives – and *Mother Jones*'s legion of subscribers were models for eliciting public support. *Mother Jones* raised more than $3 million of its $9.3 million in revenues directly from donors and subscribers (Mother Jones, n.d.). National Public Radio's member stations in 2015 obtained 37 percent of their funding – by far the biggest source of income – from individual donations (National Public Radio, n.d.).

Like National Public Radio, nonprofit organizations had to be "highly authentic to a subgroup of citizens and then [have] the ability to take an even smaller percentage of them and get them to start paying for it" (K. Davis, personal communication, January 31, 2012). Foundations also suggested that in the longer term, nonprofit sites should focus on attracting civically engaged donors and subscribers. "Communities and families who care about justice, who care about equality, who care about government transparency and accountability, one way to ensure that is to invest in these types of new startups that are covering these issues," a foundation program director said (C. Bell, personal communication, February 16, 2012).

National Public Radio and *Mother Jones* receive significant support from citizen donors but have built their support bases over many decades. In contrast, most nonprofit organizations have focused on building relations with foundations, wealthy individual donors, and publishing partners. Yet, for several of the 20 nonprofit news organizations analyzed by the Knight Foundation in 2013, individual donations and membership dues were the fastest growing source of revenue (Knight Foundation, 2015). Median annual revenue from donations almost doubled from $33,000 in 2012 to $60,000 in 2013. The average number of donors for the 20 sites increased from 498 in 2011 to 757 in 2013. Big earners of supporter donations included the *Texas Tribune*, which raised $1.4 million, and *MinnPost*, which raised $709,745. The Knight Foundation study found that the older nonprofits were, the more they received from small donors. Nonprofit organizations that were more than seven years old earned 34 percent of their revenue from donations and memberships compared with just 3 percent for organizations less than five years old, and 17 percent for organizations between five and seven years old (Knight Foundation, 2015). These figures indicate that a number of nonprofit organizations had successfully diversified their income streams but that doing so had taken time. The survey also suggests that small donors and family foundations may be more loyal than institutional foundations that regularly change their program directors and areas of focus.

> You get the letter from the foundation saying, 'we have supported you for the past four or five years … the board had a retreat last month and we have decided that we have changed our area of focus and you are no longer in it.
>
> (L. Kaplan, personal communication, April 10, 2018)

Nonprofit investigative and public interest news organizations generally placed more emphasis on trying to engage the community through events, membership experiences, workshops, and personal contact than did traditional media companies. An example of this was the *San Francisco Public Press*, which has organized daylong workshops of stakeholders and community members intent on finding solutions to local issues like affordable housing. The site then would publish the outcome of such discussions in its quarterly newspaper and online. "Readers told us repeatedly that they wanted to learn about new policy ideas that could improve their community," the nonprofit wrote (San Francisco Public Press, 2014, para. 5).

In a bid to attract funding and create communities of interest, nonprofit centers display the names of big and small donors on their websites, usually categorized by the size of the giving. Several sites also provide members civic engagement benefits such as free or cheaper entry to panel discussions on contemporary issues, talks by public figures, and cocktail parties attended by influential local identities. The *Texas Tribune*, which led the way in this type of engagement, hosted more than 50 events each year, including the Texas Tribune Festival (Texas Tribune, 2015).

Donors and subscribers to nonprofit news organizations generally were disappointed by mainstream news coverage and also supported public radio and television, according to donor profiling by researchers (Powers & Yaros, 2013). Mostly over 50 years of age, they overwhelmingly supported the Democratic Party and lived in the same metropolitan areas as the nonprofit publication they supported. Interviews with 40 nonprofit donors indicated that half felt a close personal connection or a greater sense of investment after donating. They valued a rich civic life and political participation and engagement with one another as well as with editors and reporters (Powers & Yaros, 2013). A survey of *Texas Tribune* readers in 2012 found that 91 percent were college graduates, 96 percent voted in the last election, and 52 percent had a household income of more than $100,000: a "smart, affluent audience that appeals to potential sponsors and advertisers" (Batsell, 2015, p. 20).

A survey of 465 donors to three nonprofit organizations found the most common donation was $100 or less (41 percent of total donations). The number of donors decreased as the amounts increased: between $101 and $250 (29 percent of donations), between $251 and $500 (13 percent), $501 and $999 (8 percent), $1,000 and $2,499 (3 percent), and $2,500 or more (3 percent) (Powers & Yaros, 2013). Key factors motivating giving were the quality of the journalism, including the writing, depth, timeliness, and fairness (lack of bias). Forty percent said a sense of community among readers had motivated their giving. The survey's researchers warned that foundation funding was likely to decline in future and that increasing individual donations was crucial to the long-term sustainability of nonprofit organizations. The survival of nonprofit local news centers depended on turning consumers of their digital products into habitual donors and attracting younger donors (Powers & Yaros, 2013, p. 165).

For nonprofit journalists who once worked in established media, close engagement with community members might well have been a novel experience. They had joined nonprofit news organizations to do serious journalism, not be event organizers, hand shakers, or panel participants. Nevertheless, nonprofit organizations viewed closer engagement with readers and local communities as a vital but underdeveloped area and were eager to continue experimenting with ways to enhance the relationship and revenues from that source. The development of closer community ties resonated with the public or civic journalism espoused by Jay Rosen and others in the mid-1990s as it sought to consult readers, address public concerns, and facilitate solutions (Cook, 2005; Rosen, 1999). "Not only is that important for the business model, it may well lead to better engagement, better impact, and better journalism" (McCambridge, 2013, para. 8).

Just how strongly nonprofit centers focus on local engagement in the end may depend on the size and socioeconomic profile of their local communities. A finding that only 2 percent of donors identified as Republican Party supporters (Powers & Yaros, 2013) should raise questions among nonprofit editors who insist their journalism is politically neutral. That does not appear to be the view of conservatives.

Quantifying Philanthropic Support

How much money have foundations and donors pumped into nonprofit accountability reporting? Several surveys have tried to quantify the amount (Henry-Sanchez & Koob, 2013; J-Lab, n.d.; Lewis, Butts, & Musselwhite, 2012; Media Impact Funders, 2013). The survey results differ markedly due to varying definitions of investigative journalism and a lack of consistency in research methods. The studies offer some indication of the size of foundation giving and other revenues but are not comprehensive, and often incorporate activities other than investigative and public service reporting. One of the surveys conducted by the Foundation Center, an advocacy, research, and educational organization that promotes philanthropy, places in sharp perspective the reality of funding for investigative reporting compared to other areas of media (Henry-Sanchez & Koob, 2013).

The overall journalism category, shown in Table 5.1, attracted a total of $527.3 million between 2009 and 2011. Of that, $27.8 million was directed to organizations whose primary media activity was investigative journalism. That meant that investigative journalism attracted 5.2 percent of the total for the "journalism, news and information

Table 5.1 Foundation funding of media by primary activity, 2009–2011

Primary Media Activity	Total Amount	% of Total Media Funding	Median Amount
Journalism news and information, general	$333,748,058	17.9	$50,000
Journalism education and training	$146,377,106	7.9	$50,000
Investigative journalism	$27,898,180	1.5	$52,000
Advocacy journalism	$7,345,199	0.4	$62,500
Constituency journalism	$7,270,353	0.4	$50,000
Citizen journalism	$4,673,547	0.3	$100,000
Total journalism, news, and information	$527,312,344	28.3	$50,000

Source: Henry-Sanchez and Koob (2013).

category" and just 1.5 percent of the $1.86 billion in funding for all media-related activities that included journalism, policies, applications and tools, platforms, and infrastructure.

Separate research based on the analysis of more than 32,000 relevant grants that were distributed by 6,568 foundations between 2010 and 2015 found that national nonprofit news organizations received $216 million; local nonprofits $80.1 million, and university-based sites $36 million (Nisbet, Wihbey, Kristiansen, & Jajak, 2018). This total of $332 million was compared with $796 million provided by foundations for public radio and television stations, programs, and news services (Nisbet et al., 2018, p. 24). The study, conducted for the Shorenstein Center on Media, Politics and Public Policy with the Northeastern University School of Journalism confirmed that foundation funding was the financial backbone of the nonprofit sector (Nisbet et al., 2018, p. 4). Likewise, an Institute of Nonprofit News survey of 91-member organizations found that 55 percent received the majority of their funding from foundations (Institute for Nonprofit News, 2018).

The Institute for Nonprofit News represents nonprofit organizations that use "investigative and public-interest reporting to advance their mission" (Institute for Nonprofit News, n.d.-a). The organization was created as the Investigative News Network by journalists from 27 nonprofit investigative news centers in 2009, a time of financial crisis for media. The network changed its name to the Institute for Nonprofit News in 2015 and broadened its membership to include organizations doing public service journalism. Today, 40 percent of its members focus on in-depth investigative coverage, with the remainder doing news or explanatory or analytical reporting (Institute for Nonprofit News, 2018).

The institute's members are funded mainly by foundations and wealthy donors. In order to ascertain a level of support for investigative and public interest journalism, I searched each member organization's Form 990 or equivalent document. These documents are filed with the Internal Revenue Service and show the contributions and grants made to the organizations and detail their revenue, expenditure, and assets. A condition of the institute's membership is that organizations publish their Form 990 or equivalent budget information on their websites (Institute for Nonprofit News, n.d.-b). Despite this, after searching the member websites and two Form 990 databases,[4] I could locate the revenue details of only 62 of the 120 organizations listed on the institute's website at the time.[5] Reasons why this information might not be publicly available include that the organization's budget was too small to require a form to be filed, that the organization was part of a university, had a fiscal sponsor, or simply had not bothered posting its return. The total contributions to nonprofit organizations listed below, therefore, are conservative. Despite these shortcomings, the analysis of the 62 news organizations provides a unique insight into the nonprofit news sector and of foundation and donor support.

Table 5.2 shows that between 2009 and 2015, foundations and donors gave $469.6 million to the 62 organizations. That is the sum total of the "Contributions and grants" row in the IRS's Form 990 return and includes revenue from foundations, donors, gifts, and other organizations, but excludes income earned such as program service revenue, investments, or other revenue. The good news for the nonprofit sector is that the total amounts donated increased each year. In 2009, the total for the 62 organizations was $39.6 million. That increased to $47.2 million the following year then rose each year to $100.5 million in 2015. This is an important finding in the context of the sustainability of nonprofit investigative and public interest news. It means that funders have continued to support nonprofit news organizations and have increasingly done so well beyond the turmoil of the global financial crisis. This was supported by an Institute for Nonprofit News survey that showed total revenue for 91 of its members in 2017 was $189 million (Institute for Nonprofit News, 2018).

The analysis highlights another key characteristic of the sector – its dominance by the three national nonprofit organizations – *ProPublica*, the Center for Investigative Reporting, and the Center for Public Integrity, which are profiled in coming chapters. Over the seven years examined, funding for these organizations totaled $185.4 million. In other words, just three organizations received about 40 percent of the verifiable funding in this sample. *ProPublica* received $78.3 million in grants between 2009 and 2015; the Center for Public Integrity $53.7 million, and the Center for Investigative Reporting $53.4 million.

Nonprofit	2009	2010	2011	2012	2013	2014	2015	Total
ProPublica	$6,354,979	$10,209,401	$10,115,367	$10,920,019	$13,678,241	$10,169,976	$16,882,164	$78,330,147
Center for Investigative Reporting	$4,158,035	$2,289,855	$5,403,245	$11,146,211	$7,232,248	$9,849,975	$13,330,101	$53,409,670
Center for Public Integrity	$5,610,122	$8,580,963	$5,128,583	$8,858,926	$7,464,706	$9,313,650	$8,762,615	$53,719,565
Sunlight Foundation	$7,111,704	$8,596,833	$6,186,357	$7,899,688	$8,925,077	$4,130,213	$4,940,631	$47,790,503
Mother Jones	$4,774,824	$4,725,235	$4,236,141	$5,184,690	$2,821,111	$6,259,779	$8,713,127	$36,714,907
Texas Tribune	$3,725,440	$2,127,574	$2,163,577	$3,502,370	$5,601,892	$3,736,666	$6,062,062	$26,919,581
Pulitzer Center on Crisis Reporting	$457,343	$1,985,780	$2,655,491	$1,790,205	$5,834,843	$2,325,660	$3,665,605	$18,714,927
The Better Government Association	$976,149	$986,488	$2,258,067	$2,554,743	$2,973,090	$2,359,612	$4,496,428	$16,604,577
Pacific News/New America Media			$4,603,602	$4,505,640	$1,220,441	$2,208,598	$2,015,329	$14,553,610
The Marshall Project						$5,139,255	$4,772,352	$9,911,607
Voice of San Diego	$969,286	$1,103,921	$974,109	$1,372,714	$1,293,947	$1,668,772	$1,823,041	$9,205,790
National Institute on Money in State Politics	$756,765	$947,333	$1,652,169	$858,153	$2,889,132	$1,993,413		$9,096,965
OpenSecrets/Center for Responsive Politics	$1,776,824	$163,835	$682,289	$1,120,043	$1,564,901	$1,294,038	$1,907,475	$8,509,405
Investigative Reporting Workshop				$1,500,000	$1,500,000	$1,500,000	$1,500,000	$6,000,000
MinnPost	$605,469	$812,074	$998,180	$1,033,394	$1,016,870	$1,799,591	$937,874	$7,203,452
Solutions Journalism Network					$844,608	$2,457,697	$2,679,049	$5,981,354
Women's eNews	$668,591	$711,949	$762,424	$862,581	$727,840	$1,044,903	$884,378	$5,662,666
CT Mirror	$605,995	$849,744	$892,071	$758,254	$785,289		$1,103,781	$4,995,134
IRE			$1,043,509	$1,201,372	$982,427	$2,096,455		$5,323,763
Chalkbeat						$1,276,876	$3,265,043	$4,541,919
New Haven Independent/Online J Project	$520,205	$651,190	$492,940	$544,420	$503,844	$453,760	$573,204	$3,739,563

(Continued)

Nonprofit	2009	2010	2011	2012	2013	2014	2015	Total
inewsource	$35,000	$214,800	$381,800	$403,400	$487,031	$1,015,273	$966,646	$3,503,950
Voice of OC	$60,880	$450,707	$348,333	$543,345	$542,393	$587,274	$556,412	$3,089,344
The Lens		$711,661	$214,380	$442,500	$577,027	$599,447	$478,735	$3,023,750
Food & Environment Reporting Network			$74,858	$382,669	$644,113	$688,331	$738,848	$2,528,819
Mongabay				$92,319	$527,294	$897,873	$797,421	$2,314,907
The Highlands Current		$171,888	$230,600	$277,104	$409,850	$376,560	$673,615	$2,139,617
Oklahoma Watch				$185,060	$478,685	$383,410	$1,072,869	$2,120,024
Wisconsin Center for Investigative Journalism	$172,700	$144,470	$189,767	$459,885	$264,645	$609,407	$199,143	$2,040,017
Wyofile		$265,368	$277,309	$159,081	$238,368	$464,531	$327,869	$1,732,526
VTDigger		$22,050	$234,945	$194,775	$293,384	$358,438	$565,083	$1,668,675
Charlottesville Tomorrow			$323,439	$412,143	$206,206	$302,316	$374,125	$1,618,229
Twin Cities Media Alliance (Daily Planet)	$201,413	$245,011	$209,349	$282,639	$139,325	$142,712	$114,956	$1,335,405
CALMatters						$100,000	$1,208,966	$1,308,966
Philadelphia Public School Notebook					$537,640	$535,641		$1,073,281
FairWarning				$162,255	$223,538	$288,625	$385,078	$1,059,496
The Colorado Independent					$162,621	$436,689	$365,619	$964,929
New Mexico in Depth				$122,846	$185,128	$279,218	$332,565	$919,757
Connecticut Health Investigative Team				$44,500	$14,306	$351,966	$275,637	$686,409
Maine Center for Public I. J. Pine Tree Watch		$67,317	$149,694	$175,512	$133,863	$195,199	$178,959	$900,544
InvestigateWest				$203,602	$132,096	$253,095	$244,070	$832,863
Aspen Journalism			$165,000	$50,800	$117,615	$120,554	$127,944	$581,913
Hidden City Philadelphia		$33,376	$204,097	$265,348	$141,379	$57,154		$701,354
Centro de Periodismo Inv					$90,329	$250,219	$354,576	$695,124

Organization								Total
Southern Investigative Reporting Foundation				$63,429	$163,628	$153,287	$176,012	$556,356
Midwest Center for Investigative Reporting				$160,400	$137,100	$128,246	$218,063	$643,809
Maryland Reporter	$136,244	$151,752		$139,771	$72,402	$77,130	$60,108	$637,407
Investigative Post				$113,510	$154,529	$150,704	$177,418	$596,161
Florida Center for Investigative Reporting		$172,371		$109,454	$84,115	$118,019	$100,556	$584,515
Iowa Center for Public Affairs Journalism					$131,323	$159,121	$116,679	$407,123
The Seattle Globalist	$92,556	$21,003	$11,846	$48,104	$63,848	$50,140	$38,280	$325,777
Injustice Watch							$310,009	$310,009
Austin Monitor Capital of Texas Media					$49,090	$111,504	$128,321	$288,915
Georgia Health News		$67,277		$25,484	$42,550	$50,745	$91,658	$277,714
San Francisco Public Press					$59,372	$114,481	$85,754	$259,607
Raleigh Public Record				$106,796	$110,774	$33,382		$250,952
Carolina Public Press						$99,418	$148,100	$247,518
Arizona Center for Investigative Reporting						$30,285	$144,326	$174,611
Broward Bulldog	$5,325	$12,414	$16,765	$38,278	$43,085	$57,123		$172,990
North Carolina Health News						$57,075	$23,073	$80,148
The Reporters			$5,250	$100	$28,676	$13,881	$18,601	$66,508
Scalawag							$32,749	$32,749
Totals	$39,639,605	$47,229,327	$53,686,110	$71,278,532	$75,547,835	$81,777,362	$100,523,102	$469,681,873

Source: Compiled by the author from the Form 990 and other filings provided by nonprofit organizations to the Internal Revenue Service.

Funding of the top 20 member organizations amounted to $430.8 million and included the three national organizations and others such as *Mother Jones*, *Texas Tribune*, the Sunlight Foundation, Better Government Association, the *Marshall Project*, *Voice of San Diego*, and *MinnPost*. In contrast, the bottom 20 organizations had a total income of only $7.4 million – less than 2 percent of the total for the top 20. This demonstrates the huge disparity of funding, capacity, and ultimately power and leadership that exists in the nonprofit journalism sector.

It is not possible from this research to know exactly how much was donated to the 58 institute members for which public information could not be located. The average income of the 62 organizations for which figures were found was $7.5 million over the seven-year period. That was inflated by the large incomes of the top nonprofits. The median revenue for the 62 organizations was $1.6 million over seven years. That equates to $228,500 a year – an amount that was slightly less than the Pew Research Center's median funding of $268,000 for 20 local and regional nonprofit centers in 2013 (Mitchell, Holcomb, & Weisel, 2016). When we multiply the $228,500 by the 58 organizations, we get a total of $92.8 million for the period between 2009 and 2015. Adding that to the known funding of the other 62 organizations provides a total of $562.4 million.

That total does not include funding by the Franklin Center for Government and Public Integrity, which is not a member of the Institute for Nonprofit News. The Franklin Center provided significant funding for its *Watchdog.org* centers that focus on state political reporting and other journalism programs. It is unclear from the organization's Form 990 filings how its grants were distributed through various programs but totaling the section labeled "professional journalism," the center donated almost $32 million between 2009 and 2015. Nor does this analysis include the more recent multimillion-dollar funding of investigative journalism by First Look Media, created in 2013 by eBay founder Pierre Omidyar. First Look Media funded the *Intercept*, granting it $26 million between 2013 and 2016 (First Look Media, 2013, 2014, 2015). First Look Media joined the institute in 2017 which excluded it from this analysis.

In addition, there are nonprofit organizations that produce news content but are not members of the institute such as Judicial Watch, the Project on Government Oversight, Electronic Privacy Information Center, and Consumer Reports. The Institute for Nonprofit News's executive director and CEO estimated that there were about 110 nonprofit accountability news organizations in the United States that were not members of the institute (S. Cross, personal communication, April 11, 2018).

I have adopted a conservative approach in calculating support for serious nonprofit journalism. Without analyzing the thousands of individual sites and stories produced by independent community organizations,

NGOs, and non-institute sites, there is no way of checking how well their work fits the definition of accountability reporting. I have excluded their foundation and other support from my findings. We could say that $562.4 in foundation and donor contributions was granted to institute members over the seven years to 2015. Significant funding, possibly a similar amount, was provided to accountability news projects beyond this group.

A survey conducted by the Institute for Nonprofit News in 2018 received responses from 91 nonprofit members. A breakdown of their 2017 revenue data shows that 16 percent had incomes of more than $3 million, 22 percent earned between $1 million and $3 million, 16 percent between $500,000 and $1 million, 24 percent between $200,000 and $500,000, and 22 percent made less than $200,000 (Institute for Nonprofit News, 2018). Foundations provided 53 percent of the overall funding; major donors provided 20 percent; earned revenue, 13 percent; small donations, 8 percent; other charity, 4 percent; and membership, just 2 percent.

Table 5.2 also shows that funders were selective in their support. They predominantly supported centers that published national stories, had good management structures and skilled administrators, won key awards, and whose stories were likely to attract official responses. The top foundation funders of national nonprofits between 2010 and 2015 were the Ford ($21.2 million) and the MacArthur ($18.5 million) foundations, the Omidyar Network Fund ($17.6 million), and the Knight Foundation ($11.5 million), a study of grants found (Nisbet et al., 2018, p. 44). A total of $214 million was distributed to national news nonprofits with the four main grantees being the Center for Public Integrity ($26.1 million), *ProPublica* ($23.4 million), the Sunlight Foundation ($21.3 million), and the Center for Investigative Reporting ($18.8 million) (Nisbet et al., 2018, p. 42).

Foundations also contributed to state-based nonprofits such as the *Texas Tribune* and provided solid funding for the *Voice of San Diego*, *Chicago Reporter*, and *MinnPost*. Of the $80.1 million donated to state and local news newsrooms, the Knight Foundation accounted for 20 percent of the total over the six-year period. The Knight Foundation also provided one-third of the $36 million given to journalism initiatives located at universities (Nisbet et al., 2018, p. 53).

Based on the figures in Table 5.2, the long-term futures of several news organizations look uncertain. Their survival might depend on finding new funders, additional earned revenue, or merging with other organizations. For the bigger centers, the next few years will require as much or more fundraising because "when you build it, you've got to keep it going" (R. Rosenthal, personal communication, November 3, 2010). The founder of the *Marshall Project* lamented, "We'll still be fundraising for the rest of our professional lives" (Wang, 2015, para. 21).

Democracy and the Decline of Mainstream Media

The foundation directors interviewed for this book spoke of journalism and democracy as if they were one and the same or as if the connection between them were innate or self-evident. They embraced a view about democracy and journalism that was espoused by philosophers such as John Stuart Mill, Immanuel Kant, George Hegel, and later John Dewey and journalist Walter Lippmann (Zelizer, 2012). Their comments reflected those of communications theorist James Carey who said journalism was "another name for democracy" (Carey, 1997, p. 332), and communications scholar Robert McChesney who wrote that democracy required journalism, and vice versa (McChesney, 2008, p. 54). Other scholars, however, have called on academics to retire the largely unquestioned nexus between journalism and democracy as a means of understanding journalism (Zelizer, 2012). US sociologist Michael Schudson wrote that democracy did not necessarily produce journalism, nor did journalism necessarily produce democracy (Schudson, 2008, pp. 11–13).

The foundations interviewed generally believed that economic storms had so diminished the capacity of the mainstream media to provide the public with adequate information or hold power to account that they had to help fill the information gap by funding quality reporting. "In essence we did decide to focus on investigative journalism and how we could support that, how we could make sure, given that democracy depends on it, how we can make sure that that's going to survive," one director said (S. Fischer, personal communication, February 16, 2012). At the same time, they knew that they could not provide anywhere near the amount that was cut from mainstream editorial budgets. With their own assets hit by deflating stock values, foundations could provide only a fraction of that capacity which meant they had to be selective about the areas they funded. "...our support can only go so far, so we make hard decisions" (C. Bell, personal communication, February 16, 2012).

The foundations also supported a wide range of causes in the arts and culture, education, human rights, environment, and other areas. Media funding generally was a small part of a program's overall giving. Support for media constituted 7–10 percent of a foundation program such as democracy, according to estimates by two program directors (A. Dominguez-Arms, personal communication, February 1, 2012; B. Shute, personal communication, February 13, 2012). This was consistent with a survey result that showed half the foundations said they gave 10 percent or less of their funding to media (Rosenstiel, Buzenberg, Connelly, & Loker, 2016).

The mission statements and program descriptions of the foundations were interpreted broadly enough to allow grants to be made to nonprofit investigative and public interest news centers due to their support for democracy. The James Irvine's Democracy Program's mission was to "advance effective public policy decision making" (James Irvine Foundation, n.d., para. 1); the MacArthur Foundation's program explored "ways to strengthen democracy in the US, given our perception that the political system has failed to adequately address major issues confronting the nation" (MacArthur Foundation, n.d., para. 1) and the McCormick Foundation's democracy program supported "watchdog and solutions-based reporting on government finance, ethics, responsiveness and efficiency and other issues of importance to an effective and vigorous democracy" (McCormick Foundation, n.d., para. 4). The democratic practice program of the Rockefeller Brothers Fund sought to strengthen the "vitality of democracy". Its core ideas were that for democracy to flourish, citizens had to be engaged, empowered, and assertive, and institutions must be "inclusive, transparent, accountable, and responsive" (Rockefeller Brothers Fund, 2007, para. 1). The agenda was to give citizens the information they needed to participate in democracy: "I think investigative journalism is an important piece of that," said a Rockefeller Brothers Foundation program director (B. Shute, personal communication, February 13, 2012).

Foundation program directors were concerned about the negative impact on democracy from the cutbacks in the legacy media. The James Irvine Foundation felt important policy and governance issues were going unreported because there were fewer reporters to cover state policies (A. Dominguez-Arms, personal communication, February 1, 2012). In New York, the Rockefeller Brothers Fund found that mainstream journalism was languishing in its ability to provide the type of information that people needed in a democracy (B. Shute, personal communication, February 13, 2012). In Chicago, both the MacArthur Foundation and the Richard H. Driehaus Foundation supported investigative journalism because citizens in a democracy had a right to be informed, and independent journalism was a hallmark of a healthy democracy (S. Fischer, personal communication, February 16, 2012; K. Im, personal communication, February 17, 2018). The concerns expressed extended to broader questions about the future of journalism, society, and democracy. One director asked who would provide the quality journalism that was at the core of democracy and open society if commercial media no longer did so (L. McGlinchey, personal communication, February 14, 2012).

Professional fundraisers employed by nonprofit news centers appealed directly to these sentiments when pitching for foundation funding. It was the risk to democracy rather than the possibly less palatable watchdog role that they raised when seeking funding. As one fundraiser put it,

Some foundations fund journalism, Knight funds journalism as an example, but a lot more of them, and especially in Europe, are funding accountability, good government, transparency, democracy. And so we can make the case that of course journalism is a driver of democracy, and it drives social change.

(R. Heller, personal communication, February 8, 2012)

The fundraiser outlined her approach when pitching to a foundation program director. She would start by describing the nature of nonpartisan investigative reporting. She would note its role as a pillar of democracy and state that such journalism had been devastated by economic downturns (R. Heller, personal communication, February 8, 2012). She would then show how foundations that were interested in democracy, transparency, accountability, and good governance had supported the work of nonprofit investigative organizations to try to restore democracy. "It resonates with foundations who never thought, 'gosh, I guess we could fund journalism, of all things'" (R. Heller, personal communication, February 8, 2012). Another fundraiser used a similar approach, detailing the demise of traditional media and its inability to inform people on matters of public importance. She asked foundation directors how people would know who to vote for if they did not have good information. How would they contact their local representatives? How would they be informed? (C. Parsons, personal communication, November 2, 2010).

Obtaining Grants from Foundations

Foundations and nonprofit organizations often connected at the initiative of nonprofit editorial executives or fundraisers. Once editors decided to pursue a particular story, they would ask their in-house fundraiser or development officer to try and find foundations that might fund the project. At smaller organizations, the editors would do the pitch themselves.

Foundations were approached in the first instance because of their general interest or previous funding in the area. Discussions with foundations were complicated by the fact that fundraisers and editors would provide only broad information about the stories they wanted funded (C. Parsons, personal communication, November 2, 2010; R. Heller, personal communication, February 8, 2012). There were several reasons why they felt unable to provide foundations with detail about the stories. First, the journalistic culture of independence from advertisers had transferred, along with legacy editors, to the nonprofit sector, and treated philanthropic funders in a similar way to advertisers. Even though senior nonprofit executive editors were involved in pitching to foundations, they set a veil over specific story content due to their socialization in legacy newsrooms on the importance of being independent from funder influence. For the same reason, non-profit editors also were aware that the mainstream news outlets they collaborated with would be appalled if foundations had any influence over story content.

A chief development officer at the Center for Public Integrity said that when pitching to funders, she talked mainly about the kind of stories the center did, the general area involved, and that their support might finance three stories over a year with the expectation they would also appear in the mainstream media. She talked in broad brush strokes on subjects rather than stories and did not shop around particular stories. She checked back with the relevant reporters on the type of information she could provide potential funders. "I am thoughtful about working with our journalists because I don't want to reveal anything that we're working on, so they help craft the language about what can I share with them [foundations]" (R. Heller, personal communication, February 8, 2012).

Another fundraiser said that foundations had agendas and the "tricky part" about journalism was that the nonprofit center was unable to accept funding for a specified or desired journalistic outcome. She would accept funding for a specific subject area but "we can't promise obviously what the journalism will turn up" (C. Parsons, personal communication, November 2, 2010). Before approaching a foundation for support, fundraisers researched the potential funders' interests on their websites, the composition of their boards, their funding histories, and organizational links. Fundraisers targeted foundations whose funding histories showed them to be concerned about "basic civic engagement, transparency, and accountability" or that had a specific interest such as climate change (C. Parsons, personal communication, November 2, 2010). Once they became targets, "you're basically soliciting the money from them," a veteran nonprofit founder said (C. Lewis, personal communication, November 8, 2010).

Foundations in turn undertook due diligence of the journalism organizations they looked to fund.

> Foundations do have to look behind-the-scenes, they have to look at our financials, they have to believe that we have the infrastructure to deliver, and that doesn't just mean a great reporter, that means that we have sensible HR standards, that we have a good CFO, that we have a sane development officer that they have to deal with every day. They look at your board, you know, they really do kick the tires.
> (R. Heller, personal communication, February 8, 2012)

A former journalist who became a communications officer for a large foundation noted that some foundations were "really nervous" about funding journalism projects due to concern that the reporters might investigate the foundation's directors or an area they had funded or cared about. "It's like playing with fire to them ... which was so surprising to me" (J. Fischer, personal communication, February 3, 2012).

General and Specific Foundation Funding

Foundation funding of nonprofit news organizations fell into two broad areas: the first was for particular journalism projects or reporting on a specified topic and second, for ongoing capacity building including hiring journalists, training, paying for administrative services, and so on.

San Francisco State University journalism professor Jon Funabiki spent 11 years as a program director with the Ford Foundation where he was in charge of grants that promoted "ethics, credibility and diversity in journalism; social justice journalism; and the ethnic and independent news media" (Renaissance Journalism, n.d.). In his view, while foundations talked about supporting journalism due to its role in democracy, that was not the reason they funded nonprofit journalism centers. "It's not necessarily a larger interest in investigative journalism as a function of society," he said, but more likely was due to their support of an interest such as climate change, coal mining, and health. Journalism was a way of moving the funders' agendas. "And if you get down to it, I think that's the bottom line, is the rationale" (J. Funabiki, personal communication, February 1, 2012). Funders were interested in something very specific, though not necessarily a specific outcome. They could be satisfied with just having the issue reported.

> So I can speak as a former funder, and the Ford Foundation certainly had a point of view about the world, social justice, freedom of expression, blah, blah, blah. So the first question would always be, in our case, when we've had a proposal for something is, 'Is this in our issue area?'
>
> (Personal communication, February 1, 2012)

This was consistent with a view that foundations always wanted something (R. Picard, personal communication, July 10, 2014). The *Energy News Network*, which reports on the transition to renewable energy sources, is funded by foundations with climate and clean energy programs. "They see what we do as a strategic communications initiative. They're not just funding us because they think journalism is important," the network's director explained (K. Paulman, personal communication, April 19, 2018). Foundations believed a better approach was to talk about strengthening communities and civic good rather than speaking directly about journalism: "It's almost as though they didn't make the connection" (J. Fischer, personal communication, February 3, 2012).

When former newspaper reporter Jack Fischer took a communications role at the William and Flora Hewlett Foundation in 2006, he discovered that program directors had "pretty fleshed-out agendas" on how they wanted to spend their budgets. "The place is filled with academics, a lot of Stanford [University] refugees, and they have very specific ideas about strategies for how to improve education or what the most effective way to slow global warming is" (J. Fischer, personal communication, February 3, 2012). There were periods when the Hewlett Foundation's program directors did not accept unsolicited inquiries. The foundation might also repurpose a nonprofit organization with a project grant to do something it was not doing but that the foundation wanted it to do.

Foundations often underwrote the reporting of a particular topic area. For instance, at New Jersey-based *NJ Spotlight*, the William Penn Foundation provided funds for environmental and water issues coverage; the Robert Wood Johnson Foundation funded a health-care reporter (L. Keough, personal communication, April 26, 2018). Instances of foundations directly funding reporting on specific areas at one time could be found on the *Texas Tribune*'s website though such information appears to have been removed more recently. For example, in 2014, the William and Flora Hewlett Foundation donated $175,000 for improved coverage of the Texas Congressional delegation; the Cynthia and George Mitchell Foundation provided $95,000 for stories on energy and water issues; Kaiser Health granted $60,000 for coverage and data on health-care issues; the Burdine Johnson Foundation gave $50,000 for coverage of women's issues in health, education, and the environment; Hugh A. Fitzsimmons III gave just over $11,000 for the Disappearing Rio Grande Expedition Project, and so on (Tribune Donors, 2014).

California Watch's education reporter was underwritten by the William and Flora Hewlett Foundation (L. Freedberg, personal communication, September 18, 2012). The Center for Public Integrity's founder Charles Lewis estimated that one-third of the $30 million he raised for the center between 1989 and 2004 was in general purpose grants; two-thirds was in grants to cover a specific area such as Congress (C. Lewis, personal communication, November 8, 2010).

While specific purpose grants funded reporting in areas such as climate and education, it also meant that some topics remained unfunded and unreported. Myron Levin founded *FairWarning*, an organization that focuses on consumer safety, health, and environmental issues. He had been unable to attract large grants from foundations. "The single strongest thing that we have done the most unique work on I would say is traumatic injury from shitty auto designs and things like this. No-one funds this. No-one is interested" (M. Levin, personal communication, April 9, 2017).

General purpose grants allowed nonprofit centers greater freedom in deciding how to spend the money. "This is what allows you to immediately repair the collapsed ceiling in the ladies' room. It lets you take on a story that you didn't plan for. It is essential" (Steiger, 2015). But foundations also found it "unsexy" to fund insurance premiums rather than being able to point to an investigative story and say, "I made that story happen" (M. Levin, personal communication, April 9, 2018).

Some foundations were more comfortable with general funding or building capacity rather than granting for reporting on specific subjects. The Rockefeller Brothers Fund, for instance, supported workshops on running a nonprofit organization because it believed journalists did not know how to operate a business (B. Shute, personal communication, February 13, 2012). It provided grants for training on data analysis and campaign finance reporting. This type of funding was seen as less problematic ethically than funding for journalism on specific topics, which had a greater potential for perceived interference by funders. "I'm tempted sometimes to fund content, but then the other side of that is a sense that if we fund content, and even though we are totally hands-off, but if we say, 'okay, we're going to fund climate change,' then, in a sense, that's a distortion, a distortion of the marketplace of ideas," a Rockefeller Brothers Fund program director said (B. Shute, personal communication, February 13, 2012).

The McCormick Foundation also preferred to fund noneditorial services such as tax advice or accounting assistance. Its aim was to help journalists "concentrate on journalism" and provide assistance in areas in which they had no expertise (C. Bell, personal communication, February 16, 2012). The Chicago-based MacArthur Foundation provided general support, but was interested in the issues that would be reported on when renewing a grant (E. Revere, personal communication, February 17, 2012). The foundation believed that general support helped maintain the editorial independence of nonprofit newsrooms "which we believe is critical" (K. Im, personal communication, February 17, 2018).

Measuring the Impact of Foundation Funding

The journalistic culture of loyalty to readers and independence from political and funder influence raised questions for foundations about how to assess the success or otherwise of their grants. Their ability to determine whether prospective projects would align with their interests or missions was limited in some instances because investigative center fundraisers resisted providing specific details about the stories they would be covering. This limited the ability of foundations to make standard assessments or set benchmarks for the success or otherwise of their grants. In the commercial world, profits were an obvious measure of success but were irrelevant in the not-for-profit sector. In any event, the goals of philanthropy often reached beyond concrete targets to "intangible ideals as community empowerment, justice, creativity, compassion, expression, preservation of legacies, or the like" (Jenkins, 2011, p. 788). These were more difficult to assess.

Nonprofit organizations initially used the number of unique visitors to their websites and page views to promote their organizations, usually reporting these to funders in quarterly or annual reports. They soon realized these metrics were an interesting but inadequate yardstick that measured quantity rather than quality. *MinnPost*'s chief executive officer and editor told a panel discussion that measures of unique visitors were

> worth zero. They have no relationship to the success of our business ... They will visit for 10 seconds and then after they're gone, they won't remember if you asked them where they were ... they are absolutely irrelevant to your business unless you're selling national advertising at $0.80 cost per thousand which I recommend you not do.
>
> (Pew Research Center, 2013, pp. 22–23)

One editor complained that the work involved in compiling a "dizzying array" of metrics that his donors demanded was taking huge amounts of his time, "I am not sure to what end" (Global Investigative Journalism Network, 2017, p. 16). Veteran journalists, some of whom had an inherent, almost visceral dislike of audience measurement and engagement strategies and other metrics data, had more arcane measures of success (Lewis & Niles, 2013, para. 6). A former legacy reporter working at the New Orleans nonprofit, the *Lens*, typically described impact as a city council member waving a story at a city official at the next meeting and demanding to know what would be done about it (Pew Research Center, 2013).

News organizations were wary of putting emphasis on impact "for fear of getting too close to the ethical line that supposedly separates unbiased journalism from advocacy work, or fear of the perception of straddling that line" (Pitt & Green-Barber, 2017, p. 46). Communications scholars have described three types of impact from investigative stories: "deliberative", such as debates and inquiries; "individual" such as firings and resignations; and "substantive", resulting in new laws and policies (Hamilton, 2016, p. 83). But measuring the impact of journalism proved to be maddeningly difficult given that there was no single definition of journalism together with the complexities of tracking a story once it was published. Even harder to know for certain was that any particular change had resulted directly from a story (Stray, 2012, para. 3). Audience numbers did not necessarily equate to impact – it might just mean that the story was salacious, had gone viral on social media or involved celebrities. Journalists believed that the most significant stories often were the least read, and sometimes their importance was discovered years after publication (Tofel, 2013, p. 8.). Nonprofit news advocate Charles Lewis argued that for the time being both meaningful engagement and impact measures were a long way off and urged foundations to base their judgments on original news content, character, and the news void nonprofits were filling (Lewis & Niles, 2013). Others argued that while metrics had their place and could tell you how many students enrolled in higher education or earned a degree, they could not show how a person's life had changed or if it had changed for the better (Bernstein, 2011, para. 29).

Yet, faced with a proliferation in the number of requests from organizations seeking grants, foundations wanted a system of measuring impact (Lewis & Niles, 2013). A study by the Global Investigative Journalism Network concluded that the "movement toward labeling, categorizing and charting the impact or 'impact events' of stories appears irreversible" (Global Investigative Journalism Network, 2017). Indeed, foundations in recent years have embraced many of the management techniques of large corporations. Foundation executives increasingly had business backgrounds and saw results in numbers rather than words (Tofel, 2013, p. 2).

A report by *ProPublica*'s president, Richard Tofel, says that funders often were even less precise than grantees about the impact they sought, or even what they meant by impact (Tofel, 2013). Tofel's paper, "Nonprofit journalism: Issues around impact", found that assessing the impact of investigative reporting was more difficult than other forms of journalism where reach and engagement yardsticks could be used. Impact from investigative reporting "always involves changes beyond those in the minds of readers, to changes in what journalists often term the 'real world,' actual changes in behaviors, policies, practices, legislation or some such" (Tofel, 2013, p. 6). Outcomes, in the case of investigative reporting, were harder to measure than outputs, leading to widespread confusion of means and ends. Tofel's paper made a number of valid points based on *ProPublica*'s experience about the complexities involved in trying to measure the value of investigative reporting. In its list of tentative lessons, it found that true impact was relatively rare and that not all impact was quantifiable. For example, "what is the economic value... of placing the New Orleans Police Department under federal supervision and curbing its history of official violence?" (Tofel, 2013, p. 20). Tofel was referring to the impact of A.C. Thompson's reporting for *ProPublica* on the police shootings that followed Hurricane Katrina, as described in Chapter 2. He concluded that impact was easier to identify than prove conclusively and, at times, involved a substantial measure of happenstance. Sometimes it was a long time coming – it took eight months of reporting by the *Washington Post* for Watergate to change from a crisis to a scandal. There was no single reliable measure of journalism's impact (Tofel, 2013).

The Impact that Foundations want

The impact that foundations wanted differed significantly from the journalistic aspiration of exposing corrupt public officials, scammers, and systemic failings. James Irvine Foundation program director Amy Dominguez-Arms primarily wanted journalism that provided solutions to social issues, rather than "gotcha" journalism or "here's a problem" (A. Dominguez-Arms, personal communication, February 1, 2012). Her foundation's $1.8 million donation to *California Watch*[6] came with an expectation that it would provide in-depth, substantive coverage of significant state and policy issues that were illuminating for California voters and for others.

Dominguez-Arms said she had made it clear to *California Watch*'s executive director Robert Rosenthal that her foundation's preference was for solutions-based reporting. Discussions between them had included tension between the desire for investigations into malfeasance within government and stories that provided solutions to state issues. "We go back and forth. I think we recognize there are at times differing opinions or different imperatives," she said (personal communication, February 1, 2012). Rosenthal, whose primary interest was pursuing hard-hitting investigative journalism, understood that the James Irvine Foundation's core mission was to improve the role of government and have the community more engaged in political issues. He was not unsympathetic to the desire for solutions journalism and acknowledged the argument that exposing governments as incompetent or corrupt had the potential to disengage people from politics. However, revealing corruption or incompetence, in his view, could lead to solutions: "It's a different approach and philosophy" (R. Rosenthal, personal communication, November 3, 2010; February 2, 2012). *California Watch* was obliged to highlight problems but would be comfortable with sometimes providing solutions without becoming an advocate. "What is the definition of impact? Is it informing the public, is it leading to change, is it catching the bad guys? It's all those things," Rosenthal said (personal communication, November 3, 2010; February 2, 2012).

The James Irvine Foundation paid an outside consultant to evaluate the impact of its grants. The evaluations examined story reach, surveyed both the organization's media partners and people quoted in stories, and reported on the type of stories being produced, including their fairness and impact. Dominguez-Arms was keen also to survey influential politicians and others to ascertain their sense of the value and contribution that *California Watch* was making. She had suggested the idea to Rosenthal who said he would pass it on to staff responsible for evaluation (A. Dominguez-Arms, personal communication, February 1, 2012). The James Irvine–*California Watch* case illustrates some of the tension that exists between the missions of foundations and nonprofit investigative journalism centers and the type of impact they expect. Rosenthal and Dominguez-Arms were both experienced players in their respective fields. She was motivated by her perception of decline in the mainstream media and was concerned about the impact it had on democratic processes. Creating a nonprofit state-focused journalism organization was one way of dealing with that issue. Her definition of the quality journalism she desired was for reporters to explore potential solutions to the problems they exposed. Rosenthal had an investigative editor's frame of exposing corruption, waste, and systemic failure. Nevertheless, such differences were accommodated in the broader interests of each party.

Foundations used a variety of approaches to evaluate the impact and effectiveness of their grants, with some eschewing metric assessments. An American Press Institute survey of 76 funders found that about two-thirds asked for some kind of metric, most commonly web traffic or social media activity. Forty percent requested to know about direct impact such as hearings, laws changed, or charges filed, and 14 percent did not ask for any metrics (Rosenstiel et al., 2016, What metrics and outcomes funders ask for from news organizations).

The Richard Driehaus Foundation, a small funder based in Chicago, relied on casual conversations rather than formal evaluations. Its former executive director was skeptical about the use of metrics, preferring "a matter of belief" (S. Fischer, personal communication, February 16, 2012). The McCormick Foundation, on the other hand, had developed a logic model[7] that included the number of stories published, audience reach, and website views. It was developing methods of analyzing long-term impacts such as policy changes. "We actually look and see, okay, were laws changed, were hearings held, was there an outcry, was there action taken," its program director said (C. Bell, personal communication, February 16, 2012). But such outcomes were only part of the process: other assessments were more intuitive, done from the gut and the heart, particularly with new organizations. "You've got to sometimes be a little more patient, but other times you say, you know, this group just isn't going anywhere, has no future" (C. Bell, personal communication, February 16, 2012).

Opinions on the Sustainability of Foundation Support

The sustainability of nonprofit investigative and public interest journalism organizations has been the subject of much discussion at journalism conferences and in academic and industry articles (Knight Foundation, 2015; Nee, 2013; Picard, 2014; Usher & Hindman, 2015). This is not surprising because nonprofit organizations remain dependent on foundation funding, as demonstrated earlier. Conclusions about the sector's sustainability will be reached in the final chapter; first, we will see what the protagonists and literature are saying.

In 2013, foundation grants accounted for 58 percent of the total funding of 20 nonprofit organizations studied by the Knight Foundation (Knight Foundation, 2015). The study found that two in five organizations relied on foundations for 75 percent or more of their revenue. Income from alternative sources such as advertising, events, sponsorships, training, and subscriptions contributed just 23 percent of revenue for the average site. A third of the sites generated less than 10 percent of their revenue through such income. Five of the 20 sites experienced no growth or a decline in revenue since 2011. The study concluded that while some nonprofit news organizations were inching closer to more sustainable models, for the majority of organizations "sustainability is just a premise on the distant horizon" (Knight Foundation, 2015, p. 23).

A common view was that journalistic success provided no certainty that funding would continue in the longer term because foundations, rather than being the lifeblood of news enterprises or nonprofits, sometimes operated more like venture capitalists, seeding startup organizations and then stepping away. Dan Noyes, one of the founders of the Center for Investigative Reporting, discovered that program directors did not like supporting the same area for long; they preferred to move on because the "same thing is boring after a while" (D. Noyes, personal communication, November 4, 2012). Other commentators agreed, noting that philanthropy was fad driven and impatient (Mitchell et al., 2013). "We lost a couple of foundation grants. Foundations get bored and then you have to make up for them," one nonprofit founder said (L. Keough, personal communication, April 26, 2018). Uncertainty about continued funding was a constant anxiety for nonprofit news organizations: "I don't know if some of those people are going to stick with us; just don't know. It's fickle, absolutely," another nonprofit editor said (M. Levin, personal communication, April 9, 2018).

This lack of funding assurance was apparent in a survey by former foundation program director and academic Jon Funabiki and journalist Nancy Yoshihara (Funabiki & Yoshihara, 2011). The survey sought to identify the challenges that nonprofit news organizations faced in maintaining and growing their online sites. The authors received responses from 32 organizations. The key challenge identified was that nonprofit organizations were finding it more difficult to obtain grants. Two-thirds of respondents said they were at or approaching a crossroad where it was difficult to secure a second or third round of financing. Three-quarters said they needed help in identifying and connecting with new sources of investment to remain viable and grow. As sites survived and evolved beyond journalism experiments, foundations became less interested in funding their operations (Funabiki & Yoshihara, 2011, p. 3).

Kevin Davis, the former executive director of the Institute for Nonprofit News, witnessed the challenges faced by the members of the institute. The issues at times seemed insurmountable. Foundations wanted nonprofit organizations to wean from their grants toward earned revenue streams such as advertising and subscriptions. Davis wondered if it was realistic for news organizations with few resources to earn revenue from the very area in which commercial media had failed (Davis, 2013). Investigative reporting could never be a commercial product. It was a loss leader with a civic return on investment, rather than a commercial one. Nonprofit organizations were in the midst of what venture capitalists called the "barbell effect" and some were struggling to survive. The barbell, at one end, represented money given to startups, and at the other, well-established organizations. Those in the middle, however, were most vulnerable. "We're trying to create a viable, independent outlet for accountability journalism, and it's hard. It's hard to fund, it's hard to staff and pay these people a living wage, and it's hard to get the content found" (K. Davis, personal communication, January 31, 2012).

Some foundation program directors were pessimistic about the prospects for long-term funding of investigative centers: "You can lean on the foundations but they don't have to support you... there is no mandate here," one program director said (C. Bell, personal communication, February 16, 2012). A former Knight Foundation vice president said funding was precarious because foundations found new interests and moved on: "It's still not a long-term sustainable thing to expect the MacArthur Foundation to write you a check every year for perpetuity" (J. Bracken, personal communication, February 17, 2012).

A former senior director with Open Society Foundations agreed that foundations had competing demands and directed grants elsewhere after a period. She questioned the capacity of nonprofit journalism organizations to find other consistent sources of funding that allowed them to remain independent.

> Where is this magic source of money going to come from? And is it possible that there is no source of money and that either we as a culture decide that we're okay without the levels of independent accountability and investigative journalism and beat reporting that communities really need, or we create a more comprehensive national funding solution, or foundations across the country take on this public responsibility and fund this field forever the way they fund ongoing service delivery programs or arts programs.
>
> (L. McGlinchey, personal communication, February 14, 2012)

Several funders expressed a preparedness to continue funding into the future. The MacArthur Foundation envisaged funders continuing to have a large role in supporting nonprofit media organizations. In 2016, its board renewed the journalism and media program as a long-term priority by making it an "enduring commitment" (K. Im, personal communication, February 17, 2018). The Rockefeller Brothers Fund said a number of foundations were too impatient and pushed too hard for financial sustainability. The fund would stay in a field, though not necessarily with the same grantees, for 15–20 years.

> We don't wake up next week and say we're not going to do climate change anymore, we're going to do something else. So we stick with a field for a fairly long period of time. We don't have a hard and fast rule that we will only fund a certain group for so many years ... it is iterative back and forth with us and the group; 'what are you doing, how's it going, what do you need?' But we won't be there forever.
> (B. Shute, personal communication, February 13, 2012)

The James Irvine Foundation had supported KQED, a San Francisco-based public broadcaster, for 15 years. "We understand that public media and nonprofit media probably needs foundation support ongoing" (A. Dominguez-Arms, personal communication, February 1, 2012).

Charles Lewis, who is one of the most experienced and successful fundraisers for US nonprofit investigative reporting, said that foundations were "notoriously fickle" but added that more funding was available today than when he started looking for money in the late 1980s and early 1990s. American tax laws meant that foundations had to donate 5 percent of their assets each year. "The idea that they are going to stop supporting journalism is simply not going to happen; it's going to keep happening" (C. Lewis, personal communication, November 8, 2010).

Signs are emerging that an increasing number of foundations are recognizing that accountability news organizations require financing beyond a typical startup phase. This recognition represents a new framing of nonprofit news organizations by foundations. Once seen in the same light as any commercial entity requiring startup funding, some foundations have come around to the view that journalism actually has a broad societal benefit and is a public good. That at least appears to be the case for the funders of the largest national nonprofits such as *Pro-Publica* and the Center for Public Integrity and some niche topic sites. "That doesn't fit the foundation model of being a catalyst or trying new things. I do think news is becoming like art and libraries, and hospitals and churches," Sue Cross from the Institute for Nonprofit News said (personal communication, April 11, 2018).

However, this view was not universal. The *Marshall Project*'s editor-in-chief Bill Keller thought the philanthropic community had not yet come to understand that when it came to journalism, it *was* the business model. "It is still a relatively new mindset in the philanthropy world that you are our support. You're not just our launching pad" (personal communication, April 25, 2018). The *Marshall Project* had diversified its income stream, but the reality was that all the money came from philanthropic sources as "there is a real limit in what you can do with neither membership nor advertising nor subscriptions" (personal communication, April 25, 2018).

Years after the 2007–2009 financial crisis sparked an explosion in the number of nonprofit public interest and investigative news organizations created, the vast majority of these entities continue to rely on foundation support. Though the degree of reliance has reduced for several organizations, the nonrenewal of grants by foundations has the very real potential to shut down entire operations or restrict their reporting (Browne, 2009, pp. 11–12; Lewis et al., 2012). The Santa Barbara-based site, *Mission & State* closed in July 2014, when its key local funder, the Santa Barbara Foundation, stopped funding it (Gallo, 2014). In the same year, the New Orleans-based *Lens* laid off three employees, axed a daily email newsletter, and no longer had a dedicated reporter covering state politics after a local donor who was unhappy about some of its stories withdrew a pledge of major funding and a national foundation decided to stop funding it (Lichterman, 2014). Also in 2014, the Virginia-based *Environmental Health Sciences* cut staff and moved to an aggregation model after losing funding from several foundations (Gomez, 2014). *Homicide Watch D.C.,* which created a database of reports on homicides in the District of Columbia, closed in 2014 due to lack of funding (Hasan, 2014). The *Medill Watchdog*, based at the Northwestern University's journalism school, announced in 2014 that it would cease operations due to financial issues (Exstrum, 2014). In October 2015, *Health News Colorado* closed after its key funder, the Colorado Health Foundation, did not renew its funding. The foundation said it could not make promises of funding in perpetuity (Lieberman, 2016). Several years earlier, *Capitol News Connection* ceased operating after it was unsuccessful in replacing lost foundation funding (Lewis et al., 2012). The *Chicago News Cooperative* was founded in 2009 and employed several former senior *Chicago Tribune* reporters and editors. Despite having a publishing partnership with the *New York Times*, it closed in 2012 after the MacArthur Foundation delayed a grant expected by the nonprofit (Miner, 2012).

Despite these examples, evidence suggests that the rate of failure in journalism nonprofits is well below that of other US startups, including not-for-profit organizations. Executive director and CEO of the Institute for Nonprofit News Sue Cross said her organization's data over nine years recorded a closure rate of less than 10 percent, compared with 18–20 percent for other nonprofit startups and 50 percent for commercial operations over a five-year period. "We do see quite a few eke along and then it's a long hard road but then they start to get traction. It's very hard work. They are passionate about it and I think that is a factor" (S. Cross, personal communication, April 11, 2018).

In the foreseeable future, nonprofit news organizations will continue to rely on foundation funding. One nonprofit editor summed up the situation like this: "I think bringing donors into this ecosystem is more important today, not less important, even though we're pedaling like hell trying not to be dependent upon them" (Pew Research Center, 2013, p. 31).

Notes

1 Nonprofit organizations may face income taxes on revenues from "unrelated business activities" such as advertising; see http://www.irs.gov/pub/irs-pdf/p598.pdf

2 The Institute for Nonprofit News's 2018 survey attracted responses from 91 nonprofit news organizations. At the time of writing, the analysis of the data was still under way, so the information must be considered as preliminary. It was presented to a conference in June 2018.

3 Chapter 7 has a detailed profile of *ProPublica's* founding and operation.

4 I mostly used the database of the Foundation Center, which is a nonprofit that gathers and analyzes data about philanthropic giving and has a searchable database of IRS filings. I also used the Nonprofit Explorer database developed by *ProPublica*.

5 Membership of the Institute for Nonprofit News grew rapidly since the analysis; in 2018, it had about 160 members.

6 *California Watch* was closed as an entity in 2013 when it was incorporated into its parent organization, the Center for Investigative Reporting.

7 Most evaluations employ the use of logic models – visual representations of the projects or strategies being evaluated that show how their activities are expected to lead to their desired impacts. Logic models are useful for evaluation efforts because they offer a result-oriented framework that helps focus their inquiry. From: http://www.knightfoundation.org/media/uploads/publication_pdfs/digitalTransitions.pdf

Bibliography

Acs, Z. J., & Phillips, R. J. (2002). Entrepreneurship and philanthropy in American capitalism. *Small Business Economics, 19*(3), 189–204. doi:10.1023/A:1019635015318

Austin Investigative Reporting Project. (2011). *Return of organization exempt from income tax.* Retrieved from http://www.guidestar.org/FinDocuments/2011/270/231/2011-270231463-084ef7f4-Z.pdf

Barkan, J. (2013). Plutocrats at work: How big philanthropy undermines democracy. *Social Research, 80*(2), 635–652.

Barnett, J. (2010). How two nonprofits saw the path to sustainability in 2009. Retrieved from Nieman Lab website: http://www.niemanlab.org/2010/01/how-two-nonprofits-saw-the-path-to-sustainability-in-2009/

Batsell, J. (2015). Earning their keep: Revenue strategies from the Texas Tribune and other nonprofit news startups. Retrieved from John S. and James L. Knight Foundation website: http://features.knightfoundation.org/nonprofitnews-2015/pdfs/KF-NonprofitNews2015-Tribune.pdf

Bernstein, A. (2011). Metrics mania: The growing corporatization of U.S. philanthropy. *Thought & Action, Fall,* 33–41.

Browne, H. (2009). *The promise and threat of foundation-funded journalism: In the future, when a journalist has an idea for a big story, will she talk to an editor – or write a grant application?* Paper presented at the Future of

Journalism Conference, School of Journalism, Media and Cultural Studies, Cardiff University, England.

Carey, J. (1997). Afterward: The culture in question. In E. S. Munson & C. Warren (Eds.), *James Carey: A critical Reader* (pp. 308–399). Minneapolis: University of Minnesota Press.

Cook, T. E. (2005). The functions of the press in a democracy. In G. Overholser & K. H. Jamieson (Eds.), *The press* (pp. 115–119). New York, NY: Oxford University Press.

Davis, K. (2013). *GLOBAL: Sustentabilidade para redações sem fins lucrativos.* Paper presented at the 8th Congresso da Abraji, Rio de Janeria, Brazil. Retrieved from   http://puc-riodigital.com.puc-rio.br/Videoteca/8_-Congresso-da-Abraji/GLOBAL:-Sustentabilidade-para-redacoes-sem-fins-lucrativos-23399.html

Dowie, M. (2001). *American foundations: An investigative history.* Cambridge, MA: MIT Press.

Edmonds, R. (2007). Old media meets new in Minnesota. Retrieved from Poynter website: http://www.poynter.org/latest-news/top-stories/84247/old-media-meets-new-in-minnesota/

Exstrum, O. (2014, December 18). Medill Watchdog to end amid lack of funding. *The Daily Northwestern.* Retrieved from http://dailynorthwestern.com/2014/12/18/campus/medill-watchdog-to-end-amid-lack-of-funding/

First Look Media. (2013). *Return of organization exempt from income tax.* Retrieved from http://990s.foundationcenter.org/990_pdf_archive/800/800951255/800951255_201312_990.pdf

First Look Media. (2014). *Return of organization exempt from income tax.* Retrieved from http://990s.foundationcenter.org/990_pdf_archive/800/800951255/800951255_201412_990.pdf

First Look Media. (2015). *Return of organization exempt from income tax.* Retrieved from http://990s.foundationcenter.org/990_pdf_archive/800/800951255/800951255_201512_990.pdf

First Look Media. (2016). *Return of organization exempt from income tax.* Retrieved from http://990s.foundationcenter.org/990_pdf_archive/800/80095 1255/800951255_201612_990.pdf

Foundation Center. (2014). Foundation stats: Total grantmaking foundations. Retrieved from http://data.foundationcenter.org/

Funabiki, J., & Yoshihara, N. (2011). *Online journalism enterprises: From startup to sustainability.* Retrieved from Renaissance Journalism Center website: http://renjournalism.org/wp-content/uploads/2012/04/StartuptoSustainability.pdf

Gallo, R. (2014, July 22). Mission & State closes down. *Santa Barbara Independent.* Retrieved from http://www.independent.com/news/2014/jul/22/mission-state-closes-down/

Global Investigative Journalism Network. (2017). *Investigative impact: A report on best practices in measuring the impact of investigative journalism.* Retrieved from https://drive.google.com/file/d/1o5G6O__lZ6NkWmqcY1T0APV-9xDhPhb2/view

Gomez, L. (2014). Environmental nonprofit newsroom reorganizes in face of funding reduction. Retrieved from Journo.biz website: http://journo.biz/2014/11/25/environmental-nonprofit-newsroom-reorganizes-in-face-of-funding-reduction/

Hamilton, J. T. (2016). *Democracy's detectives: The economics of investigative journalism.* Boston, MA: Harvard University Press.

Harris, E. (2012). Engelberg: ProPublica wants broader base of small donors. Retrieved from MediaShift website: http://www.pbs.org/mediashift/2012/09/engelberg-propublica-wants-broader-base-of-small-donors257/

Hasan, S. (2014, November 7). Infant mortality among nonprofit journalism sites: Homicide watch DC closes. *Nonprofit Quarterly.* Retrieved from https://nonprofitquarterly.org/management/25136-infant-mortality-among-nonprofit-journalism-sites-homicide-watch-dc-closes.html

Henry-Sanchez, B., & Koob, A. (2013). *Growth in foundation support for media in the United States.* Retrieved from Foundation Center website: http://foundationcenter.org/gainknowledge/research/pdf/mediafunding_report_2013.pdf

Institute for Nonprofit News. (2018). *INN Index: Mapping the growth of nonprofit news.* Paper presented at the INN Days, June 14, Orlando, FL.

Institute for Nonprofit News. (n.d.-a). About INN. Retrieved June 24, 2014, from http://inn.org/about/

Institute for Nonprofit News. (n.d.-b). Membership standards. Retrieved from Investigative News Network website: http://inn.org/for-members/membership-standards/

J-Lab. (n.d.). Grant funding database. Retrieved December 4, 2013, from http://www.j-lab.org/tools/grant-funding-database/

James Irvine Foundation. (n.d.). Advancing democracy in California. Retrieved from https://www.irvine.org/democracy

Jenkins, G. W. (2011). Who's afraid of philanthrocapitalism? *Case Western Reserve Law Review, 61*(3), 753–821.

Knight Foundation. (2009). Grants to Texas Tribune support online journalism launch. Retrieved from https://knightfoundation.org/press/releases/grants-to-texas-tribune-support-online-journalism

Knight Foundation. (2015). Gaining ground: How nonprofit news ventures seek sustainability. Retrieved from https://knightfoundation.org/reports/gaining-ground-how-nonprofit-news-ventures-seek-su

Lewis, C., Butts, B., & Musselwhite, K. (2012). A second look: The new journalism ecosystem. Retrieved from Investigative Reporting Workshop website: http://investigativereportingworkshop.org/ilab/story/second-look/

Lewis, C., & Niles, H. (2013). The art, science and mystery of nonprofit news assessment. Retrieved from Investigative Reporting Workshop website: http://investigativereportingworkshop.org/ilab/story/measuring-impact/

Lichterman, J. (2014). Refocusing on revenue: How The Lens is dealing with budget shortfalls in New Orleans. Retrieved from Nieman Lab website: http://www.niemanlab.org/2014/09/refocusing-on-revenue-how-the-lens-is-dealing-with-budget-shortfalls-in-new-orleans/

Lieberman, T. (2016, January). After five years of strong work, a Colorado nonprofit ran out of money at the wrong time. *Columbia Journalism Review.* Retrieved from http://www.cjr.org/the_second_opinion/health_news_colorado_closes.php

MacArthur Foundation. (n.d.). Strengthening American democracy. Retrieved from http://www.macfound.org/programs/democracy/

McCambridge, R. (2013, October 29). New report sheds a clarifying light on patterns of "enterprise" in nonprofit-based news sites. *Nonprofit Quarterly.* Retrieved from https://nonprofitquarterly.org/management/23147-new-report-a-clarifying-light-on-patterns-of-enterprise-in-nonprofit-based-news-sites. html

McChesney, R. W. (2008). *The political economy of media: Enduring issues, emerging dilemmas.* New York, NY: Monthly Review Press.

McCormick Foundation. (n.d.). Democracy program: Journalism. Retrieved from http://donate.mccormickfoundation.org/democracy/journalism

McGeveran, T. (2011, November/December). Money changes everything. *Columbia Journalism Review.* Retrieved from http://www.cjr.org/essay/money_changes_everything.php?page=all

Media Impact Funders (Producer). (2013). *Charts and stats* [Interactive data visualisation]. Retrieved from http://www.mediaimpactfunders.org/media-grants-data/

Miner, M. (2012, February 18). Why CNC is closing. *Chicago Reader.* Retrieved from http://www.chicagoreader.com/Bleader/archives/2012/02/18/why-cnc-is-closing

Mitchell, A., Holcomb, J., & Weisel, R. (2016). *State of the news media 2016.* Retrieved from Pew Research Center website: https://assets.pewresearch.org/wp-content/uploads/sites/13/2016/06/30143308/state-of-the-news-media-report-2016-final.pdf

Mitchell, A., Jurkowitz, M., Holcomb, J., Enda, J., & Anderson, M. (2013). Nonprofit journalism: A growing but fragile part of the US news system. Retrieved from Pew Research Center website: http://www.journalism.org/analysis_report/nonprofit_journalism

Mother Jones. (n.d.). MoJo's financials. Retrieved from http://www.motherjones. com/about/why-donate-mother-jones/mojos-financials

National Public Radio. (n.d.). Public radio finances. Retrieved from NPR website: http://www.npr.org/about-npr/178660742/public-radio-finances

Nee, R. C. (2013). Creative destruction: An exploratory study of how digitally native news nonprofits are innovating online journalism practices. *International Journal on Media Management, 15*(1), 3–22. doi:10.1080/14241277.2012.732153

Nisbet, M., Wihbey, J., Kristiansen, S., & Jajak, A. (2018). *Funding the news: Foundations and nonprofit media.* Cambridge, MA: Shorenstein Center on Media, Politics and Public Policy in collaboration with Northeastern University School of Journalism. Retrieved from https://shorensteincenter.org/funding-the-news-foundations-and-nonprofit-media/.

Nocera, J. (2008, March 9). Self-made philanthropists. *The New York Times.* Retrieved from http://www.nytimes.com/2008/03/09/magazine/09Sandlers-t. html?pagewanted=all&_r=0

Pew Research Center. (2013). Event transcript: Future of nonprofit journalism. Retrieved from http://www.journalism.org/files/2013/10/nonprofit-news-event-transcript.pdf

Phelps, A. (2011). For the Texas Tribune, "events are journalism"–and money makers. Retrieved from Nieman Lab website: http://www.niemanlab.org/2011/07/for-the-texas-tribune-events-are-journalism-and-money-makers/

Picard, R. (2014). Twilight or new dawn of journalism? *Journalism Studies,* 15(5), 500–510. doi:10.1080/1461670X.2014.895530

Pitt, F., & Green-Barber, L. (2017). The case for media impact: A case study of ICIJ's radical collaboration strategy. Retrieved from Columbia Journalism Review website: https://www.cjr.org/tow_center_reports/the-case-for-media-impact.php

Powers, E., & Yaros, R. (2013). Cultivating support for nonprofit news organizations: Commitment, trust and donating audiences. *Journal of Communication Management,* 17(2), 157–170. doi:10.1108/13632541311318756

Rauber, C. (2010, May 26). Bay Citizen nonprofit news producer launches, nabs $3.7M. *San Francisco Chronicle.* Retrieved from http://www.bizjournals.com/sanfrancisco/stories/2010/05/24/daily39.html

Renaissance Journalism. (n.d.). Our team. Jon Funabiki, executive director. Retrieved from https://renjournalism.org/about/staff/

Rockefeller Brothers Fund. (2007). Democratic practice. Retrieved from http://www.rbf.org/program/democratic-practice

Roelofs, J. (2007). Foundations and collaboration. *Critical Sociology, 33*(3), 479–504. doi:10.1163/156916307X188997

Rosen, J. (1999). *What are journalists for?* New Haven, CT: Yale University Press.

Rosenstiel, T., Buzenberg, B., Connelly, M., & Loker, K. (2016). Charting new ground: The ethical terrain of nonprofit journalism. Retrieved from American Press Institute website: https://www.americanpressinstitute.org/publications/reports/nonprofit-news

San Francisco Public Press. (2014, Summer). Creative solutions to San Francisco's housing crisis. Retrieved from https://sfpublicpress.org/housingsolutions

Schudson, M. (2008). *Why democracies need an unlovable press.* Cambridge, MA: Polity.

Southern Investigative Reporting Foundation. (2013). *Return of organization exempt from income tax.* Retrieved from http://sirfonline.wpengine.netdna-cdn.com/files/2013/01/SIRF_13.pdf

Steiger, P. (2015). Paul Steiger: Ten guiding principles for nonprofit investigative reporting teams. Retrieved from Netzwerk Recherche website: https://netzwerkrecherche.org/blog/paul-steiger-ten-guiding-principles-for-nonprofit-investigative-reporting-teams/

Stray, J. (2012). Metrics, metrics everywhere: How do we measure the impact of journalism? Retrieved from Nieman Lab website: http://www.niemanlab.org/2012/08/metrics-metrics-everywhere-how-do-we-measure-the-impact-of-journalism/

Texas Tribune. (2009). *Application for recognition of exemption under section 501(c)(3) of the Internal Revenue Code.* Retrieved from http://static.texastribune.org.s3.amazonaws.com/pdf/TXTribune_1023IRSExemptApplication.pdf

Texas Tribune. (2015). Texas Tribune: A brief organizational overview. Retrieved from http://www.texastribune.org/about/

Thornton, J. (2010). John Thornton: Nonprofit news outlets will be a bigger part of our future than Alan Mutter thinks. Retrieved from Nieman Lab website: http://www.niemanlab.org/2010/03/john-thornton-nonprofit-news-outlets-will-be-a-bigger-part-of-our-future-than-alan-mutter-thinks/

Tofel, R. (2013). *Non-profit journalism: Issues around impact* (A White Paper from ProPublica). Retrieved from ProPublica website: http://s3.amazonaws.com/propublica/assets/about/LFA_ProPublica-white-paper_2.1.pdf

Tribune Donors. (2014). Donors and members. Retrieved from https://web.archive.org/web/20141112120834/http://www.texastribune.org/support-us/donors-and-members

Usher, N., & Hindman, M. (2015). Gaining ground, or just treading water? Retrieved from Columbia Journalism Review website: http://www.cjr.org/analysis/the_future_of_nonprofit_news.php

Voice of OC. (2012). *Return of organization exempt from income tax*. Retrieved from http://voiceofoc.org/app/pdf/VOC9902012.pdf

Voice of OC. (2015). *Return of organization exempt from income tax*. Retrieved from https://1ccaxf2hhhbh1jcwiktlicz7-wpengine.netdna-ssl.com/wp-content/uploads/2017/01/2015990Draft.pdf

Voice of San Diego. (2013). *Return of organization exempt from income tax*. Retrieved from http://www.voiceofsandiego.org/wp-content/uploads/2015/01/990.pdf

Voice of San Diego. (2015). *Return of organization exempt from income tax*. Retrieved from http://990s.foundationcenter.org/990_pdf_arch ive/201/201585919/201585919_201512_990.pdf

Wang, S. (2015). As it grows, The Marshall Project finds plenty of partners, but fundraising is still not easy. Retrieved from Nieman Lab website: http://www.niemanlab.org/2015/08/as-it-grows-the-marshall-project-finds-plenty-of-partners-but-fundraising-is-still-not-easy/

Wisconsin990. (2013). *Return of organization exempt from income tax*. Retrieved from http://u6efc47qb7f1g5v06kf9kfdcn.wpengine.netdna-cdn.com/wp-content/uploads/2010/05/2013-Disclosure-Copy-2.pdf

Wisconsin990. (2014). *Return of organization exempt from income tax*. Retrieved from http://u6efc47qb7f1g5v06kf9kfdcn.wpengine.netdna-cdn.com/wp-content/uploads/2010/05/2014-Disclosure-Copy.pdf

Wright, K. (2002). *Generosity versus altruism: Philanthropy and charity in the US and UK*. London, England: London School of Economics and Political Science.

Zelizer, B. (2012). On the shelf life of democracy in journalism scholarship. *Journalism, 14*(4), 459–473. doi:10.1177/1464884912464179

6 Secondary Factors Promoting the Creation of Nonprofit Accountability News Centers

Twenty-four nonprofit accountability news organizations were created across the United States in 2009, potentially making it the year of the most rapid growth in the sector. A further 16 nonprofit organizations were launched the following year. The analysis in this section is based on the membership of the Institute for Nonprofit News, so it is likely that additional nonpartisan nonprofit news organizations were created in those two years at the end of the financial crisis. The analysis in this chapter includes data from pre-2000 through to and including 2017.[1] At the time the analysis was done, the Institute for Nonprofit News had 142 members. Almost 72 percent of the institute's member organizations were created between 2007 and 2017. The institute's rules require members to publish original, nonpartisan, and nonprofit public service or investigative journalism (Institute for Nonprofit News, n.d.-b). For our purposes, this requirement ensured that the organizations examined were not espousing political or religious interests or published advocacy and opinion.

Table 6.1 shows that of the 102 nonprofit news organizations launched between 2007 and 2017, 40 were created in 2009 and 2010.

Table 6.1 Institute for Nonprofit News organizations and year created

Year	Number Created	% of Total	% of Total since 2007
2007	4	3%	4%
2008	3	2%	3%
2009	24	17%	24%
2010	16	11%	16%
2011	8	6%	8%
2012	9	6%	9%
2013	11	8%	11%
2014	7	5%	7%
2015	13	9%	13%
2016	5	3%	5%
2017	2	1%	2%
Earlier	40	28%	–

Source: Compiled by the author from Institute for Nonprofit News (n.d.), the websites of individual nonprofit centers, and annual returns to the Internal Revenue Service.
Note: Due to rounding, totals may not equal 100%.

This period coincided with alarm about the future of investigative journalism in the mainstream media and demonstrates how that alarm translated into responsive action with the creation of alternative organizations to provide investigative and public service news. Table 6.1 also demonstrates that while the rate of creation slowed after 2010, new sites continued to be created each year. The numbers for 2016 and 2017 are unreliable because there is a lag between nonprofits launching and joining the institute. Nonprofit news centers are still being created today, but the sector's post-financial crisis startup phase is over and many nonprofits now are striving for sustainability.

Table 6.2 categorizes the institute's member organizations into the years they were created. It shows that 26 of the institute's members were created before 2000. Older nonprofit centers include the Center for Investigative Reporting (1977), the Center for Public Integrity (1989), *Mother Jones* (1976), and the Better Government Association, which was the oldest member having been founded in 1923.

Table 6.2 Nonprofit news organizations: year created

Year Founded	Institute for Nonprofit News Member
Pre-2000	Alicia Patterson Foundation
	Better Government Association
	Center for Investigative Reporting
	Center for Public Integrity
	Center for Responsive Politics
	Chicago Reporter
	City Limits, New York
	Current
	EdSource
	G.W. Williams Center for Independent Journalism
	Grist
	In These Times
	International Consortium of Investigative Journalists
	Investigative Fund at Nation Institute
	Mongabay
	Mother Jones
	National Institute for Computer Assisted Reporting
	National Institute on Money in State Politics
	Philadelphia Public School Notebook
	National Housing Institute/Shelterforce Magazine
	Religion News Service
	WBUR-FM
	WFYI Public Media
	WHYY
	Youth Radio
	Youth Today

Year Founded	Institute for Nonprofit News Member
2000	Newsdesk.org
2002	
2003	Women's eNews
	Global Investigative Journalism Network
2004	Inside Climate News
	Next City
	Schuster Institute for Investigative Journalism
	Voice of San Diego
2005	Charlottesville Tomorrow
	New Haven Independent
	The Reporters
	The Seattle Globalist
2006	Chicago Talks
	Pulitzer Center on Crisis Reporting
	The Crime Report
2007	Centro de Periodismo Investigativo
	MinnPost
	PolitiFact
	ProPublica
2008	Signcasts
	St Louis Beacon
	WyoFile
2009	Baltimore Brew
	Civil Eats
	Civic Story
	CT Mirror
	ecoRi News
	FairWarning
	Florida Bulldog
	Hidden City Philadelphia
	inewsource
	InvestigateWest
	Investigative Reporting Workshop at American University
	Maryland Reporter
	Midwest Center for Investigative Reporting
	New England Center for Investigative Reporting
	Pine Tree Watch
	Rocky Mountain PBS
	San Francisco Public Press
	Solitary Watch
	Texas Tribune
	The Hummel Report
	The Lens
	Tucson Sentinel
	Voice of OC
	Wisconsin Center for Investigative Journalism

(Continued)

Year Founded	Institute for Nonprofit News Member
2010	Austin Bulldog
	California Health Report
	Energy News Network
	Florida Center for Investigative Reporting
	Food and Environment Reporting Network
	Georgia Health News
	Global Investigative Journalism Network
	Highlands Current
	Honolulu Civil Beat
	Iowa Center for Public Affairs Journalism
	Juvenile Justice Information Exchange
	NJ Spotlight
	Oklahoma Watch
	The Chronicle of Social Change
	The Hechinger Report
	VTDigger
2011	100 reporters
	Aspen Journalism
	Bridge Magazine
	Carolina Public Press
	Milwaukee Neighborhood News Service
	North Carolina Health News
	PassBlue
	Public Source
2012	Arizona Center for Investigative Reporting
	BenitoLink
	Connecticut Health Investigative Team
	Economic Hardship Reporting Project
	Eye on Ohio
	Investigative Post
	New Mexico In Depth
	Rivard Report
	Southern Investigative Reporting Foundation
2013	Austin Monitor
	Colorado Independent
	Ensia
	First Look Media
	Kentucky Center for Investigative Reporting
	Chalkbeat
	Northern Kentucky Tribune
	Orb
	Retro Report
	St Louis Public Radio/St Louis Beacon (merger)
	Solutions Journalism Network
2014	Alabama Initiative for Independent Journalism
	CALMatters
	Coda Media
	Georgia News Lab
	Mountain Independent
	Scalawag
	The Marshall Project

Year Founded	Institute for Nonprofit News Member
2015	City Bureau
	Lkld Now
	Injustice Watch
	Madison365
	Mississippi Today
	Montana Free Press
	New Hampshire Center for Public Interest Reporting
	SembraMedia
	The New Food Company
	The Trace
	The War Horse
	Twin Cities Media Alliance
	Wausau Pilot and Review
2016	Indigenous Media Freedom Alliance
	Maryland Matters
	News Revenue Hub
	Searchlight New Mexico
	South Dakota News Watch
2017	Migratory Notes
	Voices of Monterey Bay

Note: Table includes members that joined up to and including 2017 based on the Institute for Nonprofit News membership list displayed online in June 2018 at https://inn.org/members/

This book identified three primary factors behind the growth of non-profit news centers after 2007. These were the financial crisis and concern about the future of quality reporting and democracy, the transfer of key legacy journalists to the nonprofit sector, and grants to the sector by foundations and wealthy donors. We now turn to four secondary factors. Each of the primary and secondary factors interacted, to varying degrees, with other factors in promoting the growth of the investigative and public interest news sector. This chapter shows that the factors and players that shaped the nonprofit sector were in a dynamic relationship: they were "structured and structuring structures" that included material, social, organizational, and personal forces (Bourdieu, 1982, as cited in Grenfell, 2004, p. 28). Each of the factors carried a form of capital: economic (billionaires, foundations, government), social (networks of editors, funders, donors, and others), or cultural (universities and centers) values.

The Internal Revenue Service

A necessary factor in the creation of nonprofit news centers was that the Internal Revenue Service (IRS) approved nonprofit status for accountability reporting organizations. This meant that donations to them were tax deductible and that the organizations were exempt from paying certain taxes. Section 501(c)(3) of the Internal Revenue Code provides exemptions for organizations involved in charitable, religious, educational, scientific, public safety testing, literary, amateur sports, and prevention of cruelty to children and animals activities (Digital Media Law Project, 2014). The IRS does not have a category for media organizations. The fact that an organization intended to benefit the public by publishing newsworthy information was not sufficient to obtain tax-exempt status (Hermes, 2012). Nor does the IRS have the authority to recognize broad new categories of tax-exempt organizations such as news outlets. Investigative and public interest news organizations had to gain nonprofit status under an education category. "The IRS ... told us to remove the word 'journalism' from anything in our corporate articles because journalism is not considered to be a charitable cause; education is," a former executive director and CEO of the Institute for Nonprofit News said (K. Davis, personal communication, January 31, 2012).

Tax law in this area is complex because the IRS applies federal laws, agency regulations, and internal guidelines to determine if applicants are eligible for 501(c)(3) status. The education category was an obvious one for news organizations to target: US federal tax regulations define educational as "the instruction of the public on subjects useful to the individual and beneficial to the community" (Council on Foundations, 2013, p. 9). The IRS had ruled that publishing investigations and analysis for the purpose of achieving higher standards "furthers an educational purpose" (Owens & Nokes, 2013, p. 27). The IRS used a four-part test to determine if activities by news organizations were educational. First, the content of the publication was educational; second, the preparation of the material followed methods generally accepted as educational in character; third, the distribution of the materials was necessary or valuable in achieving the organization's educational and scientific purposes; and fourth, the manner in which the distribution was accomplished was distinguishable from ordinary commercial publishing practices (Hermes, 2012). As will be seen, the last of these tests in which the IRS sought to distinguish distribution between nonprofit and for-profit publishing was the most troubling for nonprofit reporting organizations. The IRS imposed a further test to distinguish education from advocacy. The test correlated well with traditional approaches to journalism that eschew advocacy. The following suggested to the IRS that an organization had an advocacy role rather than an educational one:

1   Whether a significant portion of the communication consisted of "viewpoints unsupported by a relevant factual basis";
2   Whether the facts relied on are "distorted";
3   Whether the organization "makes substantial use of inflammatory and disparaging terms, expressing conclusions based more on strong emotional feelings than objective factual evaluation"; and

4 Whether the "approach to a subject matter is aimed at developing an understanding on the part of the addressees, by reflecting consideration of the extent to which they have prior background or training" (Owens & Nokes, 2013, p. 28).

In their annual returns to the IRS, many nonprofit journalism centers defined their mission as an educational one. The *Texas Tribune*, for instance, described its mission as promoting civic engagement and discourse on public policy, politics, government, and matters of statewide concern (Texas Tribune, 2013); the *Voice of San Diego* said its mission was to educate and inform residents of San Diego (Voice of San Diego, 2010); *MinnPost*'s activities were "public policy research and education" (MinnPost, 2010, p. 1); and the Center for Investigative Reporting said its mission was to expose injustice and abuse of power to provide the public with information needed to participate in democracy (Center for Investigative Reporting, 2011). The Wisconsin Center for Investigative Journalism said its mission included training current and future investigative journalists, and fostering an informed citizenry (Wisconsin990, 2013). A report by the Council on Foundations reinforced the educational role of nonprofit news organizations, arguing that academic research demonstrated that media coverage leads to higher voter turnout, better informed public opinion, and changes in public policy (Council on Foundations, 2013).

Official IRS approval as a nonprofit organization was important to nonprofit news centers because some foundations did not grant to organizations without such status; the organizations could only avoid certain taxes with such approval, and individual donors might donate, or give extra, only if they could get a tax deduction. Centers that did not have 501(c)(3) status, or were waiting for it, had to find a fiscal sponsor – another nonprofit organization with tax-exempt status – to accept donations on their behalf but had to pay fees for the service. Fiscal sponsorship was not as attractive to foundations and wealthy benefactors as centers with approved nonprofit status. Some foundations' policies prevented them from donating to fiscally sponsored projects (Griffith, 2013).

Nonprofit news organizations in 2010 and for several years after were frustrated at delays by the IRS in determining the outcome of their applications for tax deductibility and what they saw as inconsistency in the agency's determinations. The *San Francisco Public Press* waited for 27 months for IRS approval, finally achieving it in 2012 (M. Stoll, personal communication, April 16, 2018). A journalism academic at Northeastern University wrote in 2013 that the IRS had "virtually stopped" approving 501(c)(3) status for nonprofit news organizations (Kennedy, 2013, para. 2). The delays risked news organizations losing charitable revenue and generated concerns about approaching commercial partners, leaving them in an "organizational purgatory" (University of California, 2012, p. 14). The IRS had "never really fully been comfortable with granting nonprofit status to journalism outlets" (K. Davis, personal communication, January 31, 2012).

A study by the Council on Foundations, which represents 1,700 grant-making foundations and corporations, found delays of up to three years and an inconsistent approach by the IRS in dealing with applications. Rejections for tax-exempt status were based on antiquated and counter-productive standards (Council on Foundations, 2013). The Council on Foundations recommended the IRS shift its focus from operational distinctions between nonprofit media and commercial outlets. An example of the operational distinctions referred to was that the IRS framework required "the manner in which the distribution (of nonprofit media) is accomplished must be distinguishable from ordinary commercial publishing practices" (Council on Foundations, 2013, p. 3). The study said this requirement was inappropriate in the internet age. The IRS should determine whether a media organization was involved in educational activities that provided a community benefit as opposed to advancing private interests, and whether it was organized and managed as a nonprofit tax-exempt organization.

Kevin Davis, the former executive director of the Institute for Nonprofit News, asked:

> What's the difference between an investigative news network's website, the *New York Times*'s website or *Hustler*'s website? You could make the argument that they all effectively use the exact same methodology; the difference of course is the content, not the means.
>
> (K. Davis, personal communication, January 31, 2012)

The experience more recently of some nonprofits has been that applications have taken just three to four months to process. It was likely that the earlier delays were due to the IRS receiving a flood of applications in 2009 and 2010 while still determining its policy to news nonprofits (M. Levin & S. Cross, personal communication, April 9 and 11, 2018).

Kevin Davis pointed out that while foundations pressed nonprofit organizations to be more entrepreneurial and to diversify their revenue streams, the IRS frowned upon nonprofit organizations undertaking unrelated business activities such as advertising. The ability of nonprofit news organizations to advertise and raise revenue through sales or subscriptions was limited because the IRS rejected applications from organizations whose revenue models mirrored, even in part, those of their for-profit counterparts. Examples of rejections based on earned revenue, cited by the Digital Media Law Project at Harvard University, included a nonprofit organization that was formed to publish a newsletter on civic, social, business, and other news being denied an exemption even though it was distributed for free, received no contributions or grants but set a percentage of each page for advertising. A second instance was a free community newspaper that planned to unite men and women in social work but was to be supported by advertising (Hermes, 2012).

Nonprofit publications could advertise as long as the amount was considered insubstantial and the profits were counted as unrelated business income (Hermes, 2012). However, smaller organizations might struggle to understand the phrase "unrelated business income" or even what was meant by "insubstantial" (Waldman, 2011). Another potentially difficult aspect of having tax-exempt status was that nonprofit organizations were prohibited from participating or intervening in political campaigns or from substantially indulging in activities such as propaganda or otherwise attempting to influence legislation (Digital Media Law Project, 2014), though the ban on influencing legislation was not absolute (Waldman, 2011). Once again, this area of tax law was complex and concerning to many nonprofit news executives. Some feared that even publishing commentary on legislation could jeopardize their tax status. "This potentially chills free speech and makes it harder for a nonprofit media entity to do its job – covering important news and civic issues – and restricts development of sustainable business models" (Waldman, 2011, p. 353). A tax professor warned that publishing "even a small amount" of a political candidate's statements could jeopardize tax-exempt status (Waldman, 2011, p. 329). The US Federal Communications Commission recommended that policy makers recognize that removing ambiguities in the tax code was potentially a crucial step toward enabling nonprofit organizations to develop sustainable business models (Waldman, 2011). On a positive note for nonprofit news organizations, US Department of the Treasury regulations specified that making the results of nonpartisan analysis or research available to the public would not disqualify them from a tax exemption (Hermes, 2012).

The ability of media organizations to achieve tax-exempt status in the United States historically had assisted the growth of major nonprofit media organizations such as the Associated Press, *Mother Jones*, the National Review Institute, *Wikipedia*, the *Washington Monthly*, and National Public Radio. Despite the delays, confusion, and frustrations experienced by some nonprofit news organizations and the need to be educational, the IRS acceptance of tax deductibility was a critical factor in the creation and growth of nonprofit journalism centers.

University Partnerships

A different model for nonprofit accountability journalism was the creation of partnerships with universities that saw centers locating on campuses and often involved journalists teaching and working with students. At least 18 nonprofit news organizations had links to universities in 2014 under a variety of agreements. These partnerships served the dual purpose of publishing investigative and public interest stories and "inculcating core journalistic values and technical know-how in new generations of reporters and editors" (Lewis, 2014, p. 216). The centers still relied on funding from foundations and support from universities.

The partnerships that investigative centers formed with universities contributed to the expansion of the nonprofit sector and had a number of advantages over other models. "The absence of corporate interference, government control, daily deadline pressures or the need to attract advertising places universities in a strong position to produce quality investigative journalism" (Birnbauer, 2011, p. 1). Another advantage for the centers was having young energetic students working for the experience under the supervision of skilled journalists rather than working for pay. Universities provided office space for no or little cost, computing equipment, and invaluable access to library databases. For universities, the presence of professional journalists opened the possibility of reporters taking classes and creating high-profile projects with students that could attract public attention and improve educational opportunities (Houston, 2009).

A further advantage was that university-affiliated centers could channel donations through universities that already had tax deductibility for donors, thereby avoiding the process of dealing with the IRS. A university link might persuade the IRS of a center's educational credentials if it sought its own tax status as a nonprofit organization. One San Francisco nonprofit organization was told by an IRS official that nonprofit journalism would be more readily approved if it were grown out of a university or a community education center. "In other words, journalism itself is not sufficiently educational but could be tolerated if associated with an organization that was" (Council on Foundations, 2013, p. 9).

University affiliations also had potential drawbacks as the game and the players in the academic field differed markedly in what Pierre Bourdieu called habitus and doxa – intuitive disposition and conventions – from those in the field of investigative reporting (Bourdieu & Wacquant, 1992). The interests of a university and a nonprofit news center could at times diverge and create conflict, and universities might risk legal action due to the publication or partnering with investigative centers.

David Protess, a professor at Northwestern University's Medill School of Journalism for 29 years and head of the Innocence Project, departed in 2011 after falling out with the university's administration. His work with students on Innocence Project stories was credited with exonerating at least 12 wrongly convicted defendants, including five who were on death row, as well as leading to the abolition of death row in Illinois (Carr & Schwartz, 2011). The events that led to his departure are too internecine and complex to detail here. They involved personality clashes, accusations, and denials from multiple parties and legal issues. Briefly, when the Cook County State Attorney subpoenaed the notes, memos, emails, and academic transcripts of Protess's students who had investigated wrongful convictions, he refused to hand them over. The university later released the documents and accused Protess of making misleading statements to the dean and to the university's lawyers (Davis, 2012).

The Cook County State Attorney accused the students of using "alarming tactics" (Main, 2015, para. 3). A 2015 lawsuit said Northwestern had permitted a "culture of lawlessness to thrive in Protess's investigative journalism classes and investigations" (Main, 2015, para. 7). Media reports referred to a "phony crusade by Northwestern University journalism students" and described their findings as an "elaborate hoax" (Dey, 2017).

The case may be unique due to its circumstances, but it is a cautionary tale nevertheless. These unfortunate events ought to raise questions about the appropriateness of involving university students in the type of investigative journalism that Australian Emeritus Professor of political science at Sydney University, Rodney Tiffen, described as "revelations of wrong doing." Compared with the other two types of investigative reporting – of neglected issues and reconstructions or revisions of major events – that type of reporting entailed uncertainty and conflict (Tiffen, 1999, p. 33). One could readily imagine that university administrations would not regard revealing wrongdoing as a core purpose or activity.

Journalism, and particularly investigative journalism, regularly attracts legal threats from lawyers representing the targets of stories as well as subpoenas and court hearings. Media lawyers hired by news outlets work with reporters to confront and resolve the issues. It is part of the routine of serious newsrooms. However, legal threats, the prospect of public court hearings and publicity, may lead to a university administration's interests coming before those of a nonprofit journalism center. Universities, with a duty of care for students, might also be concerned about students facing the prospect of legal action arising from stories on which they had worked. University of Illinois journalism professor Brant Houston said university lawyers could be "so cautious that it is not practical to carry out some investigative projects" (Houston, 2009, p. 3). Journalists also found dealing with university bureaucracy was "like swimming in molasses" (C. Lewis, personal communication, November 9, 2010). Another potential problem was that universities might prevent nonprofit reporting centers from raising funds through sponsorships or offering other services (Lieberman, 2016). Then, there were issues such as intellectual property, editorial independence, hiring practices, employment contracts, purchasing policies, and administrative fees, each of which might have to be negotiated with the university (Houston & Hall, n.d.).

The brief examples below of university-based investigative journalism enterprises were selected to highlight a variety of models operating in the United States. It is not an exhaustive sampling. The centers are the Investigative Reporting Workshop, the Schuster Institute for Investigative Journalism, the Toni Stabile Center for Investigative Journalism, and several operations that are based on investigative reporters working in the tertiary education field.

Investigative Reporting Workshop at American University

The Investigative Reporting Workshop based at American University's School of Communication was proposed by the veteran nonprofit investigative journalist Charles Lewis in 2007 and began publishing in 2009. Lewis arrived at American University with near legendary social capital in the nonprofit investigative sector. He had created the Center for Public Integrity (see the next chapter) and the International Consortium of Investigative Journalists; he was the founding president of the Fund for Independence in Journalism, and with others helped create the forerunner to the Institute for Nonprofit News [see below]. His reputation and experience in the nonprofit journalism sector and, in particular, his long relationship with foundations resulted in the Workshop becoming the largest university-based center in the United States (Lewis, 2014, p. 216).

It is unlikely that any other player could have achieved what Lewis had over the same period of time. By 2018, he had raised $13.2 million, consisting of $7.8 million in philanthropic grants, $4.8 million from public broadcaster WGBH for 11 *Frontline* documentary projects, $234,945 in donations, and $313,457 in other earned revenue (C. Lewis, personal communication, February 16, 2018). The center employed four professional journalists, including a Pulitzer Prize winner, and several part-time staff. PBS's *Frontline* established a partnership with the center, operating a production unit for investigative documentaries at the center. Lewis's long involvement in the sector cemented multiple collaborations with legacy media and online outlets. The Investigative Reporting Workshop commissioned senior external writers to work on in-depth projects such as "What went wrong," a series by veteran journalists Don Barlett and Jim Steele and others that documented middle-class economic woes at the hands of corporations. The writers later developed it into a book, *The Betrayal of the American Dream* (Investigative Reporting Workshop, 2013).

As part of an agreement with American University, Lewis and other Workshop journalists had academic appointments to teach in the School of Communication. Graduate students could work as paid researchers and writers, pairing with professional journalists on projects. A number of graduate students from other universities were offered fellowships as paid interns. Undergraduate students could achieve academic credit for their work. Lewis also established a research arm, iLab, to report on and conduct research on trends and issues in journalism (Lewis, Butts, & Musselwhite, 2012).

Lewis found additional benefits to a university setting. Journalists Don Barlett and Jim Steele had worked as an investigative team since the early 1970s, winning dozens of national awards and two Pulitzer Prizes. Books on investigative reporting described them as the best team in the history of investigative reporting and the most systematic and thorough reporters in the United States (Barlett & Steele, n.d.). Barlett and Steele in 1991 wrote a landmark nine-part series "America: what went wrong" for the *Philadelphia Inquirer*. Lewis wanted epic-sized projects and felt more confident approaching the two reporters to revisit the "What went wrong" series than he might have if he were based at a stand-alone center.

> I had a feeling I could work with people like that, partly because of the university platform of being at a university in the nation's capital. They never really were willing or able to do stuff with me at the Center [for Public Integrity], but a group is different than a university, and so I felt that I had a stronger, bigger platform in a way, a national university in the nation's capital.
> (C. Lewis, personal communication, November 9, 2010)

In other words, the cultural capital of an institution such as American University provided the gravitas Lewis felt was needed to commission the series.

On the downside, university bureaucracies were more cumbersome and slower in making decisions than stand-alone investigative centers, resulting in frustrating delays and irritation. "The idea of going through seven people to get an answer for anything is bothersome ... To be encumbered all the time by ducks nibbling at my ankles, it sometimes drives me up the wall," Lewis lamented (C. Lewis, personal communication, November 9, 2010).

The Schuster Institute for Investigative Journalism at Brandeis University

The Schuster Institute for Investigative Journalism, launched in 2004, was the first investigative reporting center in the United States to be based at a university (Schuster Institute for Investigative Journalism, 2014). The institute focuses on issues of social justice and human rights, areas of passionate concern to its founder, Florence Graves. The institute was funded by philanthropists Elaine and Gerald Schuster, a local real estate developer with close ties to the Democratic Party (Mehta & Stone, 2011).

Much like Lewis and other nonprofit founders, the driving force behind the Schuster Institute was a seasoned investigative journalist, Florence Graves. Graves founded *Common Cause* magazine in the 1980s, which became the highest circulation investigative magazine in the nation and won a prestigious National Magazine Award. In the 1990s, she investigated a number of political scandals, most famously for the *Washington Post* complaints of sexual misconduct against Senator Bob Packwood (Investigating Power, 2011). Her stories led to the senator's censure and resignation (Graves & Konieczna, 2015).

The Schuster Institute for Investigative Journalism probes political and social problems and human rights issues including human trafficking and modern slavery. It has an Innocence Project that investigates potential wrongful convictions, and a gender and justice project. Graves cited clear advantages to being in a university environment that honored freedom of inquiry, and was independent of government and corporate influence (Schuster Institute for Investigative Journalism, 2014). Despite having only a handful of reporting and research staff, the institute's stories have been published in leading mainstream newspapers such as the *New York Times*, the *Boston Globe*, and the *Los Angeles Times*. This was achieved partly through innovative collaborations involving the institute's senior fellows and mainstream publishers. The institute's fellows have been independent journalists who investigated humanitarian issues and government accountability for the established media or in nonfiction books.

When their stories were published in mainstream outlets, the institute's website provided additional contextual information, stories, and links on related issues as well as graphics, multimedia, and other supplemental material. The model developed by Graves had advantages for independent journalists who often had little contact with busy commissioning editors in the mainstream media. Students in the journalism program at the university's American Studies Department were able to interact with the Schuster Institute for Investigative Journalism in one of three ways: by earning internship credits toward a journalism minor, being paid for partnering with a scholar on a research project, or being hired directly.

Toni Stabile Center for Investigative Journalism at Columbia University

The Graduate School of Journalism at Columbia University, New York, in 2006 established the Toni Stabile Center for Investigative Journalism, which offers students a specialized track for a Master's degree. Of the models discussed in this section, the center is the most closely integrated with a university degree. The center accepts only between 20 and 25 of the many more students who apply each year. Successful students attend investigative journalism classes, then spend six months on an investigative project, receiving advice from senior staff and experts in digital, radio, and documentary platforms (S. Coronel, personal communication, February 13, 2014).

Students who succeed in pitching their stories for publication then are eligible for a paid fellowship to continue working on their projects. Student work has been published in the *New York Times*, the *Guardian*, *BBC Magazine*, *ProPublica*, *Buzzfeed*, PBS, the *New York Daily News*, and other media. The journalism school also has a program of six-month fellowships for postgraduate students to undertake an investigative project or deep reporting on issues in immigration/migration, energy, environment, and race and equity in K-12 education. Sheila Coronel, who heads the Toni Stabile Center, was a founder of the Philippine Center for Investigative Reporting and is a highly experienced investigative editor, reporter, and author. The center is funded through an endowment from alumna and investigative reporter in the 1960s and 1970s, Toni Stabile, whose late brother was wealthy and left her money.

These ventures are examples of university-based investigative journalism models and there are others. Lowell Bergman, cofounder of the Center for Investigative Reporting and a producer and correspondent for PBS's *Frontline*, has taught investigative reporting at the University of California's Graduate School of Journalism at Berkeley for more than two decades. His students have produced content for projects that have appeared in the *New York Times* and on *Frontline* programs (University of California, 2014). Brant Houston, from the College of Media at Illinois, received a $75,000 grant from the McCormick Foundation to create a collaborative reporting network of students and lecturers at Midwest universities (Illinois College of Media, 2010). The News21 program brings together students from a dozen US universities to partner on investigative projects over 10 weeks in the midyear summer break. Under the program, students engage in a weekly webcast seminar in spring that briefs them on the topic to be investigated and produced during the summer when they would meet at the Walter Cronkite School of Journalism and Mass Communication at Arizona University. Their work has been supervised by experienced news professionals such as Professor Leonard Downie, a former executive editor of the *Washington Post* (News21, n.d.). The program is funded jointly by the Carnegie Corporation and the John S. and James L. Knight Foundation.

Institute for Nonprofit News

The Institute for Nonprofit News is a relatively small organization that has played an increasingly important role in the nonprofit journalism sector. Its board of directors has included influential players in the field such as Charles Lewis, Brant Houston, Robert Rosenthal, and others with high levels of social and cultural capital. The institute has collaborative relationships with key players including the Knight Foundation, Investigative Reporters and Editors, and the Ethics & Excellence in Journalism Foundation. The institute's membership of nonprofit investigative and public interest news organizations has grown rapidly since it was founded in 2009 with 27 members to about 160 and was still growing at the time of writing (S. Cross, personal communication, April 11, 2018). Much of the recent growth occurred because the institute broadened its membership from investigative nonprofits to include public interest and niche topic organizations. That was reflected in a name change from Investigative New Network to the Institute for Nonprofit News in 2015.

> While investigative journalism remains at the core of our organizational DNA and is considered the highest form of nonprofit journalism, the board recognizes that not all of the news and information produced by our nonprofit member organizations is purely investigative in nature.
>
> (Institute for Nonprofit News, n.d.-c)

Today, investigative reporting nonprofits constitute 40 percent of the membership (Institute for Nonprofit News, 2018a). One-third of the member organizations report on state issues, 25 percent focus on national stories, and 23 percent are local outlets. More than half publish daily. Seventy percent say they report for general audiences; the others target policy makers, age specific groups, communities of color, activist networks, and parents with school children, according to the preliminary results of a membership survey (Institute for Nonprofit News, 2018a). The institute's total income, mainly from foundations and fiscal sponsorship, was $3.2 million in 2014 and $2.5 million in 2015 (Institute for Nonprofit News, 2014, 2015).

The institute has provided practical tools and advice to journalists establishing not-for-profit newsrooms. It developed an online content management system for nonprofit organizations, provided members with a social media fundraising tool, and has acted as a fiscal 501(c)(3) sponsor for newly formed centers. The institute also made available preferred premium and subsidized insurance cover for media liability and training courses on managing nonprofit centers (Institute for Nonprofit News, n.d.-a).

Importantly, the institute also developed a framework for ethical practice in the sector. It created standards that required donors of more than $1,000 to be identified on its members' websites. Membership required organizations to have tax-exempt status or a fiscal sponsor. Their journalism and information had to be nonpartisan in character. Reports could not be based on or "influenced by or supportive of the interests or policies of any single political party or political viewpoint or any single religion or religious viewpoint." The only lobbying allowed by members was on freedom of information and press freedom issues (Institute for Nonprofit News, n.d.-d, para. 11). These standards had a subsidiary effect in that they created a brand and level of integrity that offered comfort to mainstream media partners and foundations.

The idea for an umbrella association for nonprofit investigative reporting organizations originated at a dinner in Washington that was attended by key nonprofit newsroom leaders. It was progressed with additional organizations at the Investigative Reporters and Editors conference in June 2009 and was the central issue at a meeting soon after at the Pocantino Center, north of Manhattan. It was there that Charles Lewis presented what has become known as the "Pocantino Declaration." The declaration starts with an assertion that investigative reporting "so crucial to a functioning democracy, is under threat" (Institute for Nonprofit News, 2009, para. 4). As demonstrated in Chapter 4, this reflects similar statements by nonprofit advocates, including foundations, during the financial crisis. The declaration nominated ways in which nonprofit organizations could collaborate on editorial, administrative, and financial issues.

Ever since, the institute has been a significant force in the development of business models, training, and editorial collaboration in the sector. Membership provided assurance to legacy media and foundations that a nonprofit organization was a serious player that abided by the sector's ethics and conventions.

An Investigative Vibe

The expansion of the nonprofit accountability sector after the financial crisis has led some to liken the period as the start of a golden era for investigative journalism. "My long-term belief is we're going to look back at this as potentially a new golden era … in investigative journalism, absolutely" (K. Davis, personal communication, January 31, 2012). Others argued that despite the grim outlook for newspapers, more great journalism was being produced than ever and that journalism had entered a golden age (Blodget, 2013). A more recent in-depth study challenged the conventional wisdom about the decline of investigative journalism in newspapers, finding that they had maintained their watchdog role in the digital era and that "many papers are concentrating on that role more than ever before" (Knobel, 2018, p. 8).

When media academics, historians, and journalists refer to a golden age for investigative journalism, they usually cite the muckraker era between 1902 and 1912 and the reporting from the 1960s and 1970s broadly covering the civil rights movement, the Vietnam War, and Watergate (Feldstein, 2006; Goodwin, 2013; Protess et al., 1991; Steiger, 2014). Some scholars dispute this standard version of history, noting that the traditions of investigative journalism preceded the muckrakers and that the analysis excluded the work of people such as Jessica Mitford, I. F. Stone, Rachel Carson, Ralph Nader, small-circulation opinion magazines, books, and a few newspapers following the muckraker era (Aucoin, 2005; Hamilton, 2016; Lanosga, 2011; Shapiro, 2003). Others regard the notion of a golden age as "historical fallacy" (Anderson, Bell, & Shirky, 2012, Section 1, para. 18) and still other researchers have found that the "growth in contextual journalism represents a much larger quantitative change than a reallocation of effort to investigative reporting" (Fink & Schudson, 2014, p. 16).

In any event, do these "golden eras" translate into something that is meaningful to the public or for American democracy?

Media economist Robert Picard noted that society tended to generalize eras by extraordinary performances rather than average performers: in other words, some media organizations did "some very big things while everybody else did nothing" (R. Picard, personal communication, July 10, 2014). Similarly, a 1975 study for the Urban Policy Institute in California found that several dozen newspapers and magazines were doing some investigative stories but asked, "what does this mean to the masses of readers of the 1,750 dailies, the score of news weeklies and the millions of viewers of television news?" (Levett, Churchill, & Noyes, 1975). When national stories were eliminated from the count of investigative reporting, very little was happening at state or local levels.

Whether or not the growth of nonprofit journalism has heralded a golden age or not is largely an academic argument. What is true is that concern persists today about the capacity of a decimated legacy media to provide accountability journalism in city hall, statehouse, and local community settings, while at a national level, the big media have been enthused by their adversarial relationship with President Donald Trump. Investigative and public interest nonprofits have invigorated an investigative vibe in sections of US journalism, reviving the traditional mission of journalism – accountability, the scrutiny of power, and a watchdog role – that many feared was lost to celebrity, listicles, and pop journalism. Newer online sites like *Buzzfeed*, *Vice*, and the *Huffington Post* have hired investigative journalists and some metro dailies have retained investigative teams while cutting other areas. The momentum for the media to engage in serious journalism had been growing even before the financial crisis as scholars, journalists, and engaged citizens became increasingly troubled by corporatization, cost cutting, and the trivialization of news content (Akst, 2005; Bagdikian, 1990; Meyer, 2009; Overholser, 2006). These concerns emerged in discussions, conferences, and papers that centered on saving quality journalism rather than creating new models for investigative reporting. This disquiet plowed the field for the later response involving the funding and creation of nonprofit hubs.

The factors identified in this and previous chapters coalesced to expand the nonprofit journalism sector. The field of technology played a role as it had in the muckraker era with advances in the printing and distribution of magazines, and in the Watergate era with gavel-to-gavel television coverage of the Senate hearings and later the Judiciary Committee hearings into the affair. The internet, which had so badly disrupted the business model of mainstream media, facilitated the creation of nonprofit center online platforms for the distribution of stories, databases, and interactive graphics. The creation of nonprofit investigative centers resulted in thousands of journalistic projects that otherwise would not have been produced. It led to innovations in website design, storytelling, and use of data that may not have been developed if left to the mainstream media.

The panic associated with mass layoffs, newspaper closures, and moves to digital-only publication during the financial crisis has dissipated though concern remains about the health, even survival, of local and regional mainstream media. A key question for nonprofit organizations is that in the absence of a broad perceptible crisis for journalism and democracy, will foundations and communities of American citizens in future support accountability journalism under the nonprofit model. The election of Donald Trump boosted small donations to nonprofit newsrooms (ProPublica, 2017) and subscriptions to quality newspapers. There won't always be a Trump or a financial crisis.

Note

1 The source information was accessed in June 2018 from the Institute for Nonprofit News's online list of members (Institute for Nonprofit News, 2018b). It should be noted that several nonprofit organizations that previously were listed as members no longer appeared on the member site.

Bibliography

Akst, D. (2005). Nonprofit journalism: Removing the pressure of the bottom line. *Carnegie Reporter, 3*(3). Retrieved from http://carnegie.org/publications/carnegie-reporter/single/view/article/item/138/

Anderson, C., Bell, E., & Shirky, C. (2012). *Post-industrial journalism: Adapting to the present*. Retrieved from the Tow Center for Digital Journalism website: http://towcenter.org/research/post-industrial-journalism/

Aucoin, J. (2005). *The evolution of American investigative journalism*. Columbia: University of Missouri Press.

Bagdikian, B. H. (1990). *The media monopoly* (3rd ed.). Boston, MA: Beacon Press.

Barlett, D. L., & Steele, J. B. (n.d.). Biography. Retrieved from http://www.barlettandsteele.com/about.php

Birnbauer, B. (2011). Student muckrakers: Applying lessons from non-profit investigative reporting in the US. *Pacific Journalism Review, 17*(1), 26–44. doi:10.24135/pjr.v17i1.370

Blodget, H. (2013). Journalism has entered a golden age. Retrieved from Business Insider website: http://www.businessinsider.com.au/a-golden-age-for-journalism-2013-8

Bourdieu, P., & Wacquant, L. J. D. (1992). *An invitation to reflexive sociology.* Chicago, IL: University of Chicago Press.

Carr, D., & Schwartz, J. (2011, June 17). A watchdog professor, now defending himself. *The New York Times.* Retrieved from http://www.nytimes.com/2011/06/18/business/media/18protess.html

Center for Investigative Reporting. (2011). *Return of organization exempt from income tax.* Retrieved from http://cironline.org/sites/default/files/CIR-FY11FederalForm990-Final.pdf

Council on Foundations. (2013). *The IRS and nonprofit media: Toward creating a more informed public* (Report of the Nonprofit Media Working Group). Retrieved from Nieman Lab website: http://www.niemanlab.org/pdfs/IRSandNonprofitMedia-CouncilofFoundations.pdf

Davis, K. (2012). Journalism and justice: Did student reporters in a well-known innocence project become too close to lawyers? *ABA Journal, 98*(1). Retrieved from http://www.abajournal.com/magazine/article/journalism_justice_did_innocence_project_student_reporters_get_too_close

Dey, J. (2017, May 28). Curious court rulings highlight Northwestern 'innocence' case. *The News-Gazette.* Retrieved from http://www.news-gazette.com/news/local/2017-05-28/jim-dey-curious-court-rulings-highlight-northwestern-innocence-case.html

Digital Media Law Project. (2014). How does the IRS interpret Section 501(c)(3)? Retrieved from http://www.dmlp.org/irs/section-501c3

Feldstein, M. (2006). A muckraking model: Investigative reporting cycles in American history. *Press/Politics, 11*(2), 105–120. doi:10.1177/1081180X06286780

Fink, K., & Schudson, M. (2014). The rise of contextual journalism, 1950s–2000s. *Journalism, 15*(1), 3–20. doi:10.1177/1464884913479015

Goodwin, D. K. (2013). *The bully pulpit: Theodore Roosevelt, William Howard Taft, and the golden age of journalism.* New York, NY: Simon & Schuster.

Graves, L., & Konieczna, M. (2015). Sharing the news: Journalistic collaboration as field repair. *International Journal of Communication, 9,* 1966–1984.

Grenfell, M. (2004). *Pierre Bourdieu: Agent provocateur.* London, England: Continuum.

Griffith, T. (2013, June/July). How outdated IRS policies hurt nonprofit journalism. *American Journalism Review.* Retrieved from http://ajrarchive.org/article.asp?id=5542

Hamilton, J. T. (2016). *Democracy's detectives: The economics of investigative journalism.* Boston, MA: Harvard University Press.

Hermes, J. P. (2012). Guide to the Internal Revenue Service decision-making process under section 501(c)(3) for journalism and publishing non-profit organizations. *Australian Policy Online*. Retrieved from http://apo.org.au/research/guide-internal-revenue-service-decision-making-process-under-501c3-journalism-and

Houston, B. (2009). *The first draft: Emerging models for regional and state non-profit investigative journalism centers*. Paper presented at the Duke Conference on Nonprofit Media, Duke Sanford School of Public Policy, Duke University, Durham, NC. Retrieved from http://www2.sanford.duke.edu/nonprofitmedia/documents/DWC_Conference_Report.pdf

Houston, B., & Hall, A. (n.d.). Launching a nonprofit news site. Retrieved from J-Lab, Knight Community News Network website: http://kcnn.org/learning-modules/launching-a-nonprofit-news-site/

Illinois College of Media. (2010). Illinois receives McCormick grant for journalism consortium. Retrieved from http://www.media.illinois.edu/knight/Houston-McCormickGrant

Institute for Nonprofit News. (2009). The Pocantico Declaration: Creating a nonprofit Investigative News Network. Retrieved from http://inn.org/pocantico-declaration/

Institute for Nonprofit News. (2014). *Return of organization exempt from income tax*. Retrieved from https://1l9nh32zekco14afdq2plfsw-wpengine.netdna-ssl.com/wp-content/uploads/2013/01/IRS-Form-990_2014.pdf

Institute for Nonprofit News. (2015). INN is now the Institute for Nonprofit News. Retrieved from https://inn.org/2015/03/inn-is-now-the-institute-for-nonprofit-news/

Institute for Nonprofit News. (2018a). *INN Index: Mapping the growth of nonprofit news*. Paper presented at the INN Days, June 14, Orlando, FL.

Institute for Nonprofit News. (2018b). Members directory. Retrieved June 8, 2018, from https://inn.org/members/

Institute for Nonprofit News. (n.d.-a). About INN. Retrieved June 24, 2014, from http://inn.org/about/

Institute for Nonprofit News. (n.d.-b). Ethics and practices policies. Retrieved from https://inn.org/for-members/ethics/

Institute for Nonprofit News. (n.d.-c). FAQs. Retrieved from https://inn.org/about/membership-faqs/

Institute for Nonprofit News. (n.d.-d). Membership standards. Retrieved from Investigative News Network website: http://inn.org/for-members/membership-standards/

Investigating Power. (2011). Florence Graves. Retrieved from http://www.investigatingpower.org/journalist/florence-graves/

Investigative Reporting Workshop. (2013). About the Investigative Reporting Workshop. Retrieved from http://investigativereportingworkshop.org/about/

Kennedy, D. (2013, May 16). Beyond the Tea Party: How the IRS is killing nonprofit media. *Huffington Post*. Retrieved from http://www.huffingtonpost.com/dan-kennedy/beyond-the-tea-party-how_b_3286604.html

Knobel, B. (2018). *The watchdog still barks: How accountability reporting evolved for the digital age*. New York, NY: Fordham University Press.

Lanosga, G. (2011). *The press, prizes and power: Investigative reporting in the United States, 1917–1960* (Doctoral dissertation), Indiana University, Indianapolis. Available from Proquest Dissertations and Theses database (UMI 3439578).

Levett, M., Churchill, M., & Noyes, D. (1975). *Exploring ways and means of increasing investigative journalism.* Unpublished manuscript, Urban Policy Research Institute.

Lewis, C. (2014). *935 lies: The future of truth and the decline of America's moral integrity.* New York, NY: PublicAffairs.

Lewis, C., Butts, B., & Musselwhite, K. (2012). A second look: The new journalism ecosystem. Retrieved from Investigative Reporting Workshop website: http://investigativereportingworkshop.org/ilab/story/second-look/

Lieberman, T. (2016, January). After five years of strong work, a Colorado nonprofit ran out of money at the wrong time. *Columbia Journalism Review.* Retrieved from http://www.cjr.org/the_second_opinion/health_news_colorado_closes.php

Main, F. (2015, February 17). Man sues Northwestern, others for $40 million; says prof helped frame him for double murder. *Chicago Sun Times.* Retrieved from http://chicago.suntimes.com/news-chicago/7/71/374503/man-sues-northwestern-others-40-million-says-prof-helped-frame-double-murder

Mehta, A., & Stone, P. H. (2011). Obama, first lady, VP combine for 45 fundraisers since official campaign launch. Retrieved from Center for Public Integrity website: http://www.publicintegrity.org/2011/07/05/5097/obama-first-lady-vp-combine-45-fundraisers-official-campaign-launch

Meyer, P. (2009). *The vanishing newspaper: Saving journalism in the information age* (2nd ed.). Columbia: University of Missouri Press.

MinnPost. (2010). *Return of organization exempt from income tax.* Retrieved from http://www.minnpost.com/sites/default/files/attachments/CEI%20990%20for%20FY%202011.pdf

News21. (n.d.). About us. Retrieved from http://news21.com/about-news21-more/

Overholser, G. (2006). *On behalf of journalism: A manifesto for change.* Retrieved from The Annenberg Public Policy Center, University of Pennsylvania website: http://editor.annenbergpublicpolicycenter.org/wp-content/uploads/OnBehalfjune20082.pdf

Owens, M., & Nokes, S. (2013). Overview of the Federal tax rules affecting the formation, operation, funding and structure of a tax-exempt newspaper. In Council on Foundations Nonprofit Media Working Group (Ed.), *The IRS and nonprofit media: Toward creating a more informed public.* Arlington, VA: Council on Foundations.

ProPublica. (2017, January–April). *Report to stakeholders.* Retrieved from https://assets.propublica.org/propublica-2017-1st-interim-report.pdf

Protess, D., Cook, F. L., Doppelt, J. C., Ettema, J. S., Gordon, M. T., Leff, D. R., & Miller, P. (1991). *The Journalism of outrage: Investigative reporting and agenda building in America.* New York, NY: Guilford Press.

Schuster Institute for Investigative Journalism. (2014). Welcome for the director. Retrieved from http://www.brandeis.edu/investigate/about/letter.html

Shapiro, B. (2003). *Shaking the foundations: 200 years of investigative journalism in America.* New York, NY: Thunder's Mouth Press.

Steiger, P. (2014). A closer look: Three golden ages of journalism? Retrieved from ProPublica website: http://www.propublica.org/article/a-closer-look-three-golden-ages-of-journalism

Texas Tribune. (2013). *Return of organization exempt from income tax.* Retrieved from http://static.texastribune.org.s3.amazonaws.com/media/

documents/Updated_TexasTribune990PublicDisclosureAmended_12-31-13_14Mar15.pdf

Tiffen, R. (1999). *Scandals: Media, politics and corruption in contemporary Australia*. Sydney, Australia: UNSW Press.

University of California, Berkeley. (2012). *From outsourcing to innovation: How nonprofit/commercial media partnerships can help fill the news gap.* Retrieved from John S. and James L. Knight Foundation website: http://www. knightfoundation.org/media/uploads/article_pdfs/From_Outsourcing_to_Innovation_by_UCB_for_KF_1.pdf

University of California, Berkeley. (2014). Lowell Bergman. Retrieved July 29, 2014, from http://journalism.berkeley.edu/faculty/bergman/

Voice of San Diego. (2010). *Return of organization exempt from income tax.* Retrieved from http://www.voiceofsandiego.org/wp-content/uploads/app/pdf/VOSD2010-990.pdf

Waldman, S. (2011). *The information needs of communities: The changing media landscape in a broadband age.* Retrieved from Federal Communications Commission website: www.fcc.gov/infoneedsreport

Wisconsin990. (2013). *Return of organization exempt from income tax.* Retrieved from http://u6efc47qb7f1g5v06kf9kfdcn.wpengine.netdna-cdn.com/wp-content/uploads/2010/05/2013-Disclosure-Copy-2.pdf

7 Case Studies of Four National Nonprofit Investigative Reporting Centers

The Center for Investigative Reporting, the Center for Public Integrity, *ProPublica*, and *Mother Jones* are the largest nonprofit investigative news organizations in the United States. They are prolific producers of investigative journalism and appear to have achieved financial stability. This makes them exceptions among US nonprofit news centers that are smaller and less financially secure. The circumstances in which the centers were created differed and they were launched in diverse media environments: two in the aftermath of Watergate in the 1970s, another in the late 1980s as media corporations sought to maintain big profit margins and cut costs, and the third in 2008 during the global financial crisis. This chapter analyzes their creation, progress, the reasons for their success, their finances, and the challenges they faced.

The centers operate like specialist studios with their editorial, financial, and administrative processes geared for the production of high-quality accountability journalism. The effect of these four organizations on US investigative journalism transcends the prestigious awards won, their self-described role in filling the information gap in mainstream media, and their innovative use of technology. They enlivened an idealized notion of investigative journalism as the scaffold of democracy and provided some hope to those who despaired that the tide of celebrity, spin, and the varnished statements of politicians would swamp the media, the public, and ultimately democracy itself.

They produced thousands of stories and projects in the public interest. They exposed violence and shocking conditions in private prisons, the mistreatment of miners suffering black lung disease, sexual assaults of female farm workers, patient deaths following medical interventions, campaign funding and the perks returned, thousands of doctor beneficiaries of pharmaceutical company gifts, police bungling of a rape case, inappropriate opiate prescribing, dangerous workplaces, safety risks at nuclear weapons plants, behind-the-scenes political influence by fossil fuel corporations, and scores of wrongdoings. Their journalism was distributed throughout the nation on websites, partnerships with other media, on podcasts, video documentaries, radio series, and even in stage plays and finger puppetry. However, as will be seen, these organizations also experienced financial crises, management and personality issues, and made decisions that ultimately proved to be wrong.

While the centers might be outliers in the nonprofit news sector due to their size and finances, their histories, challenges, and successes contain lessons for smaller outfits and startups. This chapter elucidates the complex legal, political, and management issues that confronted the nonprofit organizations at various stages of their development. It shows that the creation and growth of new ventures is a complex interplay of resources, opportunities, and capabilities (Thakur, 1999).

The Center for Investigative Reporting

The Center for Investigative Reporting was created in 1977, three years after the resignation of President Richard Nixon in the wake of the Watergate revelations. It was a period noted for the quantity of investigative reporting and adversarial relations between reporters and government (Protess et al., 1991, pp. 3, 20). As would be the case with some nonprofit organizations 30 years later, the Center for Investigative Reporting was created after two of its three founders lost their jobs and wanted to continue producing investigative stories. Lowell Bergman and David Weir were California-based investigative reporters for *Rolling Stone* magazine when the magazine's cofounder and publisher, Jann Wenner, announced during a Christmas party that the magazine was moving to New York and they no longer had jobs (L. Bergman, personal communication, September 2, 2014; D. Weir, personal communication, August 20, 2014). The third founder, Dan Noyes, a journalism educator and administrator, was part of a team of journalists, including Bergman, that in 1976 collaborated on an investigation into the killing of a reporter by a criminal outfit – a cooperative reporting venture that became known as the Arizona Project (Investigative Reporters and Editors, n.d.). The experience convinced Noyes that journalists from different backgrounds and jobs could work cooperatively on complex investigative stories (D. Noyes, personal communication, November 4, 2010).

In the late 1960s, Bergman wrote about corruption for alternative publications in San Diego, including the *Free Press* which later became the *Street Journal*. He moved to San Francisco in 1971 and worked with the left-wing *Ramparts* magazine before starting at *Rolling Stone* (L. Bergman, personal communication, September 2, 2014). In the mid-1970s, Bergman and another reporter faced a $522 million libel action over an article for *Penthouse* magazine in which they alleged a resort was linked to organized crime. The lawsuit was settled after 10 years of legal hearings and appeals with *Penthouse* and the resort owners meeting their own costs reportedly totaling $20 million (Acuna, 1985). Bergman had other writs seeking a total of about $1 billion in damages (L. Bergman, personal communication, September 2, 2014). Disputes with local Hearst Corporation newspapers limited his options for investigative reporting in the Bay Area. The *New York Times* was a possible employer but Bergman, like the other founders, wanted to stay in the Bay Area (personal communication, September 2, 2014).

The partners wanted to pursue stories that were too hot to handle for other publications. The Center for Investigative Reporting was launched in the garage of Bergman's Berkeley home before moving to an office in Oakland with funding that included a small grant from the Fund for Investigative Journalism – the funder that years earlier had assisted Seymour Hersh to report on the My Lai Massacre (Fund for Investigative Journalism, n.d.). The founders were not confident that the center had a long-term future or that foundations would support it.

Creating a nonprofit center for investigative journalism in the post-Watergate period appears to conflict with the view of some academics that it was a golden era with opportunities to do watchdog journalism in the mainstream media (Feldstein, 2006; Protess et al., 1991; Steiger, 2014). However, an unpublished research paper prepared in 1975 by Noyes and colleagues at the Urban Policy Research Institute concluded that while the *New York Times* and the *Washington Post* competed in Washington, only several dozen newspapers and magazines did some investigative work.

> What does this mean to the masses of readers of the 1,750 dailies, the score of news weeklies and the millions of viewers of television news? It becomes academic to try to identify those local papers which consistently do investigative work because most have not yet begun.
>
> (Levett, Churchill, & Noyes, 1975, pp. 5–6)

It is not intended to traverse the Center for Investigative Reporting's thousands of stories and projects in the decades since its formation. What is of note is that the center survived periods when investigative journalism generally was less popular; it adapted to an online environment; was among the first of the nonprofits to collaborate with mainstream outlets; charged fees for its work, pioneered a newspaper syndication model; developed multimedia storytelling and an investigative documentary site; adapted its platform and processes to focus on public radio; and was willing to experiment by presenting its findings with animation, finger puppetry, stage plays, and poetry. Constant innovation fueled the granting processes of foundations.

Early Partnerships and Recognition

The center's early stories were published in liberal magazines that were more receptive to outside contributors than newspapers, which mainly did their own reporting. Magazine editors were like-minded and interested in pursuing complex investigative stories and they paid for contributions (M. Schapiro & D. Noyes, personal communication, November 4, 2010; April 16, 2012). The center's first stories were published in progressive publications that included *Mother Jones*, *New Times*, *New West*, and *The Nation*.

Early stories on the criminal activities of the Black Panther Party, published in the *New Times* magazine (Coleman & Avery, 1978), and others in *Mother Jones* attracted the attention of Mark Schapiro, a young journalism student who had interned at the center. At the time, David Weir was investigating why chemicals banned in the United States were being used in products sold in developing countries. He had purchased a pack of Kool-Aid in a remote bazaar in Afghanistan and found that it contained cyclamates that were banned in the United States (Weir & Schapiro, 1981). *Rolling Stone* eventually published his story in February 1977 (Weir & Noyes, 1983). At the time, *Rolling Stone* was moving away from in-depth political stories to expanded coverage of music and entertainment and did not promote the story, which was overlooked by the US press (Weir & Noyes, 1983). Nevertheless, the issue of hazardous exports gained traction in Washington, DC, through Congressional hearings and conferences. *Mother Jones* asked Weir to research hazardous exports further and write about pesticides in the Third World. Schapiro joined Weir and another reporter from the center for a series of stories that were published in *Mother Jones*. "The Boomerang Crime" described how US companies shipped pesticides banned in the United States to developing countries and then imported food contaminated with poison residues (Weir, Schapiro, & Jacobs, 1979).

The stories initially were ignored or downplayed by legacy media but had substantial impact. The United Nations passed a resolution on hazardous exports, legislation was introduced in Congress, new regulatory standards for pesticides were introduced in several developing countries, and the US Environmental Protection Agency tightened the loophole that had allowed the export of banned pesticides. *Mother Jones* won a national award for the series (Weir & Noyes, 1983, pp. 171–185). Mainstream media interest increased due to the political response: dozens of reporters contacted the center to write their own versions of the story. Associated Press conducted a worldwide survey of hazardous exports, as did *Newsday*, and PBS aired a two-part documentary that relied on the center's work for a significant portion of its content (Weir & Noyes, 1983). Soon after, another investigation by the center, "The Most Captive Consumers" – about faulty wheelchairs – won a National Press Club award. The story was published in *The Progressive*, a monthly left-wing magazine (The Progressive, n.d.). The response to the pesticide series and an award from an established industry body brought the center a higher profile and some industry credibility.

The center's next phase involved partnering with commercial television stations. This represented more than a shift in platforms: it was a shift from alternative magazines to collaborations with national broadcasters that were outsourcing some of their journalistic research, story conception, and development. The shift occurred because Bergman was employed by ABC News as a reporter, producer, and head of its investigative team. He became one of the original producers on the ABC's *20/20* program and worked with the Center for Investigative Reporting on at least two stories for *20/20*. In 1979, for example, Noyes initiated a television story that identified the fundraising arm of the United Nation's International Year of the Child as a front for gunrunning and drug smuggling (Center for Investigative Reporting, n.d.). Bergman used his contacts in law enforcement to develop the story, which he also produced.

These stories led to the center contracting with ABC News, and later with CBS News's *60 Minutes* and PBS's *Frontline*, as Bergman moved to different media organizations (L. Bergman, personal communication, September 2, 2014). At the time it was unprecedented for a nonprofit organization to have a long-term content and consulting contract with a mainstream media group. The partnership brought much-needed funding to the center as several magazine outlets had closed and foundation monies were scarce (Prial, 1983).

The center published "Circle of Poison" (Weir & Schapiro, 1981), a book based on Weir and Schapiro's investigations into banned pesticide exports to developing countries. The book was commissioned by the Institute for Food and Development Policy, which asked the reporters to return to their investigations and dig deeper. The basic story had already been told in *Mother Jones* and *Rolling Stone*, so the center had low expectations about the revenue the book would earn. The story, however, led NBC News: "All of a sudden we had foundations interested in environmental issues, not so much journalism, who said 'we want to fund you to do these kinds of stories on environmental issues'," (D. Noyes, personal communication, November 4, 2010).

Despite these successes, Noyes worried about the center's future due to what he feared was a lack of long-term certainty about its funding. Commercial fees were not sufficient to recover the cost of a six-month or yearlong investigation. Weir and Noyes laid off reporters when project money ran out and there were periods when staff were not paid for a week each month (M. Schapiro, personal communication, November 4, 2010). Concern over funding shortfalls is an abiding characteristic of nonprofit journalism.

Over the next 15 years, the center's fortunes ebbed and flowed (Rosenthal, 2011, p. 2), but it consolidated its reputation and strengthened its links particularly with television networks. It continued to collaborate with broadcasters as well as progressive magazine publishers, though its stories appeared in only a small number of mainstream newspapers. In 1990, the center produced its first independent television documentary, "Global Dumping Ground." The documentary, about the traffic in hazardous wastes, was reported by Bill Moyers and produced by Lowell Bergman who took leave from *60 Minutes* to develop the documentary with others at the center (D. Noyes, personal communication, April 16, 2012). The documentary opened a new season on PBS's *Frontline* and sparked a federal investigation (Center for Investigative Reporting, n.d.). The *Frontline* partnership allowed greater editorial input by the center's journalists than did the ABC's *20/20* program or *60 Minutes*, which mainly wanted story ideas for their reporters to pursue. "Sometimes we were not sure of the story's outcome until it was ready to air" (D. Noyes, personal communication, April 16, 2012).

The early history of the Center for Investigative Reporting elicits a number of lessons about the growth, development, and sustainability of nonprofit investigative centers. Among these is the importance of personal relationships in fostering collaborations. Were it not for the relationship that Bergman had with Noyes dating back to 1975, it would have been more difficult for the center to establish ongoing partnerships with the television companies. Personal relationships, trust, and social and symbolic capital were critical to these partnerships. The financial vulnerability of the center was evident in the period before the television partnerships when the center had to lay off staff. The benefit of multiple publishing partners became apparent as several left-leaning magazines, including *Ramparts* and *New Times*, closed from the mid-1970s as the economic and political environment became more conservative. The partnership with PBS was built on the synergies that exist between public broadcasters and nonprofit centers: a similar socioeconomic audience, a capacity to produce quality journalism and finding mutual financial benefit from collaborations.

Confronting Financial Pressures and Management Issues

The MacArthur Foundation in 1993 donated $500,000 to the center in a capacity-building general grant – one of the first big contributions it received that was not tied to a specific story or project. Despite this, serious financial issues arose soon after and the center was "hanging on for dear life" (D. Noyes, personal communication, November 4, 2010). The center's executive director at the time, Rick Tulsky, was a Pulitzer Prize-winning journalist with a background of investigative reporting in newspapers that included the *San Jose Mercury News*, the *Los Angeles Times*, and the *Philadelphia Inquirer*. Tulsky, who left the position within two years on "less-than-cordial terms", complained that every project at the center had a foundation or corporate sponsor and that virtually every underwriter had an ax to grind (Edmonds, 2001).

A television documentary on mining pollution had been funded by the W. Alton Jones Foundation, an organization focused on protecting the environment and building a sustainable world. He had felt like a paid hand of the foundation, producing fodder for the foundation's environmental agenda.

Noyes later wrote that "as far as the center is concerned, he [Tulsky] left because of differences over management and performance" rather than ethical concerns (Noyes, 2001, para. 4). Foundations wanted "a person that they can talk to, that they feel inspired by, connected to, motivated to give their money to, even though obviously the work may be done by somebody else at the organization" (D. Noyes, personal communication, November 4, 2010). Noyes returned to the executive director's job and was forced to cut staff. He set about rebuilding the center, which survived due to a number of *Frontline* projects (D. Noyes, personal communication, November 4, 2010). He stayed in the role for four years until 1999 when Burt Glass was appointed, allowing Noyes to focus on journalism. He resumed the executive job with associate director Christa Scharfenberg when Glass left.

The center's next significant appointment was former veteran newspaper editor Robert Rosenthal. One of his first hires was an experienced fund raiser, a move he later described as crucial to securing the center's finances (Rosenthal, 2011). Rosenthal arrived during the global financial crisis and found the center was at risk financially. It had seven staff and a budget of about $1 million, most of which was dedicated to a documentary project. Foundations and traditional funders of nonprofits were "going backwards, cutting all their funding" (R. Rosenthal, personal communication, November 3, 2010).

Rosenthal was determined to change the way the center operated, though he lacked unanimous support from the board (Rosenthal, 2011). Rather than working with individual outlets like PBS's *Frontline*, he envisaged a news organization that would publish stories on multiple partnering platforms to reach bigger and more diverse audiences. The strategy was "create-once-distribute-many, realizing the digital cost of the second copy is nil" (Doctor, 2011, para. 20). Funders, however, also remained wary. "There were doubts and challenging questions about the necessity of creating new models out of small existing nonprofits" (Rosenthal, 2011, p. 3). With funding from the James Irvine Foundation, the John S. and James L. Knight Foundation, and the William and Flora Hewlett Foundation,[1] in early 2010, Rosenthal and a partner launched *California Watch* as a project of the Center for Investigative Reporting. *California Watch* would report on local issues and distribute its stories to local and regional newspaper partners, as well as public broadcasters and ethnic media.[2] When *California Watch* advertised for staff, nearly 700 journalists applied including multiple Pulitzer Prize winners (Rosenthal, 2011). Agreement was reached with public broadcaster

KQED to share the salary of a reporter who would produce radio versions of the site's stories; the ethnic media organization, New America Media, would translate some of the stories and provide them to its media members and an in-house video production unit was established. Some of the more creative and innovative storytelling involved developing a coloring book on earthquake safety for children, the use of animation and finger puppets to illustrate the dangers of imported toys, and partnering with a theater company to produce one-act plays based on its investigative reports. Under a syndication deal with city newspapers, editors shaped stories for relevance and appropriate local detail, depending on a paper's location in California.

It would not have been possible to engage competing media in the same state were it not for the conjunction of several factors. First, the center had an established reputation for quality journalism. Local editors were aware that the center had produced good stories over a significant period. Second, Rosenthal had a background in the mainstream press and the same journalistic intuition, ethics, practice, and culture as local editors. The center's then editorial director, Mark Katches, also had a background in newspapers as a Pulitzer Prize-winning editor. Third, staff cuts in local media made well-edited and locally relevant stories attractive at little cost. Fourth, even in good economic times for newspapers, few could devote the time or had the resources to do complex investigative projects such as "On shaky ground," a series on school earthquake safety. Media now had access to projects, some of which cost hundreds of thousands of dollars to produce, for a fraction of the cost. The fifth factor was the erosion of a newsroom culture that once would have rather missed a story than run another organization's work. Rosenthal was surprised at how easily the need for exclusivity "once so sacrosanct throughout print as well as broadcast, fell by the wayside" (Rosenthal, 2011, p. 11). The same story could be published simultaneously on 30–40 websites including those of competing Bay Area newspapers such as the *San Francisco Chronicle*, the *Oakland Tribune*, the *Contra Costa Times*, and the *San Jose Mercury News* (R. Rosenthal, personal communication, November 3, 2010).

In its first year, *California Watch* partnered with almost 80 news organizations and reached an audience estimated at 25 million people. Revenue from these news organizations remained negligible: the center earned just $27,375 from sales but, on a positive note, it established the "principle of payment" for content (Rosenthal, 2011, p. 14). In 2010, Rosenthal anticipated that within three to five years, the center would raise 25 percent of its total revenue from sources other than foundation funding (R. Rosenthal, personal communication, November 3, 2010). In 2015, the center made $512,190 in earned revenue – $476,490 from content fees, $30,344 in fiscal sponsorship, and $5,356 from publications and advertising plus an additional $57,219 in other revenues. While this earned revenue was substantially bigger than that of most nonprofit news organizations, it was only 4 percent of the center's total revenue of $13.8 million (Center for Investigative Reporting, 2015). The percentage of revenue from big and small donors more recently "has increased greatly" (R. Rosenthal, personal communication, June 27, 2018).

Create Once, Distribute Often

An example of the center's publication and multiple platform distribution model was a project called "On Shaky Ground." This was a 19-month investigation that involved analyzing tens of thousands of documents about earthquake safety inspections of school buildings. The project, depicted in Figure 7.1, resulted in a three-part series of about 20,000 words, with video and audio content, a searchable database of more than 10,000 school inspection reports, a coloring book explaining seismic safety to children, and an iPhone app pinpointing earthquake fault locations (California Watch, 2011). The project cost $550,000 to produce, mostly in staff salaries (Doctor, 2011). Almost 30 newspapers, radio programs, and television outlets ran either parts or the entire series. Two Korean newspapers, a Chinese newspaper, and a Chinese television station ran the stories; twelve PBS affiliates broadcast a 30-minute special (Doctor, 2011). The multimedia series won the Investigative Reporters and Editors Medal, the top honor available at the Investigative Reporters and Editors organization (Center for Investigative Reporting, 2014a).

Another example of Rosenthal's vision for multiple publishing partners was a series on the sexual harassment of migrant female laborers working on farming properties (Center for Investigative Reporting, 2014b). The "Rape in the Fields" series was produced by the center in collaboration with Univision, *Frontline*, and the Investigative Reporting Program at the University of California Berkeley's Graduate School of Journalism. It included a one-hour documentary, multiple written stories, radio segments, and graphic animation (Green-Barber, 2014). The stories reached an estimated six million people. The documentary aired on *Frontline* with 3.3 million viewers, was reported in seven daily newspapers, a four-part series ran on radio KQED, and it had about 100 screenings in local communities. Parts of the series were presented in both English and Spanish. Stakeholders met for a solutions summit to discuss the issues and in May 2014, the Californian Senate passed a bill under which a farm contractor's license could be revoked if it hired a supervisor who had sexually harassed workers in the past three years.

Despite these successes, Rosenthal still worried about the sustainability of the nonprofit venture. Much of his time was spent visiting foundations and giving talks rather than doing journalism (Rosenthal, 2011).

Figure 7.1 California Watch's On Shaky Ground published in 30 different media.

Source: California Watch (2011).

"What I need to do is keep raising money, because when you build it, you've got to keep it going" (R. Rosenthal, personal communication, November 3, 2010). The center continued to depend on foundation support. The revenue earned by *California Watch* for its "On Shaky Ground" stories, which cost an estimated $550,000, was between $35,000 and $40,000 (Rowe, 2011).

In early 2012, the MacArthur Foundation announced it had awarded the center its $1 million Award for Creative and Effective Institutions. Rosenthal again expressed concern about financial issues. "The challenges really for all of us in this sector is how to sustain it. No-one has figured out the business model" (MacArthur Foundation, 2012). The center merged with a local online news site, the *Bay Citizen*, which had launched two years earlier, and the *California Watch* platform was subsumed into the Center for Investigative Reporting. The mergers created the biggest nonprofit reporting organization in the United States at the time with almost 70 staff. The center had the capacity to produce Bay Area news, statewide news as well as national and potentially international stories. In April 2012, the Knight Foundation, in line with its emphasis on supporting innovation, announced it would give the center $800,000 to curate an investigative journalism channel on YouTube.

Further changes to the center's operations soon followed. A new brand and platform called *Reveal* was created with a focus of presenting its projects to a national audience through regular programming on NPR's public radio stations. The center partnered with PRX, a nonprofit public media company, to produce what would become weekly one-hour radio programs and podcasts featuring its own projects and stories produced by other news outlets and public radio partners. *Reveal* was launched with three one-hour-long pilots in 2013 and 2014, tackling multiple investigative stories, and winning a Peabody Award with its first story. By mid-2018, the program aired on about 470 public radio stations and had 1.5 million podcast downloads a month (R. Rosenthal, personal communication, June 27, 2018).

The strategy shifted the center's vision of "one story, many audiences" into the mobile platform and apps era. It recognized that audiences increasingly were using their smartphones, iPads, and other mobile devices not just for music but for more serious content. The *Reveal* program provided the center its own audience, rather than having to depend on other media to distribute its projects. The center's *Reveal* platform and branding was funded by a three-year $3 million grant from the Reva & David Logan Foundation and a $500,000 grant from the Ford Foundation (Ellis, 2014).

As mentioned in this chapter's introduction, the center and the other nonprofit organizations profiled here were the exceptions – the leading exponents – in the sector of nonprofit investigative reporting. But the center's longevity provides evidence that investigative nonprofit organizations can survive in the United States with good leadership, productive partnerships, and some risk taking. Noyes and Bergman forged partnerships with television broadcasters at a time when programs like *60 Minutes* and *Frontline* were at the height of their popularity. Rosenthal took a risk in abandoning the system of working with individual media, instead taking stories wherever an audience could be found. *Reveal* built on that vision. "CIR [Center for Investigative Reporting] has consistently adapted, grown and taken risks," Rosenthal said (Salladay, 2015, para. 8). The center's history shows that innovation and constant project renewal are needed to draw new grants from foundations. Foundations supported the creation of *California Watch*, funded the *I-Files* collaboration between the center and YouTube, and financed the *Reveal* project. The MacArthur Foundation's $1 million award recognized organizations that "provide new ways of addressing problems, generate provocative ideas, innovate within their field, reframe the debate and have impact altogether disproportionate to their size" (Rosenthal, 2012, para. 2).

The Center for Public Integrity

The Center for Public Integrity is located in Washington, DC, and was founded 12 years after the Center for Investigative Reporting. Its launch, focus, and early method of investigative story production and distribution differed significantly from that of the Center for Investigative Reporting. Like the Center for Investigative Reporting, it would face financial and management challenges and develop innovative models of investigative reporting. The Center for Public Integrity has been at the forefront of the evolving nonprofit investigative sector for 30 years. Like the Center for Investigative Reporting, it launched in the home of its founder, Charles "Chuck" Lewis (2014, p. 201).

Lewis had been a researcher and producer on CBS's high-rating *60 Minutes* program, working with its top journalist and drawcard Mike Wallace. After several of his ideas were rejected by the program's executives, he became embroiled in an argument with his superiors over a story involving former US government officials who worked in Japan as agents for mergers and acquisitions in the United States (Lewis, 2014, p. 195). One of those implicated in the story was a former Commerce Secretary who had close ties with senior people at CBS and *60 Minutes*. In the fallout, Lewis resigned the day after the program, "Foreign Agent", screened (Lewis, 2014, pp. 194–195).

With two political science degrees and located in Washington, DC, Lewis was curious about how political power structures and influence might be better reported. As he considered the best model for doing that, and needing to support a young family, he joined the "dark side" (C. Lewis, personal communication, November 10, 2010) – working for nine months as a consultant for Kroll, a global finance and intelligence management company (Kroll, n.d.). The experience alerted him to how much more information was available to lawyers, forensic financial analysts, historians, and other investigators than to journalists. He had witnessed a financial takeover investigation that involved 60 people around the world working for several months and produced 36 volumes of data: "The stuff they were amassing was jaw dropping" (C. Lewis, personal communication, November 10, 2010).

The model of journalism that the Center for Public Integrity would adopt in its early days and the later creation of a global network of investigative reporters reflected the model of intense research that Lewis had seen at Kroll. The model he developed for the center was unique in journalism: it melded a political science approach with established in-vestigative journalism techniques. Projects would take months or years to research, involve large teams of journalists, academics, and interns, and the results would be released in detailed reports to the media. Lewis believed, and this proved to be the case, that the impact of releasing the center's findings at press conferences would be greater than if the center were to partner with one or two news outlets. The question was how to fund such a "journalistic utopia" (Lewis, 2007, p. 8) while avoiding conflicts of interest and pressure from corporate interests.

Lewis took his idea for an investigative center to influential Washington identities and well-known journalists including the historian and writer Arthur Schlesinger; the president of the University of Notre Dame, the Reverend Theodore Hesburgh; a former head of the *New York Times'* Washington bureau, Bill Kovach; Pulitzer Prize winner, Hodding Carter; and Kathleen Hall Jamieson, later a professor of communication and director of the Annenberg Public Policy Center. He received positive feedback and they agreed to be on the center's advisory board (Lewis, 2014, p. 201).

Lewis and two partners, Alejandro Benes, with whom he had worked at ABC News, and Charles Piller, a journalist on the West Coast, ruled out a for-profit model because corporate entities could withdraw their support if the stories offended them. They settled on a mixture of sup-port from foundations, corporate sponsors, and unions, though Lewis "didn't know anything about this world" of fundraising (C. Lewis, per-sonal communication, November 10, 2010). The founders favored trying to win foundation support in preference to donations from companies and unions but relented and accepted such funding until 1994 when they decided the conflict of interest risk was too great.

The center was launched in October 1989 and moved from Lewis's guest bedroom to an office. Its first budget of $200,000 was raised from union and corporate donations and a small consulting contract with ABC News (Lewis, 2000, p. 8). Its first project returned to the issue that had aggrieved Lewis at *60 Minutes*. In December 1990, at the National Press Club, Lewis released a 201-page study entitled "America's Front-line Trade Officials" (Lewis, 1990). The report found that 47 percent of former US trade officials had personally registered or registered their firms as foreign agents working with countries or overseas corporations: a revolving door issue that encouraged serving government officials into cozy relations with groups they ought to be regulating in the hope of landing lucrative roles after leaving office (Lewis, 1990, 2014). The re-port's findings were covered by CNN, *Frontline*, ABC News, and other networks. The study sparked an investigation by the General Account-ing Office and a Justice Department ruling and was referred to by four presidential candidates in 1992 (Lewis, 2000, p. 5).

Over the next three years, Lewis and his partners, with the assistance of hundreds of undergraduate and graduate interns and freelance reporters, wrote 13 detailed reports about money, power, political influence, and corruption in Washington and by the 1992 election "we were being called daily for quotes about the candidates and ethics-related situations" (Lewis, 2000, p. 9). What Lewis called the center's first prototypical study was released in 1994 amid controversy over the Clinton Administration's health-care reforms. Written by 17 researchers and more than 200 pages long, it exhaustively tracked the lobbying activities of 662 health-care interests (Lewis, 1994). The findings included everything from privately funded trips and revolving door examples to campaign contributions and personal investments. More than 50 reporters covered the news conference when Lewis released the findings. In 1996, Avon Books published "The Buying of the President" by Lewis and the Center for Public Integrity, which tracked the relationships between presidential candidates and their career patron supporters. The book's findings received wide media coverage and triggered a PBS *Frontline* documentary called, "So you want to buy a President?" (PBS Frontline, 1996).

Similarly, themed books were published in the 2000, 2004, and 2008 election years. Extensive investigations also were conducted into corruption, lobbying, and conflicts of interest in state legislatures, the beneficiaries of US government contracts in the Afghanistan and Iraq conflicts, and media ownership and lobbying by telecom companies. A separate project spawned a new nonprofit organization, Global Integrity, which assessed and monitored government transparency and corruption around the world. The first report in 2004 was 750,000 words and examined government integrity issues in 25 countries (Lewis, 2000, p. 211).

The center's investigative think-tank methodology of comprehensive reports and media releases reflected both its location in the heart of national politics and Lewis's political science background and experience at Kroll. The center published stories on its own website from 1999 and books extended its reach: the 2004 edition of "The Buying of the President" was on the *New York Times* best seller list for three months (Lewis, 2014, p. 205). The center's methodology changed after Lewis departed in 2004 to a more conventional approach of multimedia display and a faster turnover of stories. The following section describes some of the key financial and legal challenges faced by the organization. There also were personality clashes, management issues, executive incompetence, and the sort of ups and downs found in any organization. For instance, relations after many years finally broke down between the center and its project, the International Consortium of Investigative Journalists,[3] which Lewis founded so that reporters in different countries could investigate common concerns and provide a global picture of issues that do not stop at a nation's borders.

Costly Internal Ructions

The consortium's successes bred a desire among its senior editors for independence from its parent organization. Several years after its launch in 1997, Lewis clashed with the consortium's then director who "felt strongly from the first week on the job that the International Consortium of Investigative Journalists should be a stand-alone nonprofit; it should not be within the center" (C. Lewis, personal communication, November 10, 2010). The same issue erupted in a more explosive way many years later. By 2016, the consortium had 190 journalists in 65 countries and had published its Pulitzer Prize-winning *Panama Papers* project, exposing the offshore holdings of 140 world leaders and senior public officials (International Consortium of Investigative Journalists, 2016). In late 2017, it followed up with the *Paradise Papers* revelations of the offshore interests and activities of world leaders and multinational corporations.

Behind the scenes, however, relations between senior editors at the consortium and the Center for Public Integrity soured to the degree that one almost punched another's lights out: "It was getting real ugly inside the place" (C. Lewis, personal communication, February 23, 2018). By then, the International Consortium of Investigative Journalists had sufficient foundation support to stand on its own and after a series of crisis meetings between senior players, the consortium, still elated at the success of its recent investigations, was launched as a separate entity in 2017. Charles Lewis, who once had regarded the consortium as the "family jewel" of the center recognized that "at some point the separation and differentiation of the two was almost essential" (C. Lewis, personal communication, November 10, 2010; February 23, 2018).

The most serious issues, however, were financial. In 2010, the center's board and executive director Bill Buzenberg embraced a radical change of direction proposed by a relatively new arrival at the center, former Associated Press and *Washington Times* and *Washington Post* reporter John Solomon. His strategy, as outlined in the executive summary of the business plan entitled "A Digital Strategy for Expanding and Monetizing CPI's Investigative Reporting" (Center for Public Integrity, 2010), recommended a realignment of the center's operations. Instead of focusing on the extended deadline journalism pursued by Lewis and others, the emphasis would be on breaking news daily. The aim was to develop the center into a primary destination for readers and boost revenue through advertising, email marketing, e-publication, subscriptions, and content syndication (Center for Public Integrity, 2010). A subscription publication would update throughout the day. The strategy predicted a massive jump in revenues. By the end of the fifth year, the center would gross $11.8 million in revenue, web traffic would grow to 20 million views, and an e-edition of stories would have 100,000 subscribers, according to the strategy document (Center for Public Integrity, 2010). The number of reporting staff would double, as would the capacity to produce long-form investigative projects. At the same time, daily news would be read by millions of people. "Instead of producing content that others use and monetize … the Center would transform itself into a destination news source able to command and monetize a national audience…" (Center for Public Integrity, 2010, para. 34). In the first two years, approximately two dozen additional staff would be needed for content generation, web development, and digital development at an additional annual cost of about $4 million. The plan was evaluated by an outside consultancy and agreed to by the board (Blake, 2012). The Knight Foundation provided a $1.7 million grant toward a redesign of the center's website and the creation of new revenue streams (Knight Foundation, 2014).

A dozen staff were hired and in May 2011, the *iWatch News* website was launched at Washington's National Press Club. The site provided greater social media interaction with readers through mobile devices and interactive screens, giving them access to data, documents, and videos. It boosted audience numbers, raising the prospect of bigger earned revenues: "Within this next five years, we'd like to be earning one dollar for every dollar that's donated," Buzenberg said (Masters, 2011). The plan was to publish 10–12 original stories each day and to provide paying members a multiplatform reader that flipped rather than scrolled pages and enhanced the visual display of stories (Blake, 2012). The future must have looked bright, particularly as the *Huffington Post*'s Investigative Fund, then believed to have $2 million, merged with the center, providing additional staff and funding, and the promise of a large new audience by driving page views to the center's site (Blake, 2012).

But not all the staff were convinced. Investigative editor David Kaplan, then director of the International Consortium of Investigative Journalists, "thought the push toward a more daily journalism model was a terrible idea, and he let that be known, in meetings and to Buzenberg" (Hagey, 2011, p. 2). Kaplan worried that Solomon's "dubious revenue-generating schemes" would result in financial chaos and compromise the center's ability to do the investigative reporting it was founded to do (Blake, 2012, para. 20). An acrimonious relationship developed between Kaplan and Solomon that involved "full-scale warfare, and fierce shouting matches began erupting in the newsroom" (Blake, 2012, para. 32).

Kaplan's concern about the projected income the scheme would generate proved to be well placed. Implementation of the plan led to million-dollar budget deficits, staff cuts, and Buzenberg having to reassure funders that the center's "story is a good story" (B. Buzenberg, personal communication, February 8, 2012). In November 2010, as the strategy was embraced, Buzenberg was enthusiastic about the new direction and believed the total staff might grow from 50 to 70 in the next few years. Fifteen months later, he conceded the plan was "way overly optimistic" and that many of the targets and aims either were not met or dropped. "We were too optimistic, the numbers were completely exaggerated frankly, and I'm glad John Solomon is not here anymore" (B. Buzenberg, personal communication, February 8, 2012).

The strategy document envisaged that circulation of a premium e-edition of the site, essentially the site without advertisements, would grow from 30,000 to 100,000 member donors by the end of year five. Buzenberg later revised this, saying he would be happy if membership reached 10,000. Advertising revenue projected at $500,000 earned just $10,000 (R. Heller, personal communication, February 8, 2011). Buzenberg had to dismiss an advertising staff member because the income she made did not even recoup her salary. The *iWatch*-themed brand was dumped in favor of the original "public integrity" label. Buzenberg reflected:

> We are all trying to figure out what is the way ... there's a big transition underway, how is it going to work? And no one has figured it out. We thought we had a way to figure it out. We did get some very nice grants from people like the Knight Foundation, but in truth we spent more than they even gave us ....
> (B. Buzenberg, personal communication, February 8, 2012)

The center's experience highlights the importance foundations and other major funders placed on the organization's leadership. The revenue trends in Table 7.1 and in Figure 7.2 demonstrate the importance of the

Table 7.1 Center for Public Integrity finances, 2002–2010

Year	Program services	Gifts and grants	Expenses	Revenue	Surplus/ deficit
2002	$3.2 million	$2.9 million	$3.6 million	$2.9 million	–$747,953
2003	$3.3 million	$4.2 million	$4.3 million	$4.3 million	–$48,695
2004	$3.4 million	$6.4 million	$4.5 million	$6.4 million	$1.9 million
2005	$3.1 million	$3 million	$4.4 million	$3.1 million	–$1.2 million
2006	$3.3 million	$3.1 million	$4.7 million	$3.2 million	–$1.5 million
2007	$3 million	$3.8 million	$4.2 million	$4.1 million	–$78,476
2008	$3.1 million	$7.6 million	$3.9 million	$8.2 million	$4.3 million
2009	$4.1 million	$5.6 million	$4.9 million	$6 million	$1.1 million
2010	$6.4 million	$8.8 million	$7.7 million	$9.2 million	$1.5 million
Total	$33 million	$40 million	$42 million	$48 million	$5.3 million

Source: Compiled by the author from 990 Forms filed with Internal Revenue Service and retrieved from http://www.publicintegrity.org/about/our-organization/annual-tax-returns

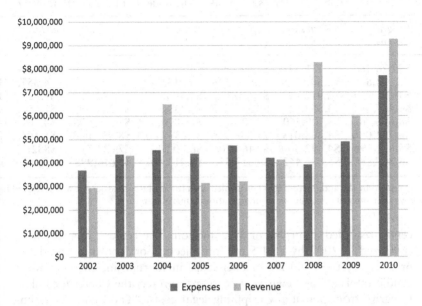

Figure 7.2 Center for Public Integrity's revenue and expenses, 2002–2010.
Source: Compiled by the author from 990 Forms filed with Internal Revenue Service and retrieved from http://www.publicintegrity.org/about/our-organization/annual-tax-returns.

executive director's role in fundraising and show the sensitivity foundations have to internal issues in their grantees' organizations.

The data in Table 7.1 and Figure 7.2 were drawn from the Form 990 documents that the center was required to lodge each year with the Internal Revenue Service (IRS). In Table 7.1, "Gifts and grants" represent donations made predominantly by foundations and wealthy donors. 'Revenue' includes those contributions in addition to extra income from contractual services, publication sales, investment income, and other revenues. "Expenses" is total spending on salaries and entitlements, fundraising fees, promotion, leases, travel, and so on, and "Program Services" is the amount spent directly on producing journalism projects. The table and chart show that after Charles Lewis left in 2004, revenues fell and did not recover until after 2007 when Bill Buzenberg, a former vice president for news at National Public Radio, was appointed executive director. Revenue of $6.4 million in 2004 dropped to $3.1 million in 2005 and a similar amount the following year. Despite the revenue declines, the center's expenses remained fairly constant, resulting in three consecutive years in which spending outdid revenue. The 2005 deficit of $1.2 million represented a turnaround of $3 million in the center's budget. Following his appointment in 2007, Buzenberg managed to double revenues from $4.1 million to $8.2 million. In 2008, the

Table 7.2 Center for Public Integrity's financial results under Bill Buzenberg's leadership

Year	Program expenses	Salaries and benefits	Gifts and grants	Expenses	Revenue	Surplus/ deficit
2007	$3,076,464	$2,781,395	$3,870,985	$4,212,835	$4,134,359	−$78,476
2008	$3,112,639	$2,600,929	$7,692,526	$3,913,389	$8,271,362	$4,357,973
2009	$4,191,710	$2,912,517	$5,610,122	$4,903,472	$6,024,115	$1,120,643
2010	$6,487,393	$3,863,196	$8,845,667	$7,708,349	$9,264,997	$1,556,648
2011	$8,666,767	$5,700,760	$5,128,583	$10,076,320	$5,371,676	−$4,704,644
2012	$6,732,000	$4,363,015	$8,858,926	$7,633,950	$8,998,063	$1,364,113
2013	$5,631,896	$4,692,500	$7,464,706	$6,802,136	$7,634,713	$832,577
2014	$6,887,886	$5,632,462	$9,313,650	$8,413,507	$9,616,998	$1,203,491

Source: Compiled by the author from 990 Forms filed with Internal Revenue Service and retrieved fro
http://www.publicintegrity.org/about/our-organization/annual-tax-returns

center recorded a surplus of $4.3 million. The center's finances were stabilized in 2007 by a $1.5 million injection of "transition funding" provided by the Fund for Independence in Journalism, an endowment fund established by Lewis years earlier to protect the Center for Public Integrity from potentially crippling legal costs. "The Center was thus saved by the Fund, enabling the organization to get its expenses and revenue in balance" (Fund for Independence in Journalism, 2008, para. 8). Table 7.2 shows the second financial issue faced by the center – the impact of the *iWatch News* strategy.

The center recorded a $4.7 million deficit in 2011 as it struggled to contain the fallout of the additional staff hiring, web redesign, and other costs of implementing the strategy. Expenses rose by $2.3 million on the 2010 total while revenues fell by $3.8 million. Buzenberg said that while 2010 was the center's most successful fundraising year, the costs associated with the plan together with a big shortfall of anticipated revenue meant that in 2011 the center had to dip into its reserves, take out a loan, and cut staff (B. Buzenberg, personal communication, February 8, 2012). Ten positions were eliminated and five other people lost their jobs. Figure 7.3 depicts the two periods discussed here when financial challenges occurred between 2004 and 2007 and in 2011.

This analysis, using an Excel spreadsheet and data from the annual Form 990 documents, showed that between 2002 and 2015 inclusive, the Center for Public Integrity spent $85 million on the production of investigative journalism and received about the same amount from foundation and individual grants. The center earned $1.6 million in program service revenue over that period, or just 1.9 percent of total funding. When it was suggested to Buzenberg that the mainstream media loved the cake but wouldn't pay for the ingredients, he responded, "You got it in one" (B. Buzenberg, personal communication, February 8, 2012).

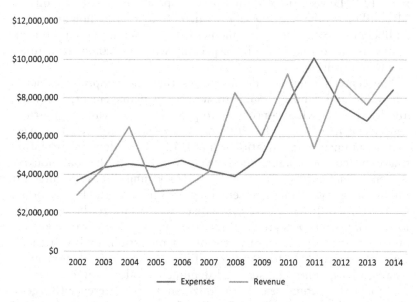

Figure 7.3 Financial crises affected the Center for Public Integrity twice since 2004.

Source: Compiled by the author from 990 Forms filed with Internal Revenue Service and retrieved from http://www.publicintegrity.org/about/our-organization/annual-tax-returns.

The second key threat to the center was legal action by the organizations and individuals it investigated. In 2000–2001, the center faced three libel writs including one from two Russian oligarchs who were represented by a prestigious Washington law firm (Lewis, 2007; Sullivan, 2010). The center had published an article about links between the multinational corporation, Halliburton Company, and a Russian oil conglomerate whose "roots are imbedded in a legacy of KGB and Communist Party corruption, as well as drug trafficking and organized crime funds" (Royce & Heller, 2000, para. 2). The allegations were "hotly disputed" by the Russian company (Royce & Heller, 2000, para. 3). The case of Alfa Bank v. Center for Public Integrity led to one of the longest discovery processes in recent US history, involving five years of hearings, 20 depositions, and 107,000 documents (Lewis, 2007). The suit was unsuccessful, though the judge found that at least some of the allegations in the story were exaggerated or inaccurate. The lapses amounted to negligence or bad journalism rather than actual malice. "To ensure the ascertainment and publication of the truth about public affairs, it is essential that the First Amendment protect some erroneous publications as well as true ones," the judge found (Leagle, 2005, para. 122). Lewis estimated the Russians spent between $8 million and $10 million on the case; the center's defense cost $4 million and it lost its libel insurance. The case demonstrated the fragility of nonprofit investigative reporting generally, especially when big commercial interests were involved.

The center's longevity demonstrates that the nonprofit model is adaptable and robust enough to withstand management, financial, and legal issues while continuing to produce award-winning journalism. The center won its first Pulitzer Prize – the third by a US investigative nonprofit organization – in 2014 for a yearlong investigation that exposed how doctors and lawyers worked with the coal industry to deny benefits to workers who had black lung disease (Center for Public Integrity, 2014). The center's global project, the International Consortium of Investigative Journalists, won a Pulitzer Prize in 2017 for the *Panama Papers* project. In partnership with a software company and data specialists, the International Consortium of Investigative Journalists was able to convert millions of different documents – emails, PDFs, contracts, scanned documents, tables – into a dataset that journalists could search, organize, and cross reference (Burgess, 2016). It followed up with the *Paradise Papers*, a project that involved a leak of 13.4 million files that were analyzed by 380 journalists from 90 media organizations around the world and sparked numerous inquiries by tax authorities and criminal investigations as well as reforms (Fitzgibbon & Starkman, 2017). The consortium, with its unique model of investigative reporters around the world collaborating on projects, also produced hundreds of stories on tax havens, the trade in human tissue, exploitation of fishing grounds, and tobacco smuggling.

As mentioned, the Center for Public Integrity is one of a handful of outliers in the nonprofit accountability news sector due to its financial strength, focus on national issues, and location in Washington, DC. Still, we can draw broad understandings from its history. The case study highlights the importance of the organizational leader, in terms of dealing with internal issues and outside perceptions. Both relate directly to funding, the key challenge for nonprofit organizations. Word of internal ructions in nonprofit organizations spreads quickly to funders in what is a small niche sector of journalism.

The center had transformed itself over three decades from an organization focused on investigative books and reports that suited the times into a modern, online multimedia organization. It broadened its areas of interest from national politics – albeit still providing investigations of the interests behind President Trump and his appointees – to issues of national security, immigration, the environment, workers' rights, and business. It proved to be financially sustainable through a combination of loyal and ongoing foundation supporters and new funders.

ProPublica

ProPublica was founded during the global financial crisis when numerous nonprofit organizations were launching or preparing to do so. What distinguished it from the others was that it started with substantial funding that allowed it to concentrate on journalism projects and build its business model without concern over its short- to medium-term survival. Billionaire former banker Herbert Sandler and his wife, Marion, launched *ProPublica* with a commitment to spend tens of millions of dollars supporting the organization (Perez-Pena, 2007). The funding effectively insulated *ProPublica* from the financial crisis that affected both the mainstream media and the wealth of foundations and individual funders.

The Sandlers had sold Golden West Financial Corporation, a company they had built into the second biggest savings and loan organization in the United States, to Wachovia Corporation for $25 billion. They received $2.4 billion for their stake and deposited $1.4 billion in the Sandler Foundation (Nocera, 2008). The Sandlers had thought about establishing a journalism outlet for over a decade (Perry, 2007). Herbert Sandler was frustrated by the media's focus on celebrities rather than issues like global warming and the war in Iraq. He was critical of the coverage of the 1980s savings and loan scandal, and subprime mortgage issues during the financial crisis. Like some other funders of nonprofit reporting, Sandler was concerned at the erosion of the mainstream media and wanted to create an organization that would produce stories with "moral force" that sustained democracy (Perry, 2007).

In contrast to the Center for Investigative Reporting and the Center for Public Integrity, which started in their founders' homes, *ProPublica* was launched in a tower in Manhattan's financial district, not far from Wall Street. Unlike most accountability news organizations, the upfront funding meant that *ProPublica* was "born on third base" (R. Tofel, personal communication, April 24, 2018).

The Sandler money enabled the organization to employ several of the United States' top journalists and media executives. Paul Steiger, a former long-serving managing editor of the *Wall Street Journal*, was employed to establish *ProPublica*. As the managing editor of a national newspaper that was awarded 16 Pulitzer Prizes during his tenure, Steiger arrived with enormous social and symbolic capital. Stephen Engelberg, a former managing editor of the *Oregonian* in Portland, Oregon, who earlier had founded the *New York Times* investigative unit, was appointed managing editor. Richard Tofel, who had previously been an assistant publisher and assistant managing editor of the *Wall Street Journal*, became *ProPublica*'s founding general manager. "Between the three of us, we knew most everybody in American journalism" (R. Tofel, personal communication, April 24, 2018). When *ProPublica* sought to staff its newsroom, hundreds of journalists, including high-profile award winners, applied.

The Sandler funding allowed *ProPublica* to compensate its senior editors and reporters at significantly higher rates than other nonprofits. Steiger was paid $571,689 and Engelberg's salary soon after starting was $341,181 (ProPublica, 2010). A journalism advisory board that included Jill Abramson, who would become executive editor of the *New York Times* in 2011 and journalist and biographer, Robert Caro, as well as other high-profile editors, funders, and academics was established. Influential venture capitalists and executives from equity investment, public relations, and corporate advice firms were appointed to provide guidance on business issues (ProPublica, n.d.-a). By spring 2008, Steiger and the editors were working through 850 job applications (Steiger, 2008). The initial staff of 28 editors and reporters included seven Pulitzer Prize winners. The strategy of hiring top journalists rapidly brought the organization recognition for quality journalism. It won the first ever Pulitzer Prize awarded to an online news organization in 2010, a second Pulitzer Prize in 2011, and two more in 2016 and 2017 (ProPublica, n.d.-b).

The Sandler money, totaling $19.7 million in the first four years, enabled *ProPublica* to produce high-quality stories and data; its editors' mainstream media networks facilitated partnerships with prestigious mainstream publishers; it won major awards; and the organization's journalistic success and leadership attracted other funders. Its senior executives embraced hardheaded business discipline. "Very few nonprofits are run like businesses and they suffer for it. They don't have a very good handle on what their revenue prospects are, they don't engage in a terribly rigorous budgeting process, they don't have much of a strategic planning process, they don't have terribly strong controls on expense, they don't have great support systems to infrastructure of all sorts," president Richard Tofel said (personal communication, April 24, 2018). Herbert Sandler not only continued supporting *ProPublica* through the Sandler Foundation, but as a former chairman and current board member he has an ongoing involvement on the business side. "He helps us raise money, he was a spectacular businessman and he's given me and us enormous practical advice about how to run this place as a business. I speak to him most work days" (R. Tofel, personal communication, April 24, 2018).[4]

The Sandlers' involvement, however, had some reputational cost. Their support of the Democratic Party and liberal organizations attracted criticism from conservative commentators, as described in Chapter 9. Their former corporate activities at the World Savings Bank drew scrutiny and criticism in the mainstream media. A *New York Times* article accused the bank of aggressively marketing risky loans at the height of the housing bubble (Moss & Fabrikant, 2008). The Sandlers defended their bank's behavior in the article and in a long letter to the *New York Times'* then executive editor Bill Keller in which they highlighted what they regarded as inaccuracies and distortions. They maintained their business careers had always been based on ethics, integrity, discipline, and fair dealing (Sandler & Sandler, 2009, p. 1). The *Times* published four corrections based on the information the Sandlers provided (Keller, 2009). At about the same time, the Sandlers were parodied as greedy bankers on *Saturday Night Live*, a skit that later was removed from the internet after complaints and an apology (Moss & Fabrikant, 2008). *60 Minutes* featured a World Savings Bank whistleblower who said he had warned senior executives that the bank was "sitting on an Enron" and was breaking the law by issuing loans to people who could not afford them (Pelley, 2009, paras. 6, 4). And *Time* included the Sandlers on its list of people to blame for the financial crisis (Horowitz, 2010). The critics extended their condemnation to *ProPublica* itself, suggesting it had a hidden political agenda. *ProPublica* was described as a vehicle for left-wing hit pieces financed by donors who wanted to promote "radical left-leaning change in American society" (Chumley, 2009, paras. 3, 10). One article noted that *ProPublica*'s stories on foreclosures contained little to no information about the Sandlers' role in the 2008 market crash. "This is perhaps not coincidental" it said, noting the "obvious conflict created by the incongruent interests of *ProPublica*'s chairman" (Gabbay, 2012, para. 4). Another critic asked, "What do the Sandlers want for their millions? Perhaps to return us to the days of the partisan press" (Shafer, 2009, para. 6).

The table below shows that the Sandlers' proportion of total funding of the nonprofit declined each year since 2008, except in 2014. The returns that *ProPublica* submitted to the IRS, in Table 7.3, show that the percentage of funding provided by the Sandlers decreased from 94 percent in 2008 to less than 30 percent in 2013, but rose to almost 40 percent in 2014 before dropping significantly in 2015 (ProPublica, n.d.-d). The percentage dropped to 11 or 12 percent in 2017 due to a large increase in total revenues (R. Tofel, personal communication, April 24, 2018).

Table 7.3 The Sandlers' support of *ProPublica*

Year	Sandler	Total	% of total
2007	$1.2 million	$1.4 million	85.7
2008	$8 million	$8.5 million	94.1
2009	$4.5 million	$6.3 million	71.4
2010	$6 million	$10.2 million	58.8
2011	$5 million	$10.1 million	49.5
2012	$4 million	$10.9 million	36.7
2013	$4 million	$13.6 million	29.4
2014	$4 million	$10.1 million	39.6
2015	$3 million	$16.8 million	17.8
Total	$39.7 million	$87.9 million	45.1

Source: Compiled by the author from Form 990 returns to the Internal Revenue Service and retrieved from https://www.propublica.org/reports/

The Sandler Foundation donated $39.7 million to *ProPublica* between 2007 and 2015, which was 45.1 percent of its total funding. After launching the site, senior staff had no clear sense of where other funding might come from (Engelberg, Tofel, & Fields, 2018). They need not have worried: big donors have included the MacArthur Foundation, the Knight Foundation, Ford Foundation, Pew Charitable Trusts, and the Bill & Melinda Gates Foundation. Total donations over the same period amounted to $87.9 million. The majority of the funding was donated by wealthy individuals and private and family foundations (R. Tofel, personal communication, April 24, 2018).

While *ProPublica* attracted other significant donors, this analysis puts in perspective the value of the Sandlers' support. Without it, *ProPublica*'s funding between 2007 and 2015 would have totaled $48.2 million (rather than $87.9 million) and it is likely to have been less because its early editorial success, funded almost solely by the Sandlers, attracted other funders. *ProPublica*'s general manager Richard Tofel believed having a diversified funding base was an important market indicator of success. "If the only people you can convince to give you money are the founding donors, that's not terrific in terms of what that would say about convincing people of the importance of the work that we're doing" (R. Tofel, personal communication, November 17, 2010). In 2017, on the heels of Donald Trump's election as President, the number of individual donors to *ProPublica* exploded. In 2015, the organization had fewer than 4,000 donors who were not individually solicited and gave less than $10,000. Two years later, the number had jumped to 34,000 (ProPublica, 2017a). *ProPublica* gained almost $7 million in individual contributions in 2017 compared with $3.8 million in the preceding year (ProPublica, 2017b). At the same time, funding by foundations jumped from $9.8 million in 2016 to $36 million in 2017 (ProPublica, 2017b).

Unlike the Center for Investigative Reporting, which charged some of its media partners a small fee for its stories, and the Center for Public Integrity, which would like to charge, *ProPublica* invited anyone to "steal our stories" (ProPublica, n.d.-c). Where it had collaborated with publishers in partnership deals, media were welcome to run the stories following publication on *ProPublica*'s site (Editors Weblog, 2009). When the organization was launched, doubts were expressed that established news outlets would partner with a nonprofit site on exclusive stories (Ellis, 2013; Miner, 2007; ProPublica, 2014). Those doubts proved incorrect. Since launching, *ProPublica* has had 156 different partners distribute its stories (ProPublica, 2017a). It has had exclusive deals with media such as the *New York Times*, National Public Radio, the *Washington Post*, *Frontline*, the *Atlantic* magazine, and *This American Life* (Ellis, 2013) and has collaborated with nonprofits such as the *Marshall Project* and *Texas Tribune*. It seems extraordinary today that when *ProPublica* launched none of us were sure we would be able to overcome ... news organizations' historic skepticism toward investigative reporting done by outsiders. Given that our web traffic at the time consisted, basically, of our families and friends, the question of what we would do if no one wanted to partner with us was not trivial.

(Engelberg et al., 2018)

ProPublica pioneered innovation in data journalism. It was a key developer of accessible and searchable databases that often also provided the key findings of its stories. The online databases enabled readers to customize searches for information that was relevant to them. For example, they could look up their doctors' prescribing habits or list the payments individual doctors had received from drug and medical device companies. The "Dollars for Docs" database recorded more than 20 million page views and spawned local stories in 175 news organizations (ProPublica, 2013). Another database enabled readers to check the average waiting times at emergency departments. The database provided the average time patients spent in emergency rooms before being sent home, the average wait to receive pain-relieving medication for broken bones, and how long they had to wait before being taken to their rooms (Groega, Tigas, & Wei, 2014). *ProPublica* used such applications to leverage its journalism, with local, regional, and national media cherry picking the data for their own stories (Ellis, 2013).

In 2017, *ProPublica* affirmed its leadership in the nonprofit journalism sector by launching projects aimed at improving accountability reporting at local and regional outlets. It provided salary and benefits for reporters at seven local and regional news organizations to spend a year pursuing investigative projects in their newsrooms with guidance from *ProPublica* editors. It received applications from 239 reporters wanting to participate in the scheme (ProPublica, 2017c). Separately with seed funding from the Ford Foundation, *ProPublica* launched what may be the first of several state-based newsrooms dedicated to local investigative reporting. *ProPublica* spent two or three years researching the feasibility of the project and chose to open in Chicago due to the stories likely to be found there, the decline of local media, and the availability of publishing partners and local philanthropic support. *ProPublica Illinois* was treated as an experiment that could be repeated in other states if it were successful and local funders could be found (R. Tofel, personal communication, April 24, 2018). *ProPublica Illinois*'s first major story exposed serious issues in Cook County's property assessment system and was published in partnership with the *Chicago Tribune*. It was a Pulitzer Prize finalist and an example of how nonprofits complement commercial media rather than compete with them (ProPublica, 2017a).

ProPublica was the first of a new generation of well-funded national accountability news organizations in the nonprofit investigative reporting sector. It was followed by the *Intercept*, funded by Pierre Omidyar, and the *Marshall Project*, headed by former *New York Times* editor Bill Keller, and funded initially by a former reporter and success-ful hedge fund manager. *ProPublica*'s success, both journalistically with Pulitzer Prizes and other awards, and financially through foundation and donor support, demonstrates that it is feasible for well-resourced noncommercial organizations to undertake and distribute high-quality investigative stories. Its ability to find new funders and retain older ones suggests that funders may not be as fickle as some observers initially proposed, at least for nationally focused organizations. Whether that is true for the funders of local and regional investigative and public interest journalism remains to be seen. Scholars and journalists have lamented the popularity of celebrity journalism and the dumbing down of newspa-pers, but *ProPublica*'s visitor numbers suggest that substantial demand exists for serious journalism, compellingly presented. In 2017, its web-site averaged 3.9 million page views a month with another 1.2 million page views off its platform. It had an average of 2.1 million unique visi-tors monthly. *ProPublica* attracted 712,000 Twitter followers, 374,000 Facebook members, and 118,000 plus email subscribers (ProPublica, 2017a). In 2018, the organization employed 120 staff at its New York and Illinois sites.

Mother Jones

Like the Center for Investigative Reporting, *Mother Jones* was founded in San Francisco in the mid-1970s in the wake of the *Washington Post*'s Watergate revelations and Richard Nixon's resignation as president. It was a divisive time in the country with millions of people who supported civil rights, feminism and environmentalism, and who had opposed the Vietnam War, wanting change. "We were still living in the afterglow of the 1960s ..." wrote Adam Hochschild, one of *Mother Jones*'s founders (Hochschild, 2001).

Despite the public sentiment, *Mother Jones*'s founders were uncertain even after launching that there would be sufficient demand for a new progressive magazine (A. Hochschild, personal communication, May 12, 2018). Left-leaning publications such as *New Times*, *Politicks*, and *Seven Days* were struggling financially and *Ramparts*, which had been active during the 1960s with front-page scoops on the Vietnam War and the CIA's funding of front organizations, produced its final issue in 1975 (Armstrong, 1999, pp. 307–309).

The founding editors of *Mother Jones* – Adam Hochschild, Richard Parker, and Paul Jacobs – left *Ramparts* shortly before its demise and started planning the new publication as the *Washington Post* was break-ing its Watergate stories. Their dream was to create a magazine of progres-sive politics, and their hope was that accurate investigative stories, good art, photographs, and design would attract a wider audience than the small-circulation progressive publications then available (A. Hochschild, personal communication, May 19, 2018).

Mother Jones launched with a print run of 80,000 in February 1976 through the efforts of 17 staff who worked in a cramped office above a McDonald's outlet. At least three staff had worked at *Ramparts* at one time, and half were concerned with advertising, circulation, and accounts rather than editorial. Most of the stories were done by outside writers who were commissioned by the editors (A. Hochschild, personal communication, May 18, 2018).

Staff used the mailing lists of *Ramparts* and other magazines in early promotions and gained support from people such as Burt Lancaster and others in the Hollywood film community (Armstrong, 1999, p. 315; Hochschild, 2001; A. Hochschild, personal commuication, May 12, 2018). The investigative focus of the magazine was on "the great unelected power wielders of our time – multinational corporations" (Hochschild, 2001). *Mother Jones* was a project of the Foundation for National Progress, a tax-exempt nonprofit established to fund the magazine.

The founders named the magazine after Mary Harris Jones, who had helped workers fight low pay, long workdays, high mortality rates, child labor, and other labor-related issues in the late 1800s and early 1900s. She was commonly known as Mother Jones and

> was one of the most famous women in America. Articles about her regularly appeared in magazines and newspapers, and for many working Americans, she had achieved legendary, even iconic, status … For a quarter of a century, she roamed America, the Johnny Appleseed of activists.
>
> (Gorn, 2001, para. 3, 9)

The founding editors chose the name due to her "spirit, energy, assertiveness, and optimism and because the things she fought for represent the values we believe in" (Mother Jones, 1977, para. 7).

Mother Jones quickly became recognized for the quality and impact of its journalism. Its first issue in February/March 1976 published a story about safety issues in an India-based atomic reactor built with US aid. The story resulted in the aid being cut (Armstrong, 1999, p. 311). A story about the communist entry into Peking won a National Magazine Award. Investigative stories about misleading marketing and deaths from complications of the Dalkon Shield, 500 or more deaths from ruptured fuel tanks on the Ford Pinto exploding after being rear-ended, and "The Boomerang Crime", described earlier in this chapter, exemplified *Mother Jones*'s approach: thoroughly documented, understated, with a tone of "tightly focused anger," and grounded in personal anecdote and description (Armstrong, 1999, p. 312). "Muckraking, as practised by *Mother Jones* and other alternative media outlets, differs from pure documentary in that it doesn't passively present a set of facts or outline a problem, but advocates a solution. Muckraking is purposeful, political, moralistic reporting" (Armstrong, 1999, p. 305).

More recently, *Mother Jones* published the biggest investigative project it had ever undertaken, 18 months in the making. Reporter Shane Bauer worked undercover as a prison guard for four months investigating shocking conditions and prisoner mistreatment in a corporate-run prison, after which a team of editors and producers spent a year fact checking and researching a 35,000-word piece that was accompanied by videos, a radio documentary, and graphics. The project, published in 2016, won multiple awards including *Mother Jones* taking out the 2017 Magazine of the Year from the American Society of Magazine Editors and Bauer winning a prize for his reporting in the same awards.

In common with several other lengthy projects by nonprofit news centers, the costs by far outweighed any revenue gains. "My four months as a private prison guard" (Bauer, 2016) cost an estimated $350,000 to produce; advertising accompanying the project on *Mother Jones*'s website raised about $5000, and three foundations had provided some funding for criminal justice reporting (Bauerlein & Jeffery, 2016). The Justice Department soon after publication announced it would no longer contract with private prisons (Bauerlein & Jeffery, 2016).

Mother Jones's founders had three principle beliefs that hold true today. First, *Mother Jones* would be an organization that produced reliable, accurate journalism. Second, it would have a point of view: "our mission includes words like justice and democracy, and ... we were going to go after big institutions with political or economic power and hold them accountable and we would name names" (S. Katz, personal communication, April 12, 2018). Third, the organization would primarily be funded by readers.

Its point of view being a publicly stated grounding in progressive values and its reliance on reader support differentiated *Mother Jones* from other nonprofit news organizations that embraced journalistic neutrality and pitched to wealthy funders and foundations for support. Unsung at times by media and political commentators due to a perceived leftist perspective, *Mother Jones* stories nevertheless won prestigious journalism awards, set news agendas, and nonprofit editors grew increasingly envious of its support from individual donors.

Mother Jones did not rely as heavily on foundations for its revenue as most other news nonprofits. Foundations contributed 15–18 percent of its income (S. Katz, personal communication, April 12, 2018). This contrasted with some other nonprofits that depended on foundations for almost 60 percent of total revenues (Knight Foundation, 2015). Two-thirds of *Mother Jones*'s $16.3 million budget in 2017–2018 derived from 200,000 subscribers to its bimonthly print magazine and 50,000 individual donors. Advertising in the magazine and digital site contributed the remainder. "We found that people are happy to give us money, because we tell them that they should, and it's important to support journalism, and they do," *Mother Jones*'s editor-in-chief said (Kafka, 2017). Unlike some other nonprofit editors, Clara Jeffery was confident that the organization's business model was one of the few "that's gonna last long-term" (Kafka, 2017). Like NPR, *Mother Jones* regularly asked readers for donations, often talking to them directly about future projects it wanted to fund.

Foundations, whose funding decisions generally tend to be risk averse, in the past were hesitant to fund the nonprofit. "I think we were perceived by the major foundations as partisan and that their brand and our brand would not support each other," publisher Steve Katz said (personal communication, April 12, 2018). The attitude of foundation program directors and media critics changed after the commercial model for journalism collapsed, triggering a recognition that alternative models had to be found to fund quality journalism. The perspectives of media critics, journalism pundits, writers, and philanthropic players had shifted closer and closer to "what we have been doing and are for years" (S. Katz, personal communication, April 12, 2018).

Spurring recent interest in *Mother Jones* has been an extraordinary growth in audience and potential donors. In 2006, its print magazine and website had a combined readership of about 600,000. At the time of writing, its monthly audience across all platforms, including 1.2 million on Facebook and Twitter and 250,000 newsletter recipients, exceeded 10 million (Bauerlein & Jeffery, 2016; S. Katz, personal communication, April 12, 2018). The key factors behind the growth were a reorganization of its digital coverage, described below, and the heightened political climate associated with Donald Trump's presidency.

Other than being less dependent on foundation support, the size of *Mother Jones*'s audience and donor base meant it could operate as a publisher rather than depend on collaborations and distribution of its stories by legacy media. It demonstrated that readers desired and were prepared to support the type of journalism it produced. CEO Monika Bauerlein believed *Mother Jones* was the most advanced nonprofit in building a hybrid business model that combined traditional revenue streams and reader support (personal communication, April 12, 2018).

Senior editors insist the organization's journalism is not driven by partisanship. Rather, it is motivated by probing areas of interest such as exposing abuses of power and injustice. Key stories were fact checked and rigorously edited (M. Bauerlein, personal communication, April 12, 2018). "I would say that we are primarily an investigative journalism shop, but we are informed by progressive values, as many muckrakers are," editor-in-chief Clara Jeffery said (Kafka, 2017). Unverified data from its social media sites suggest that 18 percent of its Facebook users were politically conservative and 28 percent of its Twitter audience identified as conservative (S. Katz, personal communication, April 12, 2018).

Media scholars at times have labeled its journalism as "predictably liberal" and its readers as "left-leaning" and have not rated its journalism in the same class as that of legacy outlets such as the *New York Times* or *Washington Post* (Shirky, 2017). In 2012, *Mother Jones*'s Washington bureau chief David Corn obtained a secretly recorded video of Republican presidential contender Mitt Romney at a private fundraiser where he described the 47 percent of the population who supported President Barack Obama as being dependent on government, and who believed they were victims and that the government had a responsibility to care for them. They paid no income tax and believed they were entitled to health care, food, housing, "to you name it" (Corn, 2012). *Mother Jones* posted the video and accompanying story on its website, igniting a media storm that damaged Romney's candidacy (Sivek, 2014). *Mother Jones* won the 2013 National Magazine Award for its scoop. The story generated nine million page views and was credited with adding 14,000 Twitter followers and 12,000 new Facebook fans to *Mother Jones*'s social media sites. Donations jumped by 53 percent (Sturdivant, 2013).

It is perhaps unsurprising that in the politicized, divisive climate of US politics that *Mother Jones*'s journalism would be typecast, ignored, or dismissed as biased. One scholar attributed the impact of the 47 percent story to the fact of the video rather than *Mother Jones*'s journalism saying "the fact of the recording meant *Mother Jones*'s reputation didn't become a serious point of contention. Because people had to trust only the recording, not the publication, the veracity of the remarks was never seriously challenged" (Shirky, 2017). Others, however, lamented that the magazine no longer represented the politics of its namesake and produced "centrist, neoliberal, bourgeois-minded pieces" (LaChance, 2016) or acted "as a mask for the soft power of liberal elites and their not-for-profit corporations" (Barker, 2010).

While these sentiments may be viewed as part of free speech and debate in a robust democracy, *Mother Jones* also faced several serious threats to its operations. In 1981, the IRS at first disputed the Foundation for National Progress's nonprofit status and later targeted the magazine. In 1982, the IRS ruled that *Mother Jones* was unrelated to the foundation's purposes because it was a commercial enterprise and was not eligible for a tax exemption (English, 1983; Project Censored, 2017). Editors were convinced that the IRS had acted "after a number of our stories irked authorities in Washington" (Hochschild, 2001). Its executive editor in 1983 wrote that the IRS is

> out to get us. The Reagan administration 'proposes to end the threat that *Mother Jones* poses by putting it out of business': that's the

conclusion our legal counsel has reached after two years of arguing our case with the IRS.

(English, 1983)

The IRS finally dropped the case, but not until it had cost the magazine a large legal bill.

Mother Jones battled other costly law suits, in one case spending $2.5 million in lawyers' fees defending itself successfully against a defamation action brought by an Idaho billionaire (Global Freedom of Expression, 2015; Jeffery & Bauerlein, 2015). In a separate case, it was sued for $2 million by now documentary filmmaker Michael Moore over his dismissal as editor. Moore and Adam Hochschild, then chairman of the Foundation for National Progress, presented divergent reasons for Moore's removal in what became a publicly reported disagreement (Jones, 1986). In the end, Moore received $58,000 which he invested in the making of *Roger & Me*, his depiction of the decline of Flint, Michigan (MacFarquhar, 2004). There have been times also when the magazine has had to appeal to readers beyond its regular plea for funds due to circulation declines and revenues not meeting its expenses (Furlong, 1985).

Pivoting to Digital

In 1993, *Mother Jones* became the first general interest magazine to publish on the internet (Hochschild, 2001). By the mid-2000s, editors and business staff believed that while the print magazine had loyal subscribers, a more aggressive online approach to news might hold the potential for a much bigger audience (M. Bauerlein, personal communication, April 25, 2018). Senior editors Monika Bauerlein and Clara Jeffery were appointed coeditors, and working with business staff, recommended significant changes to the organization's operations. Editorial emphasis would broaden from deep dive stories written for the magazine, which would continue, to a redesigned website that would carry fresh content daily. Journalists would write for both the website and develop appropriate stories further into in-depth features for the site and the magazine. There would be additional full-time staff with reporters covering beats and less reliance on freelancers.

The coeditors established a bureau in Washington, DC, in anticipation of the 2008 presidential election. *Mother Jones* had several reporters in Washington but the editors felt that the reporting of national politics in the run up to the Iraq War had been "captured by the established political conversation" and that *Mother Jones*'s audience would welcome a stronger alternative voice (M. Bauerlein, personal communication, April 12, 2018). The board agreed. As metropolitan daily newspapers cut staff and closed foreign and expensive Washington bureaus during the global financial crisis, *Mother Jones* expanded its bureau to 15 staff. "People were like, 'you're out of your fucking mind.' But it worked" (S. Katz, personal communication, April 12, 2018).

The changes increased costs and were possible during the recession because the organization was not dependent on advertising or foundation support. "For us there was an obvious path because we felt that reader support had a better chance of translating to digital channels than advertising did," CEO Bauerlein said (personal communication, April 12, 2018). Readership jumped in line with the greater emphasis on more frequent news stories and the fact that *Mother Jones* pursued issues that media on The Hill did not cover.

The bimonthly print-version magazine was retained because it catered to an engaged audience that supported *Mother Jones* financially and attracted advertising. The magazine boosted the credibility of *Mother Jones* in the media, political, and donor worlds and differentiated the organization from an online-only publication, as well as generating a subscriber list (Sturdivant, 2013). In 2018, *Mother Jones* had a team of about 100, including eight Ben Bagdikian Fellows, a program named after the investigative reporter who helped the *Washington Post* publish parts of the "Pentagon Papers" in 1971.

More than any other news nonprofit organization, with the exception of National Public Radio, *Mother Jones*'s longevity and large donor list demonstrates that there are viable alternatives to foundation funding for accountability journalism. That may be true only for national news organizations with a particular perspective, but it does indicate that nonprofit news organizations can become publishers over time. *Mother Jones*'s CEO, Monika Bauerlein: "Your relationship with the audience is almost a sacred trust; your relationship with advertisers is a business-to-business relationship" (personal communication, April 12, 2018).

The Lessons Gained

The four organizations profiled in this chapter were power players in terms of economic, political, and cultural capital in the nonprofit accountability news sector. They attracted the bulk of the funding, had networks of mainstream media publishers, won key industry awards, and employed some of the nation's leading journalists. The organizations were founded by people who believed that better investigative journalism could be done in the nonprofit sector than in a commercial media environment. The organizations developed under the leadership of visionary founders, many of whom had experience in legacy media. Their symbolic capital facilitated collaborations with legacy media and attracted foundation funding. Despite concerns expressed by observers, including foundation program directors, that foundations might lose interest in investigative reporting, to date there is no evidence of that occurring at this level. The substantial ongoing funding by foundations, wealthy philanthropists, and a growing number of individual donors reflects both an appreciation of the journalism created and a conservatism by larger funders who prefer to stay with known entities. Yet, some nonprofits that rely on foundations remain hesitant about predicting the prospect of funding in the longer term.

The histories and funding experiences of these organizations suggest the following about the state of the nonprofit sector. First, foundations and wealthy philanthropists are willing to fund the ongoing operation of successful national nonprofit organizations. Second, funders are sensitive to the internal affairs and the activities of nonprofits and their program directors and will respond accordingly. Third, significant upfront funding is a preferred start because it gives organizations time to prove the concept journalistically and locate other revenue streams. Fourth, a sizeable audience of readers appreciates high-quality journalism and is willing to support it. Fifth, nonprofit organizations need to innovate constantly and develop new projects to attract foundation grants. Sixth, nonprofit organizations must be active in seeking new audiences as well as media partners. Seventh, public broadcasters are a natural partner for collaborative projects as they have similar missions and audiences. Eighth, mainstream media will publish nonprofit stories but are reluctant to pay for them. Earned revenue remains hard earned, though the Center for Investigative Reporting has succeeded in raising significant revenue from content fees. Ninth, difficult issues involving human relations and finances will challenge from time to time. Tenth, while major funding by a wealthy individual might provide initial stability, robust criticism and scrutiny will surely follow due to the United States' contested political climate.

Notes

1 Chapter 9 examines some of the ethical issues raised by the Hewlett Foundation's underwriting of reporters at *California Watch*.
2 Chapters 3 and 9 have more detail about the funding and launch of *California Watch*.
3 Bill Birnbauer has been a member of the International Consortium of Investigative Journalists since 1998 and has been involved in two major projects for the organization. He is the vice chair of the consortium's network committee.
4 Richard Tofel made clear that Herbert Sandler and other board members did not know in advance of publication the stories that *ProPublica* was working on (R. Tofel, personal communication, April 24, 2018).

Bibliography

Acuna, A. (1985, December 21). Each side to pay own costs: Penthouse, La Costa settle 10-year suit out of court. *Los Angeles Times*. Retrieved from http://articles.latimes.com/1985-12-21/news/mn-2902_1_la-costa

Armstrong, D. (1999). *A trumpet to arms: Alternative media in America.* Boston, MA: South End Press.

Barker, M. (2010). Mother Jones and the defence of liberal elites. Retrieved from http://www.swans.com/library/art16/barker47.html

Bauer, S. (2016, July/August). My four months as a private prison guard. *Mother Jones.* Retrieved from https://www.motherjones.com/politics/2016/06/cca-private-prisons-corrections-corporation-inmates-investigation-bauer/

Bauerlein, M., & Jeffery, C. (2016). This is what's missing from journalism right now: And a slightly scary experiment to try and fix it. Retrieved from Mother Jones website: https://www.motherjones.com/media/2016/08/whats-missing-from-journalism/

Blake, M. (2012, July/August). Something fishy? John Solomon had grand plans for the digital future of the Center for Public Integrity. But there was always a catch.... *Columbia Journalism Review.* Retrieved from http://www.cjr.org/feature/something_fishy.php?page=all

Burgess, M. (2016). How the 11.5 million Panama Papers were analysed. Retrieved from Wired website: http://www.wired.co.uk/article/panama-papers-data-leak-how-analysed-amount

California Watch. (2011). On shaky ground. Retrieved from http://californiawatch.org/earthquakes

Center for Investigative Reporting. (2014a). Awards. Retrieved from http://cironline.org/cir-awards

Center for Investigative Reporting. (2014b). Rape in the fields. Retrieved September 3, 2014, from http://cironline.org/rapeinthefields

Center for Investigative Reporting. (2015). *Return of organization exempt from income tax.* Retrieved from https://s3-us-west-2.amazonaws.com/revealnews.org/uploads/CIR+Dec+2015+Tax+Returns+-+Final+-+Form+990+Only+For+Public+Inspection.pdf

Center for Investigative Reporting. (n.d.). Our history. Retrieved from the Center for Investigative Reporting website: http://cironline.org/about/cir-history

Center for Public Integrity. (2010). *A digital strategy for expanding and monetizing CPI's investigative reporting.* Unpublished manuscript, The Center for Public Integrity.

Center for Public Integrity. (2014). Center wins first Pulitzer Prize. Retrieved from http://www.publicintegrity.org/2014/04/14/14593/center-wins-first-pulitzer-prize

Chumley, C. K. (2009). ProPublica: Investigative journalism or liberal spin? *Foundation Watch.* Retrieved from Capital Research Center website: http://capitalresearch.org/2009/05/propublica-investigative-journalism-or-liberal-spin/

Coleman, K., & Avery, P. (1978, July 10). The party's over. *New Times,* 23–47.

Corn, D. (2012). SECRET VIDEO: Romney tells millionaire donors what he REALLY thinks of Obama voters. When he doesn't know a camera's rolling, the GOP candidate shows his disdain for half of America. Retrieved from Mother Jones website: https://www.motherjones.com/politics/2012/09/secret-video-romney-private-fundraiser/

Doctor, K. (2011). The newsonomics of a single investigative story. Retrieved from Nieman Lab website: http://www.niemanlab.org/2011/04/the-newsonomics-of-a-single-investigative-story/

Editors Weblog. (2009). ProPublica: Could the non-profit model be the saviour of the newspaper industry? Retrieved from http://www.editorsweblog. org/2009/02/06/propublica-could-the-non-profit-model-be-the-saviour-of-the-newspaper-industry

Edmonds, R. (2001). Foundations and journalism: An awkward fit. *Chronicle of Philanthropy, 13*(16). Retrieved from https://philanthropy.com/article/ FoundationsJournalism-an/180037

Ellis, J. (2013). ProPublica at five: How the nonprofit collaborates, builds apps, and measures impact. Retrieved from Nieman Lab website: http://www. niemanlab.org/2013/06/propublica-at-five-how-the-nonprofit-collaborates-builds-apps-and-measures-impact/

Ellis, J. (2014). CIR wants to turn investigative reporting into a weekly public radio show with Reveal. Retrieved from Nieman Lab website: http://www. niemanlab.org/2014/07/cir-wants-to-turn-investigative-reporting-into-a-weekly-public-radio-show-with-reveal

Engelberg, S., Tofel, R., & Fields, R. (2018). Welcome to our second decade. Retrieved from ProPublica website: https://www.propublica.org/ article/propublica-10th-anniversary-welcome-to-our-second-decade?utm_ campaign=sprout&utm_medium=social&utm_source=twitter&utm_ content=1528650544

English, D. (1983). Say it isn't so, Uncle Sam. *Mother Jones, 8*(1), 7.

Feldstein, M. (2006). A muckraking model: Investigative reporting cycles in American history. *Press/Politics, 11*(2), 105–120. doi:10.1177/1081180X 06286780

Fitzgibbon, W., & Starkman, D. (2017). The "Paradise Papers" and the long twilight struggle against offshore secrecy. Retrieved from International Consortium of Investigative Journalists website: https://www.icij.org/investigations/ paradise-papers/paradise-papers-long-twilight-struggle-offshore-secrecy/

Fund for Independence in Journalism. (2008). A letter from Charles Lewis. Retrieved from https://web.archive.org/web/20090914154449/

Fund for Investigative Journalism. (n.d.). About us. Retrieved from http://fij. org/about/

Furlong, T. (1985, October 1). Mother Jones magazine seeks $197,000 in aid. *Los Angeles Times.* Retrieved from http://articles.latimes.com/1985-10-01/ business/fi-19367_1_mother-jones

Gabbay, T. (2012). Why is mainstream investigative journalism outfit *ProPublica* funded by Soros-affiliated donors? Retrieved from The Blaze website: http:// www.theblaze.com/stories/2012/04/03/why-is-mainstream-investigative-journalism-outfit-propublica-funded-by-soros-affiliates/

Global Freedom of Expression. (2015). Vandersloot v. Mother Jones. Retrieved from https://globalfreedomofexpression.columbia.edu/cases/ vandersloot-v-mother-jones/

Gorn, E. J. (2001, May/June). Mother Jones: The woman. *Mother Jones.* Retrieved from https://www.motherjones.com/about/history/

Green-Barber, L. (2014). 3 things CIR learned from analyzing the impact of Rape in the Fields [Blog post]. Retrieved from Center for Investigative Reporting website: https://www.revealnews.org/article-legacy/3-things-cir-learned-from-analyzing-the-impact-of-rape-in-the-fields/

Groega, L., Tigas, M., & Wei, S. (2014). State-by-state waiting times. Retrieved from ProPublica website: http://projects.propublica.org/emergency/

Hagey, K. (2011, December 5). Tuna and turmoil at CPI. *Politico*. Retrieved from http://www.politico.com/news/stories/1211/69763.html

Hochschild, A. (2001, May/June). Mother Jones: The magazine. *Mother Jones*. Retrieved from https://www.motherjones.com/about/history/

Horowitz, J. (2010, March/April). The education of Herb and Marion Sandler. *Columbia Journalism Review*. Retrieved from http://www.cjr.org/feature/the_education_of_herb_and_marion.php?page=all

International Consortium of Investigative Journalists. (2016). The Panama Papers: About this project. Retrieved from https://panamapapers.icij.org/about.html

Investigative Reporters and Editors. (n.d.). Arizona Project. Retrieved from http://www.ire.org/about/history/

Jeffery, C., & Bauerlein, M. (2015). We were sued by a billionaire political donor. We won. Here's what happened. The backstory of the massive lawsuit against Mother Jones. Retrieved from Mother Jones website: https://www.motherjones.com/media/2015/10/mother-jones-vandersloot-melaleuca-lawsuit/

Jones, A. S. (1986, September 27). Radical magazine removes editor setting off a widening political debate. *The New York Times*. Retrieved from https://www.nytimes.com/1986/09/27/us/radical-magazine-removes-editor-setting-off-a-widening-political-debate.html

Kafka, P. (2017). Full transcript: Mother Jones Editor in Chief Clara Jeffery on Recode Media. Retrieved from Recode website: https://www.recode.net/2017/9/15/16316750/transcript-mother-jones-editor-clara-jeffery-nonprofit-progressive-left-magazine-recode-media

Keller, B. (2009). *Letter to Herbert and Marion Sandler*. Retrieved from http://graphics8.nytimes.com/packages/pdf/business/2579_001.pdf

Knight Foundation. (2014). Knight Foundation awards $1.4 million to enhance DocumentCloud. Retrieved from http://www.knightfoundation.org/pressroom/press-mention/knight-foundation-awards-14-million-enhance-docume/

Knight Foundation. (2015). Gaining ground: How nonprofit news ventures seek sustainability. Retrieved from https://knightfoundation.org/reports/gaining-ground-how-nonprofit-news-ventures-seek-su

Kroll. (n.d.). History. Retrieved April 23, 2012, from http://www.kroll.com/about/history/

LaChance, N. (2016). Mother Jones' legacy is haunting Mother Jones as the magazine embraces neoliberalism. Retrieved from Paste website: https://www.pastemagazine.com/articles/2016/12/the-legacy-of-mother-jones-is-haunting-mother-jone.html

Leagle. (2005). OAO Alfa Bank v. Center for Public Integrity. Retrieved from http://www.leagle.com/decision/2005407387FSupp2d20_1403

Levett, M., Churchill, M., & Noyes, D. (1975). *Exploring ways and means of increasing investigative journalism*. Unpublished manuscript, Urban Policy Research Institute.

Lewis, C. (1990). *Office of the United States Trade Representative: America's frontline trade officials*. Washington, DC: Center for Public Integrity.

Lewis, C. (1994). *Well-healed: Inside lobbying for health care reform*. Washington, DC: Center for Public Integrity.

Lewis, C. (2000). *Annual report*. Retrieved from The Center for Public Integrity website: http://www.publicintegrity.org/files/manual/pdf/corporate/2000_CPI_Annual_Report.pdf

Lewis, C. (2007). *The growing importance of nonprofit journalism* (Working Paper Series #2007-3). Retrieved from the Shorenstein Center on Media, Politics and Public Policy website: http://shorensteincenter.org/wp-content/uploads/2012/03/2007_03_lewis.pdf

Lewis, C. (2014). *935 lies: The future of truth and the decline of America's moral integrity*. New York, NY: PublicAffairs.

MacArthur Foundation (Producer). (2012). *Center for Investigative Reporting, 2012 MacArthur Award for creative and effective institutions* [Video file]. Retrieved from https://www.macfound.org/videos/88/

MacFarquhar, L. (2004). The populist: Michael Moore can make you cry. *New Yorker*. Retrieved from https://www.newyorker.com/magazine/2004/02/16/the-populist

Masters, G. (2011). Digital transformation. Retrieved from American Journalism Review website: http://ajrarchive.org/Article.asp?id=5089

Miner, M. (2007, October 25). A Federal Bureau of Investigation: Can two dozen reporters in Manhattan fill the void left by newspapers across the country? *Chicago Reader*. Retrieved from http://www.chicagoreader.com/chicago/a-federal-bureau-of-investigation/Content?oid=926179

Moss, M., & Fabrikant, G. (2008, December 24). Once trusted mortgage pioneers, now scrutinized. *The New York Times*. Retrieved from http://www.nytimes.com/2008/12/25/business/25sandler.html?_r=0

Mother Jones. (1977). Four questions about Mother Jones. *Mother Jones, 2*(6), i.

Nocera, J. (2008, March 9). Self-made philanthropists. *The New York Times*. Retrieved from http://www.nytimes.com/2008/03/09/magazine/09Sandlers-t.html?pagewanted=all&_r=0

Noyes, D. (2001). Commentary was misguided. *Chronicle of Philanthropy, 28 June 2001. Academic OneFile*, Retrieved from http://link.galegroup.com/apps/doc/A147060481/AONE?u=monash&sid=AONE&xid=954bde7c

PBS Frontline. (1996). So you want to buy a President? Retrieved from http://www.pbs.org/wgbh/pages/frontline/president/

Pelley, S. (2009). World of trouble. Retrieved from CBS News website: http://www.cbsnews.com/news/world-of-trouble/

Perez-Pena, R. (2007, October 15). Group plans to provide investigative journalism. *The New York Times*. Retrieved from http://www.nytimes.com/2007/10/15/business/media/15publica.html

Perry, S. (2007). Financier backs project to beef up investigative reporting. *Chronicle of Philanthropy, 20*(2), 3.

Prial, F. (1983, September 10). Freelance unit thrives in TV reports. *The New York Times*. Retrieved from http://www.nytimes.com/1983/09/10/us/coast-freelance-unit-thrives-on-reporting-for-tv.html

Project Censored. (2017). 17. The IRS censors Mother Jones. Retrieved from http://projectcensored.org/17-the-irs-censors-mother-jones/

ProPublica. (2010). *Return of organization exempt from income tax*. Retrieved from http://s3.amazonaws.com/propublica/assets/about/propublica_990_2010.pdf?_ga=1.101534465.1802018135.1422211603

ProPublica. (2013). *Tackling the toughest stories, five years on*. Retrieved from http://s3.amazonaws.com/propublica/assets/about/propublica_2013report_final.pdf

ProPublica. (2014). *ProPublica report to stakeholders.* Retrieved from https://s3.amazonaws.com/propublica/assets/about/propublica-2014-2nd-interim-report.pdf?_ga=1.187860653.488934625.1427193785

ProPublica. (2017a). *2017 annual report: The next frontier is local.* Retrieved from https://assets.propublica.org/propublica-2017-annual-report.pdf

ProPublica. (2017b). *Financial statements, December 31, 2017.* Retrieved from https://assets.propublica.org/2017-Financial-Statements-for-Pro-Publica-Inc.pdf

ProPublica. (2017c). *Join ProPublica's new project to work with local news-rooms.* Retrieved from https://www.propublica.org/article/join-propublicas-new-project-to-work-with-local-newsrooms

ProPublica. (n.d.-a). About us. Retrieved from http://www.propublica.org/about/

ProPublica. (n.d.-b). Awards and honors. Retrieved from https://www.propublica.org/awards

ProPublica. (n.d.-c). ProPublica: Journalism in the public interest. Retrieved from http://www.propublica.org

ProPublica. (n.d.-d). *Reports & financials.* Retrieved from https://www.propublica.org/reports/

Protess, D., Cook, F. L., Doppelt, J. C., Ettema, J. S., Gordon, M. T., Leff, D. R., & Miller, P. (1991). *The Journalism of outrage: Investigative reporting and agenda building in America.* New York, NY: Guilford Press.

Rosenthal, R. (2011). *Reinventing journalism: An unexpected personal journey from journalist to publisher.* Retrieved from the Center for Investigative Reporting website: http://www.knightfoundation.org/media/uploads/publication_pdfs/CIR_IndustryReport_FINAL.pdf

Rosenthal, R. (2012). CIR receives $1 million MacArthur Award for Creative and Effective Institutions. *Reveal: The Center for Investigative Reporting.* Retrieved from https://www.revealnews.org/article/cir-receives-1-million-macarthur-award-for-creative-and-effective-institutions/

Rowe, S. (2011). *Partners of necessity: The case for collaboration in local investigative reporting* (Discussion Paper Series #D-62, June 2011). Retrieved from the Shorenstein Center on Media, Politics and Public Policy website: http://shorensteincenter.org/wp-content/uploads/2012/03/d62_rowe.pdf

Royce, K., & Heller, N. (2000). Cheney led Halliburton to feast at federal trough. State Department questioned with firm linked to Russian Mob. Retrieved from The Center for Public Integrity website: http://www.publicintegrity.org/2000/08/02/3279/cheney-led-halliburton-feast-federal-trough

Salladay, R. (2015). Reveal brings together all of CIR's journalism. Retrieved from Reveal website: http://www.revealnews.org/article/revealnews-org-brings-together-all-of-cirs-journalism/

Sandler, H., & Sandler, M. (2009). *Letter from the Sandlers to The Times.* Retrieved from http://www.goldenwestworld.com/wp-content/uploads/2009_042209_letter-from-the-sandlers-to-the-times-_april-22-2009.pdf

Shafer, J. (2009). What do Herbert and Marion Sandler want? Retrieved from Slate website: http://www.slate.com/articles/news_and_politics/press_box/2007/10/what_do_herbert_and_marion_sandler_want.html

Shirky, C. (2017, Winter). Political journalism in a networked age. "Journalism after Snowden: the future of the free press in the surveillance state" examines the challenging power dynamics between reporters and governments. *Nieman Reports.* Retrieved from http://niemanreports.org/articles/the-shadow-of-the-future/

Sivek, S. C. (2014). Political magazines on Twitter during the US Presidential election 2012. Framing, uniting, dividing. *Digital Journalism, 2*(4), 596–614.

Steiger, P. (2008, Spring). Going online with watchdog journalism. *Nieman Reports.* Retrieved from http://niemanreports.org/articles/going-online-with-watchdog-journalism/

Steiger, P. (2014). A closer look: Three golden ages of journalism? Retrieved from ProPublica website: http://www.propublica.org/article/a-closer-look-three-golden-ages-of-journalism

Sturdivant, J. (2013). Mother knows best. Retrieved from Publishing Executive website: https://www.pubexec.com/article/mother-jones-magazine-builds-2012-success/all/

Sullivan, D. (2010). *Libel tourism: Silencing the press through transnational legal threats.* Retrieved from Center for International Media Assistance website: http://cima.ned.org/publications/research-reports/libel-tourism-silencing-press-through-transnational-legal-threats

Thakur, S. P. (1999). Size of investment, opportunity choice and human resources in new venture growth: Some typologies. *Journal of Business Venturing, 14*(3), 283–309. doi:10.1016/S0883-9026(98)00002-0

The Progressive. (n.d.). About us. Retrieved from http://www.progressive.org/content/about-us

Weir, D., & Noyes, D. (1983). *Raising hell: How the Center for Investigative Reporting gets the story.* Reading, MA: Addison-Wesley.

Weir, D., & Schapiro, M. (1981). *Circle of poison: Pesticides and people in a hungry world.* San Francisco, CA: Food First Books.

Weir, D., Schapiro, M., & Jacobs, T. (1979, November/December). The boomerang crime. *Mother Jones.* Retrieved from http://motherjones.com/politics/1979/11/boomerang-crime?page=2

8　On the Ground with Smaller Nonprofit News Organizations

Most nonprofit investigative and public interest news organizations in the United States employed fewer staff and had far smaller budgets than the sector's better-known national players, *ProPublica*, *Mother Jones*, the Center for Investigative Reporting, and the Center for Public Integrity. The day-to-day operations of many smaller organizations depended on the "sweat equity, heart and hope" of journalists who struggled to raise funds and were ill prepared to run a nonprofit organization (Lewis, Butts & Musselwhite, 2012, para. 6).

Mc Nelly Torres, a cofounder of the Florida Center for Investigative Reporting, rated her chances of receiving a big grant from a national foundation as "one to a million" (personal communication, February 6, 2012). Instead, she had to focus on cultivating relationships with local community foundations that typically supported schools, environmental initiatives, and disaster relief. Torres, a former newspaper reporter, found the biggest challenge was that "we are journalists, we're not business people." She did not have the fundraising skills of some of the bigger nonprofit news organizations. "The big guys are always on top … so the little guys always struggle" (personal communication, February 6, 2012).

Former commercial television reporter Mark Saxenmeyer established *The Reporters* as a nonprofit organization in 2004 with the aim of producing independent television documentaries on issues that were underreported or not covered by the media. Dealing with potential funders left him exhausted and demoralized. "It's like you are in this vacuum trying to make people listen to you and begging for money. I just couldn't do it" (personal communication, April 19, 2018). He turned instead to crowdfunding, Facebook promotions, ticket sales to screenings, and hoped to sell his documentaries to domestic and international television networks.

The journalists who established nonprofit accountability news organizations were true believers in the media's watchdog role and the public's right to independently verified information. Often through dogged perseverance, they obtained information and documents that exposed illegal or immoral behavior by powerful entities. Some conceived or canvassed solutions to pressing environmental, social, and human rights issues.

Much of the time, like Torres and Saxenmeyer, they worried about having sufficient funds to do their work. This chapter presents case studies of several small- to medium-sized organizations in the nonprofit sector in the United States. The organizations are members of the Institute for Nonprofit News, which means they practice nonpartisan investigative or public service reporting. They were selected for the diversity of their areas of focus.

FairWarning

When newspaper reporter Myron Levin left the *Los Angeles Times* after 23 years, he was frustrated by his editors' story choices and dismayed at the newspaper's demise under billionaire owner Sam Zell. He took a buyout in 2008 without having a job to go to. Aged 59, he wanted to work fewer hours and enjoy semiretirement. Starting a nonprofit news organization was not on his mind. "I didn't want to do it because I knew I would be working like a donkey into my senior years" (personal communication, April 9, 2018).

Levin had written extensively about the tobacco industry since the 1980s. Based on his previous reporting and with newfound availability, he was hired as a consultant by filmmaker Charles Evans to work on "Addiction Incorporated", a documentary about tobacco company whistleblower Victor DeNoble. Evans then offered him a $250,000 grant from his family foundation should he want to continue writing the consumer-focused stories he had done in better days at the *Los Angeles Times*. The startup funding swayed Levin to incorporate *FairWarning* in April 2009 as a nonprofit organization. Less than a year later, it began publishing in-depth stories focused on "public health, consumer and environmental issues and related topics of government and business accountability" (FairWarning, n.d.). Levin, who had never raised money, had to find new donors, and do some of the reporting, assigning, and editing: "everything got done in a mediocre way" (personal communication, April 9, 2018).

Nevertheless, between 2012 and 2016, the nonprofit raised a total of $1.4 million from about 30 different foundations, some of which had renewed their grants. It had 200 small donors, but had attracted no funding from major foundations (FairWarning, 2016). Story sales, typically at $150–$200 each, generated income, though not much (M. Levin, personal communication, April 9, 2018). Levin favored unrestricted funding rather than grants for specific projects. It limited the amount of revenue he raised from donors but meant he was not "bound by anybody's expectations" (personal communication, April 9, 2018).

Levin recruited a board from among his journalist colleagues, rather than appoint one consisting of wealthy donors as some other nonprofits had.

This is the original sin of recruiting our board: some of them said, 'Myron, I would like to help you but I'm not going to raise money'. And instead of saying, 'well thanks anyway, bye', I said, 'oh that's okay.'
(Personal communication, April 9, 2018)

FairWarning has employed up to four staff depending on funding and paid several "old dogs from the *LA Times*" to write stories, some of which were copublished in the *Washington Post, Chicago Tribune, Mother Jones, CBS News, McClatchy DC, Salon,* and other media. Levin was reluctant to collaborate with media partners from the start of a project, preferring that they published *FairWarning*'s stories at the same time as he did. "I don't ever want to be the tail of some bigger dog ... we have probably lost some opportunities this way" (personal communication, April 9, 2018).

FairWarning's office is located in a historic mansion that houses the Western Justice Center in Old Town Pasadena, just a block from what was once called Millionaire's Row. Levin would like to increase the budget to $1 million, double the staff, and ensure the nonprofit's future. But if he were to leave for whatever reason "editorially we would be screwed ... there's nobody really to step in. I don't know what we would do" (personal communication, April 9, 2018).

The Marshall Project

The opportunity and challenge of creating a nonprofit accountability organization was too tempting for Bill Keller to resist. Keller had a job that most journalists would envy. As a columnist at the *New York Times,* his audience was assured and he could write about anything he wanted. A Pulitzer Prize-winning foreign correspondent and executive editor of the *Times* between 2003 and 2011, Keller might well have finished his long career in journalism writing opinion pieces.

Neil Barsky was a reporter at the *Wall Street Journal* before becoming an equity analyst and a successful hedge fund founder and manager. He shut the hedge fund in the financial crisis year of 2009 after it had lost 20 percent of its value the previous year. Financially, he could have continued but the stress was too great. "You can never escape it. You are never free" (Nocera, 2009). Barsky was wealthy enough to do anything he wanted.

Books such as *Devil in the Grove: Thurgood Marshall, the Groveland Boys, and the Dawn of a New America,* and *The New Jim Crow: Mass Incarceration in the Age of Colorblindness* revealed to Barsky how expensive, ineffective, and racially biased the US system of crime and punishment was and how inured the public had become about the overuse of solitary confinement, prison rape, and the jailing of teens with hardened adults (The Marshall Project, n.d.-b). The books were like a "whack on the cheek" and the lack of urgency to resolve the issues amazed him (Barsky, 2017, 7.45 min).

Barsky had considered starting a nonprofit news organization that would report on civil rights abuses and had sought advice from friends at *ProPublica* but now wanted to create a sense of national urgency about the criminal justice system. Margaret Sullivan, then public editor at the *New York Times*, organized a breakfast meeting between her friend Barsky and Keller at which Keller was asked if he would be interested in leading the editorial team at a nonprofit startup focused on criminal justice (B. Keller, personal communication, April 25, 2018). Barsky later would say he had an inkling that Keller may have been restless at the *Times* (Barsky, 2017, 13 min).

Keller had written several columns about criminal justice and was intrigued by the idea: "building something from scratch was something that doesn't happen every day" (personal communication, April 25, 2018). It felt like a natural evolution so he quit the *Times* where he had worked for 30 years. Eight months later in November 2014, the *Marshall Project* was launched. Keller's transfer to the nonprofit sector attracted wide media and funder interest (Calderone, 2014, para 5). The organization was named after Thurgood Marshall, the first African-American justice of the Supreme Court and the civil rights lawyer who in 1954 had paved the way for a landmark decision that declared unconstitutional segregation in the nation's public schools (The Marshall Project, n.d.-c).

The first challenge was to get funders to donate to an area that did not attract much reader or media interest. Barsky hired the chief financial officer at his former hedge fund to run the budget, and Keller set about hiring editorial staff. Barsky invested $1 million a year for the first two years and persuaded several wealthy colleagues to donate toward a $5 million budget (Barsky, 2017, 13.40 min; B. Keller, personal communication, April 25, 2018). The *Marshall Project* today is one of the better resourced organizations in the nonprofit sector, both in terms of staffing and funding. Revenues for fiscal year 2019 were expected to be more than $6 million with foundations providing about two-thirds of the income, and wealthy individuals and 1,700 smaller donors contributing the rest. In 2018, the nonprofit employed 35 full-time staff, including 12 staff writers and two journalism fellows.

Reform of the US criminal justice system falls within the missions of numerous NGOs, activists, lawyers' groups, and human rights organizations. But Keller said he had not accepted funding for specific projects other than for a small number of topic areas where the initiative had been his own. He would not partner with an activist organization and would reject funding to do a specific story. "I don't have a moral or ethical sense that that is wrong, it's just that it's a lot easier to establish your independence if you are talking about a broad purpose than a very focused purpose" (personal communication, April 25, 2018).

Keller initially hired a news manager and a digital manager from the *New York Times* but later employed younger digital and reporting staff. Website designers built a new content management system then moved to new ventures and were replaced by staff who could service the site: "We hired people who don't necessarily build the car but can repair it and drive it" (B. Keller, personal communication, April 25, 2018). He favored a younger reporting team that was energetic and passionate about online reporting and trained them to do *New York Times*-style reporting.

In 2016, the *Marshall Project* and *ProPublica* won the Pulitzer Prize for Explanatory Reporting for a 12,000-word story about the rape of a woman that was not believed by police (Armstrong & Miller, 2015). The *Marshall Project* also was a finalist in the Pulitzer Prize's Investigative Reporting category for a collaboration with the *New York Times* on violence by corrections officers at New York state prisons (The Pulitzer Prizes, 2016).

Finding publication partners was relatively easy for Keller due to his career at the *New York Times* and the contacts he had in the industry. Senior editors would take his calls.

> Marty Baron who is the editor of the *Washington Post* had worked with me at the *Times* ... Dean Baquet, [executive editor at the *New York Times*] I hired back after he had left the *Times* to go and work at the *Los Angeles Times* and I knew a lot of the subeditors. It was very helpful in persuading them to work with us.
>
> (Personal communication, April 25, 2018)

The *Marshall Project* has partnered with more than 100 organizations since its launch.

Another factor in securing collaborations with legacy media was that mainstream editors did not regard Keller or the *Marshall Project* as advocates. Rather, they were seen as professional journalists who upheld the disciplines of independence, verification, accuracy, and so on. That was despite the *Marshall Project*'s mission to "create and sustain a sense of national urgency about the US criminal justice system" (The Marshall Project, n.d.-a). "It's very challenging when you have a mission of criminal justice reform and then you have independence ... how do those two sides relate to each other?" Barsky wondered (Barsky, 2017, 33.30 min). Keller said the nonprofit's stories did not prescribe solutions to issues, but presented the views of people who believed they had some answers and then applied the "same degree of skepticism that we apply to the failures of the system" (personal communication, April 25, 2018).

Despite the site's relatively large income and its rapid growth, Keller was concerned about its long-term sustainability.

For now we are growing and funders are enthusiastic about the work we do. I do worry about five years from now or 10 years from now whether they're gonna say, 'well we got you started, now diversify your income stream'. We have diversified our income stream, but it's all philanthropy. The philanthropy community has to learn that when it comes to journalism, they are the business model.

(Personal communication, April 25, 2018)

San Francisco Public Press

The founder and executive director of *San Francisco Public Press*, Michael Stoll, developed an unconventional but effective way of covering intractable local issues such as homelessness, racial segregation in schools, and immigration. He commissioned stories that identified potential solutions then asked why those solutions had not been implemented. It was like doing investigative reporting in reverse (personal communication, April 16, 2018). For example, in 2017, the site's reporters identified 1,827 vacant rooms in privately owned single-room occupancy hotels and probed the reasons why they were not used to house some of San Francisco's 4,353 homeless people. "We went and asked why this had not been done. We didn't really get good answers from city departments" (M. Stoll, personal communication, April 16, 2018).

With several years of experience reporting mainly local issues in mainstream media and working for a university pilot project that assessed the quality of news in the Bay Area (Grade the News, n.d.), Stoll started drafting proposals in mid-2000 for a startup that would cover underreported public interest stories. He was drawn to the idea of merging quality reporting with a public broadcasting revenue model that would be accountable to readers rather than advertisers. After two years of planning, the *San Francisco Public Press* was launched officially in 2009.

Attracting funders was difficult because the organization had no reputation. Stoll was inspired by local public television and radio broadcaster KQED, which raised about $40 million a year from its 200,000 members and donors (KQED, 2016). "It showed what is possible" (personal communication, April 16, 2018). *San Francisco Public Press*'s first grant, just $20,000, was approved by a San Francisco Foundation officer who wanted to "take a chance on us" (M. Stoll, personal communication, April 16, 2018). It was barely enough to hire an editor and pay freelancers and the rent for a short time. An unexpected challenge arose when the Internal Revenue Service took 27 months to approve the organization's nonprofit status, further delaying funding opportunities.

By 2016, total annual revenue had increased to $163,393 (San Francisco Public Press, 2016). The organization's publisher, Lila LaHood, expected this would jump to about $450,000 in 2018 (L. LaHood, personal communication, April 16, 2018). Stoll, however, was in no hurry to grow the organization, preferring incremental growth and stability. "I would rather do it slowly and deliberately than try to make money in any way possible and risk tainting our reputation" (personal communication, April 16, 2018).

Community and family foundations have provided two-thirds of the *Public Press*'s funding and 550 individual donors contributed the remainder. LaHood would like to increase funding from readers in order to ensure long-term sustainability through a broad base of public support rather than depending on foundation grants (personal communication, April 16, 2018).

Another early challenge was retaining staff as there was not enough money to secure stable employment. The constant turnover and need to train people created a "sense of perpetual institutional amnesia" (M. Stoll, personal communication, April 16, 2018). The organization now has a core group of about five full-time staff and 20 freelance reporters, editors, designers, proof readers, photographers, and graphic designers.

The *Public Press*'s major investigative stories typically take three to six months to produce and focus on issues affecting minority groups, the poor, dispossessed, and people falling through the social safety net. They cover issues like labor, health care, education, politics, campaign finance, and the environment. Stoll and his team have developed a model in which major investigations of up to 10,000 words are published in a quarterly newspaper, complete with graphics, photographs, and side-bars, as well as being posted on the organization's website. The news-paper sells for $1 in about 40 retail outlets and is home delivered to a small number of subscribers. With a circulation of 10,000, it is also dis-tributed free of charge to community centers, health outlets, low income districts, festivals, and events. Each edition costs about $22,000 to print and distribute: "If you look at this as a product that we are trying to sell, it makes no sense at all – we do not make money off this" (L. LaHood, personal communication, April 16, 2018).

Michael Stoll always envisaged having a newspaper as well as a web-site. He reasoned that the newspaper reached readers who had no inter-net access, it provided a large canvas for infographics, it could be sold, it was a local touchstone, it could be used for marketing, it provided a sense of stability and commitment, it was a membership benefit, and every copy contained a donation envelope (M. Stoll, personal communi-cation, April 16, 2018).

The newspaper is distributed to every office at city hall. In early 2018, a mayoral candidate published an election platform that promised to end street homelessness. He noted that 1,500 single-room occupancy units were vacant in San Francisco and promised to investigate why the rooms were not leased so that homeless people could move into them (Leno, 2018). "We are read by influencers. We take free copies over to city hall and give them to every office and, lo and behold, we see our reporting seep into activity at city hall" (L. LaHood, personal communication, April 16, 2018).

NJ Spotlight

One of the first things the founders of *NJ Spotlight* had to settle was what not to cover. New Jersey has more than 600 school districts, 566 municipalities, and nine million people. The main deficit in accountability news, according to cofounder Lee Keough, was reporting state issues and the statehouse at New Jersey's capital in Trenton (personal communication, April 26, 2018). "When it came to state-wide issues, there used to be a lot of different voices covering them and now there aren't" (L. Keough, personal communication, April 26, 2018).

NJ Spotlight was launched in 2010 with the intention of filling that gap. Keough, who had edited computer magazines and websites, and three colleagues raised $150,000 from the Community Foundation of New Jersey and the Knight Foundation to launch the project. By 2018, the nonprofit had an annual budget of about $1.1 million, half of which was provided by foundations. Large and small donors contributed about 35 percent of its revenue, with the remainder raised through advertising and sponsorship (L. Keough, personal communication, April 26, 2018).

The nonprofit pays freelance writers and has seven staff reporters who break hard news in beats such as education, the environment, state financial issues, health care, transportation, and politics. The reporters are underwritten by foundations: the William Penn Foundation funds environment and water coverage, the Robert Wood Johnson Foundation finances the healthcare reporter, and so on. While such specific funding was not ideal, the foundations were hands off and had not interfered in editorial processes; the problem was that several had stopped their support. "They get bored and then you have to make up for them" (L. Keough, personal communication, April 26, 2018).

The *Spotlight* publishes about six stories a day and attracts around 150,000 unique readers each month. Its readers include bureaucrats, administration and legislature officials, lobbyists, advocacy communities, and "people who really care about the issues" (L. Keough, personal communication, April 26, 2018). At the time of writing, Keough was finalizing the details of a merger with public broadcaster NJTV. "We'll have the same focus and are determined not to be subsumed the way perhaps some others have once mergers have occurred" (L. Keough, personal communication, April 26, 2018).

Energy News Network and Ensia

The *Energy News Network* and *Ensia* are nonprofit news and magazine publications that are linked to larger not-for-profit organizations.

Located about 12 kilometers apart in St Paul and Minneapolis, Minnesota, both report on issues relating to global warming but their story paths rarely cross.

The *Energy News Network* was established to report news on state energy economies. It is published by Fresh Energy, a nonprofit organization that advocates for clean energy policy. The news organization is editorially independent from its parent organization, but director Ken Paulman has no conflict with Fresh Energy's mission: "As a news organization our viewpoint is that climate change is a problem and we should do something about it. We have that bias. This is an existential crisis facing humanity" (personal communication, April 19, 2018).

Ensia is published with the support of the Institute on the Environment at the University of Minnesota where it is based. Publisher and director Todd Reubold and editor-in-chief Mary Hoff worked in the institute's communications division before launching *Ensia* in 2013 to report more broadly on issues impacting the environment. The institute provides about 35 percent of the nonprofit's $325,000 annual budget but has no say on the stories it publishes. "We have published stories the institute didn't like" (T. Reubold, personal communication, April 18, 2018).

The *Energy News Network* also determined its own stories: "There's never been a situation where I've been told what to publish or when" (K. Paulman, personal communication, April 19, 2018). The network was created as an energy news aggregator for the Midwest region of the United States in 2010. Since then, it has expanded its coverage with separate websites for the Southeast, Northeast, and Southwest regions. In 2017, it was granted $1.5 million over three years by the MacArthur Foundation to move its coverage across 50 states (MacArthur Foundation, 2017). It employs eight part-time reporters based in regional areas and has three full-time staff in its main office.

The network's budget of almost $1 million is provided by eight or nine foundations, several of which have climate and clean energy programs (K. Paulman, personal communication, April 19, 2018). "They [foundations] see what we do as a strategic communications initiative. They're not just funding us because they think journalism is important" (personal communication, April 19, 2018). The association with the Fresh Energy nonprofit, which was founded in 1992, had made funding easier because the organization was well known to philanthropists and the clean energy sector.

The *Energy News Network* publishes about 400 stories a year and expects that to increase to about 600 when new regional reporters are hired. It attracts 50,000 unique visitors every month: one-third work in power utilities, solar firms, and energy distributors; 20 percent at other nonprofits and advocacy groups; and the remainder work for regulators, government agencies, or communications areas. "People have described us as a trade publication ... I guess it's true in a way" (K. Paulman, personal communication, April 19, 2018).

Ensia's model differs in that it focuses on in-depth magazine stories and hires freelance reporters to write them. Foundations with environmental and science programs and major donors provide about 60 percent of its budget. The site publishes two stories a week and attracts a million readers a year, with half living outside the United States (T. Reubold, personal communication, April 18, 2018). *Ensia*, whose name is derived from 'environmental solutions in action', also publishes a high-quality print magazine that it uses as a marketing tool and sends to members, donors, and foundations.

Conclusion

The case studies described above are a small sample of the nonprofit news organizations that operate in the United States and are not comprehensive in the description of their histories, funding, operations, or the challenges they have faced. The case studies were drawn from interviews with their founders and other staff as well as information on their websites but involved little observation or detailed research. Caution is required when generalizing findings to the broader sector of nonprofit accountability reporting. Having said that, a number of common features were observed.

First, many of the founders had experienced challenges when dealing with foundations. Their comments revealed a range of funding issues.

"The chances of us getting a grant from the national foundations are one to a million" (M. Torres, personal communication, February 6, 2012). "We've never got anywhere with Open Society [Foundations], Carnegie, Rockefeller, with Ford" (M. Levin, personal communication, April 9, 2018). The reality for Florida-based Mc Nelly Torres and Myron Levin in Pasadena was that the biggest funders of nonprofit news donate to nationally focused nonprofits such as *ProPublica*, the Center for Investigative Reporting, the Center for Public Integrity, NPR, and PBS rather than smaller enterprises. It meant that the nonprofits had to attract funding from community and family foundations that may not consider journalism as an area of need.

Nonprofit center founders also worried about the lack of ongoing support from foundations. "Even when foundations like you, sometimes after a couple of years they say, 'there's going to be a break in funding'. Each grant is not guaranteed from year to year," one publisher said (L. LaHood, personal communication, April 16, 2018). *NJ Spotlight* editor-in-chief Lee Keough added: "Foundations get bored and then you have to make up for them" (personal communication, April 26, 2018). Bill Keller worried that foundations after several years would expect nonprofits to diversify their incomes away from philanthropy (personal communication, April 25, 2018). Myron Levin from *FairWarning* said he didn't know "if some of those people are going to stick with us; just don't know. It's fickle, absolutely" (personal communication, April 9, 2018). However, Ken Paulman from the *Energy News Network* said several foundations had renewed funding the nonprofit over its first eight years, balking the conventional wisdom "that you can only use foundations for startup costs then somehow you must sustain yourself after that" (personal communication, April 19, 2018).

Nonprofit leaders expressed a strong desire to be less reliant on foundations by increasing revenue from individual donors. The *Energy News Network* was 99.9 percent foundation funded but wanted to boost small donors to between 5 and 10 percent of revenues (K. Paulman, personal communication, April 19, 2018). *Ensia* had about 100 small donors who provided about 5 percent of its income: "We're slowly coming around to where people realize if you want quality news you have to pay for it. But that shift is taking a while" (T. Reubold, personal communication, April 18, 2018).

San Francisco Public Press is two-thirds foundation funded, with 550 small donors providing the other third. Publisher Lila LaHood would prefer the ratios to be flipped so that donors provided the majority of the income. "I think it would speak of our relevance to the community if we could build that level of support from individual donors" (personal communication, April 16, 2018). *FairWarning* had about 200 individual donors that provided seven to eight percent of its income. Founder Myron Levin believed a larger funding base would ensure the nonprofit's sustainability but was not sure how that could be achieved (M. Levin, personal communication, April 9, 2018). The *Marshall Project* also attracted few small individual donations but editor Bill Keller hoped that could be increased to between 5 and 10 percent of its budget.

It was apparent even in this small sample that having a wealthy individual or institutional backer from the start enabled newly created organizations to focus on building their editorial teams and business models without a pressing concern about survival in the short term. That was particularly the case for the *Marshall Project* where wealthy philanthropists provided a multimillion-dollar base, and *FairWarning*, which received a $250,000 upfront grant. The *Energy News Network* was supported by the well-established Fresh Energy organization, and *Ensia* had institutional support from a university department.

Organizations that were established by journalists who were well known in the broad sector of mainstream journalism found it easy to partner with mainstream media. Bill Keller was one of the highest profile reporters and editors in the United States before forming the *Marshall Project*. "It helped that I could start by calling the editors. I started with some reservoir of trust and relationships that had developed over the years" (personal communication, April 25, 2018). Having reported for and edited the *New York Times* over 30 years, he had established networks and a strong reputation centered on journalistic values. Myron Levin, a journalist at the *Los Angeles Times* for 23 years, the *Kansas City Star* for five years, and at other newspapers before that, also could call editors and copublish with media such as *Mother Jones*, the *Oregonian*, the *Washington Post, Chicago Tribune*, and others. In contrast, the *San Francisco Public Press* mainly partnered with other nonprofit media organizations. The *Energy News Network* hardly collaborated with for-profit media because its relationship with advocacy group, Fresh Energy, was "still a little bit toxic for newspapers" (K. Paulman, personal communication, April 19, 2018).

Most positive was that these nonprofit organizations produced quality accountability reporting on issues that otherwise may not have received media attention. As metropolitan and local newspapers cut their budgets and reporting staff, the resources and expertise available to report on issues such as energy policy, environmental issues, statehouse politics, and criminal justice diminished. The Institute for Nonprofit News has 160 nonprofit journalism organizations and its executive director and CEO has estimated that another 110 nonprofit news organizations exist in the United States (S. Cross, personal communication, April 11, 2018). That means there are 270 relatively small nonprofit news organizations across the United States that produce national, regional, local, and niche topic stories, without which there would be less scrutiny of powerful interests and independently produced information available to the public.

Bibliography

Armstrong, K., & Miller, T. C. (2015). An unbelievable story of rape. Retrieved from The Marshall Project website: https://www.themarshallproject. org/2015/12/16/an-unbelievable-story-of-rape?utm_campaign=-interstitial&utm_source=internal&utm_medium=referral&utm_term=-victim

Barsky, N. (Producer). (2017). The Marshall Project: Shedding light and heat on criminal (in) justice [video]. Sol Price School of Public Policy. Retrieved from https://www.youtube.com/watch?v=ikxyPKWfi2U

Calderone, M. (2014, November 16). The Marshall Project aims spotlight on "abysmal status" of criminal justice. *Huffington Post*. Retrieved from http://www.huffingtonpost.com/2014/11/16/the-marshall-project-barsky-keller_n_6163504.html

FairWarning. (2016). *Return of organization exempt from income tax*. Retrieved from http://990s.foundationcenter.org/990_pdf_archive/264/264615038/264615038_201612_990.pdf

FairWarning. (n.d.). About FairWarning. Retrieved from https://www.fairwarning.org/about-fairwarning/

Grade the News. (n.d.). Evaluating print and broadcast news in the San Francisco Bay Area from A to F. Retrieved from http://www.gradethenews.org/index.htm

KQED. (2016). *Local content and service report to the community 2016.* Retrieved from https://issuu.com/kqed/docs/kqed-annualreport-2016-issuu

Leno, M. (2018). Issues. Retrieved from http://www.markleno.com/issues#homelessness

Lewis, C., Butts, B., & Musselwhite, K. (2012). A second look: The new journalism ecosystem. Retrieved from Investigative Reporting Workshop website: http://investigativereportingworkshop.org/ilab/story/second-look/

MacArthur Foundation. (2017). Fresh energy. Retrieved from https://www.macfound.org/grantees/2626/

Nocera, J. (2009, May 16). Hedge fund manager's farewell. *The New York Times.* Retrieved from https://www.nytimes.com/2009/05/16/business/16nocera.html

San Francisco Public Press. (2016). *Public charity status and public support.* Retrieved from https://projects.propublica.org/nonprofits/organizations/271275141/201713189349204631/IRS990ScheduleA

The Marshall Project. (n.d.-a). About. Mission statement. Retrieved from https://www.themarshallproject.org/about

The Marshall Project. (n.d.-b). A letter from our founder. Retrieved from https://www.themarshallproject.org/about/our-founder

The Marshall Project. (n.d.-c). Why the "Marshall" Project? Retrieved from https://www.themarshallproject.org/about/thurgood-marshall

The Pulitzer Prizes. (2016). Tom Robbins of The Marshall Project and Michael Schwirtz and Michael Winerip of *The New York Times.* Retrieved from http://www.pulitzer.org/finalists/tom-robbins-marshall-project-and-michael-schwirtz-and-michael-winerip

9   Ethical Issues in Foundation Funding of Journalism

The predominant ethical concerns in nonprofit journalism relate to the agendas and influence of funders. Two factors motivate these concerns. First, nonprofit news organizations are heavily dependent on philanthropic funding. Unlike the established media with multiple advertisers, subscription income, and other revenue sources, nonprofit organizations, particularly smaller ones, rely on a limited number of foundations to provide a large percentage of their income. With limited alternative sources of funding, this power imbalance has the potential to make nonprofits susceptible to the whims of their funders. Second, foundations fund other causes and use their media donations to generate coverage of issues in those areas. This may propel journalism toward advocacy.

Common rejoinders to the ethical issues posed by foundation-funded journalism in essence are: from nonprofit editors – we have a firewall; and from foundations – we are hands-off on stories. Nonprofit news organizations fail to acknowledge that their reliance on a philosophical firewall between their journalism and their funders borrows an ideal from mainstream media that does not translate easily into the nonprofit sector. There, senior managers are responsible for both the journalism and the funding. In any event, the concept of a firewall has applied unevenly across the established media. As for foundations being hands-off stories, their influence could be more subtle than blatantly demanding a particular story or angle, though such cases exist. Simply raising an issue in the public sphere may be sufficient return for a donation.

Ethical questions arise constantly in journalistic practice. Who to interview, when to interview them, how much to tell them about the story, who not to interview, and how to frame an issue are questions faced daily by journalists. Editors may be pressed to cover real estate matters to attract more advertising or retailers may sponsor a section, blurring journalism into advertorial content. Various codes of ethics and traditional practice provide guidance but, in the end, it is up to journalists themselves and their organizations to decide what is acceptable or not. This is true for commercial, public, and nonprofit journalism.

Is the Piper Playing an Ethical Tune?

If we accepted the assertions of foundations that they supported accountability reporting organizations in order to strengthen democracy and were hands-off on stories, there would be few ethical issues. But the relationship is more complex and questions remain about the degree to which foundations influence, or even have a right to influence, story selection and content.

One foundation director I interviewed recalled having donated to a nonprofit investigative organization because they believed that watchdog media were crucial to democracy. The nonprofit organization's subsequent investigations led to the resignation of a key government agency executive over what appeared to be a relatively minor financial matter. The foundation had been planning a cooperative venture with the government agency and had a high regard for the executive who was the target of the investigative stories. The foundation director, who asked that the foundation not be identified, said only a small sum was involved and that the government executive had done nothing wrong. The foundation program director complained to the nonprofit organization that the issue had been blown out of proportion. The experience raised questions in the program director's mind about the relationship between foundations and nonprofit news organizations. How might a foundation take on its grantees without stomping on freedom of the press? What rights did funders have to object? What did nonprofits owe their funders? Was it a good idea to have nonprofit journalism that relied on donations?

These were difficult questions that remain largely unaddressed in the nonprofit sector other than in broad guidelines for funders and nonprofit newsrooms developed by the American Press Institute and a standard reference to a firewall by the Institute for Nonprofit News (American Press Institute, 2017; Institute for Nonprofit News, n.d.-a). The Institute for Nonprofit News encourages its members to display an editorial independence policy on their websites. The policy says in part:

> Our organization may consider donations to support the coverage of particular topics, but our organization maintains editorial control of the coverage. We will cede no right of review or influence of editorial content, nor of unauthorized distribution of editorial content.
>
> (Institute for Nonprofit News, n.d.-a)

Firewalls are boundaries between journalistic activity and the business side of media companies, supposedly ensuring that news decisions are not economically motivated (Cotter, 2010, p. 61). In the mainstream media, the firewall has been "one of the foremost professional markers of journalism, a principle that is reinforced most strongly in the central sites of its socialization – journalism schools, textbooks, and reviews, not to mention thousands of newsrooms large and small" (Coddington, 2015). Concerned journalists have guarded against advertising or commercial considerations intruding on the independence of the journalism, either by publicizing transgressions or demanding adherence to a code of ethics or conduct. In practice, however, the operation of the firewall has varied from company to company depending on the organization's size and financial status, the leverage of its staff and their union, the political will of publishers and proprietors, and the demands of advertisers and sales staff. "The wall was either impenetrable, high, and thick, or it didn't exist at all. Its presence, or lack of presence, was determined by the owners ..." (Merritt, 2005, p. 123). It was the owners and CEOs who selected, hired, and fired newsroom editors and reporters, determined budgets, the space for news or advertising, and ultimately determined quality (Kovach & Rosenstiel, 2007, pp. 63–64). This power imbalance left journalists with only a porous philosophical firewall to protect their ethical standards.

In the nineteenth century, the *Chicago Tribune* had separate elevators for editorial and business staff. Today, such a physical separation appears quaint. Editors and other news staff regularly share meetings with marketing and advertising managers; they share overlapping management by objectives targets and journalists experience direct and very personal pressure to align their standards with those of the business (Merritt, 2005, p. 124). There has been a growing recognition that newspapers have dual characteristics, both as a service and a product (Lacy & Simon, 1993, pp. 4–5). "A nasty, unreported truth about journalism is this: journalism is a business. Journalists like to pretend this is not so, but it is" (Serrin, 2000, p. vii). Today, the firewall may be "seen as a rather anachronistic relic of a time when the news industry's survival wasn't threatened" (Coddington, 2015).

In the nonprofit sector, senior editorial executives often attend meetings with foundations or big donors, further eroding the firewall concept: "A good deal of the protection of journalistic independence in the realm of nonprofit media is left to good intentions" (Rosenstiel, Buzenberg, Connelly, & Loker, 2016). Like most editors, Robert Rosenthal from the Center for Investigative Reporting would prefer to devote all his time to journalism. But he has wider responsibilities.

I am a publisher in the sense that I'm responsible for keeping people employed. I have to bring in the money, and the money in our model, 95 percent plus ... comes from foundations, and the foundations want to all deal with me.

(R. Rosenthal, personal communication, November 3, 2010)

When he stepped down as head of the Center of Public Integrity in early 2015, Bill Buzenberg wrote about both the award-winning journalism he had overseen and the $50 million he had raised (Buzenberg, 2015).

Despite these dual responsibilities, the ideal of a firewall has transferred from mainstream journalism to the nonprofit sector. Many senior nonprofit journalists began their careers in traditional newsrooms and were imbued with conventions that included independence from business influence. While they now pitched for funding, they insisted that the resultant stories were not swayed by funders. This assertion is critical to the credibility of nonprofit journalism. If nonprofit stories were perceived by readers or the industry as having been influenced by funders, trust would be lost and the stories would be considered something other than journalism. That would be disastrous for nonprofit media organizations. It would immediately end collaborations with mainstream and public media.

Some reporters in the mainstream media still retain a definite skepticism about partnering with a nonprofit organization (Kaplan, 2008, p. 119). This is not surprising because the professional distance between funders and journalists in nonprofit newsrooms is significantly less than in traditional newsrooms (Cutbirth, 2016). Responding to a questionnaire, investigative reporters in the mainstream media said that before agreeing to partner with a nonprofit organization, they would want to know its history and funding sources. They expected to have full transparency and access to all the documents and sources used in the nonprofit story (Kaplan, 2008, pp. 120–124). Similarly, former *Boston Globe* investigative editor Tom Farragher said he would want to see the "innards of the work as it's being done." The nonprofit organization's funding had to be untainted to the degree that the story was not crippled or could be dismissed as part of an agenda. "That's the central problem: what is the agenda of the people with the money? Once the reader concludes, 'oh, yes, they investigated X but they would never investigate Y because the funder wouldn't allow it,' then you're in trouble" (T. Farragher, personal communication, February 25, 2014).

While mainstream reporters considered their organizations not beholden to commercial interests, a study by journalism professor Philip Meyer found that editors representing 79 percent of daily newspaper circulation in the United States reported sometimes being pressured by advertising to the extent that it was serious enough to "require a newsroom conversation to resolve the issue" (Meyer, 2009, p. 226). Other media critics pointed out that most newspapers received about 75 percent of their revenue from two dozen advertisers, and in many cases five or six advertisers provided about half of the advertising revenue. Significant financial damage would occur if an advertiser reduced or withdrew funding because it was offended by a paper's content (Picard, 2005, p. 342). Professor Meyer downplayed the idea that foundation funding of journalism was more ethically fraught than taking advertising dollars. "Allowing charitable foundations to pay for the news might be risky, but it is probably no worse than a system in which advertisers pay for it" (Meyer, 2009, p. 226). Veteran nonprofit sector advocate Brant Houston said the idea of "purity of purpose is a daily job, whether you are in a for-profit or not and to think otherwise is naïve" (B. Houston, personal communication, November 19, 2010).

Most nonprofit organizations have smaller budgets than newspapers and are reliant on a more limited number of funders. "No one is in a financial position to say, 'You know what, thank you for offering that $300,000, $400,000 to us, we're okay; ethically we feel that is troubling'," a former nonprofit executive said (K. Davis, personal communication, January 31, 2012). In the real world of competitive funding, where to draw the line ethically may be somewhat flexible. A veteran nonprofit organization founder put it this way:

> My line for many, many years at the center was 'ethics are what you have the ability to pay for.' If you can finance yourself travelling all around the country on a story you can have great ethics, but if you don't have the money you might have to scrape together some things that aren't quite as ethical. But are you going to not do the story?
> (D. Noyes, personal communication, November 4, 2012)

Nonprofit organizations limited the amount of detail they gave funders about the projects they wished to pursue in the belief it would lessen the potential for funder influence. Some also told foundations not to contact reporters, and instructed reporting staff not to talk to funders. A chief development officer at the Center for Public Integrity said her contact with foundations consisted of only very broad brushstroke discussions about topic areas rather than story content (R. Heller, personal communication, February 8, 2012). *ProPublica*'s Paul Steiger said the organization's key funders, Herbert and Marion Sandler, and other members of the board did not know in advance what stories its journalists were working on, nor were they to have contact with reporters (Schilders, 2008). Despite these assurances, a survey of funders, nonprofits, and commercial media showed that funders were three times as likely as their grantees to say they discuss with some specificity the work being produced such as specific stories and the issues to be exposed (Rosenstiel et al., 2016). Funders also were less likely to say they discussed coverage in only general terms than their grantees. These responses indicate that a gap exists between how funders and nonprofits interpret their discussions around the expected outcomes of funding.

That there have been attempts by foundations and wealthy individuals to initiate and influence stories, there can be no doubt. The Center for Investigative Reporting's Robert Rosenthal said: "I have had foundations approach me and want us to work with advocates for considerable amounts of money ..." (R. Rosenthal, personal communication, November 3, 2012). Nonprofit veteran Charles Lewis said:

> I had murky characters come to me offering me money. I have had donors that I didn't feel comfortable with ... I've had other cases of ideological people who feel strongly about something. After the 2000 election, I had liberals who were very upset about [Democratic candidate Al] Gore losing wanting us to investigate voting machines and offering money, like, in my face, checks waving almost in my face, they were so upset with what had happened.
>
> (C. Lewis, personal communication, November 8, 2012)

Lewis rejected these offers which he felt would turn him into an "adjunct to the Democratic Party." During the 2004 Presidential campaign, billionaire George Soros became active in the Democratic campaign and offered the Center for Public Integrity $750,000, which Lewis also rejected (Schilders, 2008). One funder asked a reporter at the Center for Investigative Reporting to provide information in advance of publication to an advocacy group that the funder was supporting. That approach was refused by the center's fundraiser:

> What we could say we would do is we would be happy to put those advocates on a story alerts list, and as soon as the story is published they can get access to it immediately, but we can't do anything in advance, we can't favor one constituency over another.
>
> (C. Parsons, personal communication, November 2, 2010)

Several nonprofit executives said they had rejected ethically dubious grants. This proved, they said, that their firewall was effective.

Nonprofit editors said they looked for an alignment between offers of funding and their areas of interest. For example, the Center for Public Integrity might talk to foundations that want to fund environmental stories but would accept such projects only if it had already decided that the environment was an area of interest (B. Buzenberg, personal communication, November 11, 2012). The Investigative Reporting Workshop at American University might look at the super fund program of the Environmental Protection Agency but would not look at a story in "Secaucus, New Jersey, because the next-door neighbor is pissed off and wants to give us $30,000" (C. Lewis, personal communication, November 8, 2012). The Center for Investigative Reporting would cover clean water issues in California, but would not work with an advocacy group or provide information they could then use. "If we publish a story and they see it and want to take the information and use it as they like, sure" (R. Rosenthal, personal communication, November 3, 2010). These examples involve executives with many decades of experience and so-cialization in journalistic culture and practice. But what might happen when they retire and are replaced by people with a more corporate out-look and little or no journalistic culture? Might a wink and a nod to foundations guarantee funding?

Foundations and Editorial Influence

The John D. and Catherine T. MacArthur Foundation, one of the big-gest independent foundations in the United States, has been a generous funder of accountability news organizations for many years. Data sup-plied by the foundation show that MacArthur donated $36.6 million to US nonprofit investigative organizations between 2003 and 2015. In addition, it gave National Public Radio $15.5 million and $1.7 million to international news organizations (K. Im, personal communication, January 9, 2018). The donations show that the MacArthur Foundation has favored large investigative centers: the Center for Public Integrity, the Center for Investigative Reporting, *ProPublica*, and documentary makers at *Frontline*, reflecting a national focus in its grant making. The foundation also supports a large number of other areas, including re-form of state juvenile justice systems, human rights programs, the en-vironment, and initiatives to provide affordable rental accommodation (MacArthur Foundation, n.d.). But the foundation kept separate its me-dia grant making from its other investments. "Our media funding ... is not designed to bring more visibility to the fields we otherwise support. It's designed to strengthen the quality of information that citizens in a democracy get to experience," a former media program director said (E. Revere, personal communication, February 17, 2012). The foundation provided general funding rather than grants for specific projects. She added, however, that it was useful to know about a nonprofit center's area of reporting and to have "some overlap in interest. We just try to make sure that it's not one-dimensional or very narrow in an area that we're just not interested in supporting" (E. Revere, personal communi-cation, February 17, 2012).

I asked MacArthur's program director about the question raised ear-lier in this chapter by the unidentified foundation director on the extent to which foundations might object to the reporting of nonprofit centers they had funded. She responded that she had never objected about a news organization's reporting:

> I don't think that would be proper for us. I think that we both ex-press our confidence in the ... professional editorial leadership of the place and put the money in, or we don't feel confident and we don't put the money in.
> (E. Revere, personal communication, February 17, 2012)

The foundation had donated to a newsroom whose stories had conflicted with the foundation's other support, but "we're big enough, we can live with it" (E. Revere, personal communication, February 17, 2012).

However, the unidentified program director's uncertainty about the extent to which foundations could challenge or question the reporting of nonprofits remains a subterranean issue, buried under vague assurances of editorial freedom and firewalls. Yet, the director clearly had concerns about the whole process.

> We funded them [the nonprofit] big-time and they are doing really well and we are part of the reason they're doing really well, and there are things that they are doing that make me crazy. They make me crazy; so upset about it. It is a real question of what rights do we have as funders to say 'we hate what you're doing and we're funding it', or object to something that we think is unjust.

Jon Funabiki was the deputy director of the Ford Foundation's media fund between 1995 and 2006. The foundation was "hands-off on the editorial process. We believed in the independence of the media maker, the journalist or the filmmaker" (J. Funabiki, personal communication, February 1, 2012). However, there were funders, especially individual donors, who had a different ethic and

> that's where it starts to get pretty nasty. There are lots of stories out there where a donor says, 'I want you to cover this and this is what I want you to say.' So that's an education process for the donors.

Most foundations were interested in a return that was very specific.

> I can speak as a former funder, and the Ford Foundation certainly had a point of view about the world, social justice, freedom of expression, blah, blah, blah. But when we funded journalism or, say, documentary projects, we didn't necessarily fund because we thought that this would lead to a very specific action. We funded because we thought that raising the issue would be useful. Funders ... may be happy with just having the issue reported on.
> (J. Funabiki, personal communication, February 1, 2012)

Foundation Advocacy for Policy Reform and Transparency

Survey responses by 63 nonprofit funders showed that 52 percent made media grants on issues where they did policy work, 59 percent funded specific subjects, and 61 percent funded investigations into specific problems or a particular series of stories. Forty-one percent of nonprofit media organizations said they had received offers from funders to conduct specific investigations. Of those, 80 percent had accepted such offers. Three-quarters of these nonprofits said the investigation had been on their to-do list (Rosenstiel et al., 2016). In the same survey, 54 percent of funders said they were mainly interested in strengthening a free press, but 44 percent said they engaged in media funding to advance larger strategic goals. Over 40 percent of grantees recognized that funders wanted to drive some agenda other than improving journalism (Rosenstiel et al., 2016).

For some journalists, these sorts of findings were sufficient to make them suspicious of foundation agendas. The retired broadcaster and journalist Ted Koppel once said: "When a soap company sponsors 'Nightline,' I know what they want – so many million eyes on an ad for their soap. But when the money is from Pew [Foundation], what is it you're looking for?" (Edmonds, 2002, para. 6). Journalists are right to ask such questions. However, that foundations have agendas should be neither surprising nor seen as a negative. Foundations want to change or improve things in their areas of interest; funding journalism often was a small part of a larger strategy for doing that. One funder explained it this way

> Now, other people here might wake up in the morning and say, I want to create great journalism and I hope it has an impact. I get here and I say, I want to make an impact, and journalism is a great way to do that.
>
> (Funt, 2015)

The ability of nonprofit investigative organizations to report deeply on issues and have an impact, given sufficient funding, is where and how the interests of the nonprofit news and foundation sectors intersect. As one fundraiser put it,

> So they [foundations] have an agenda. I don't mind that, I'm not troubled by that. They're looking to impact and often we can talk with them about ways that policy or laws have literally changed [due to stories]. They want to see the discourse elevated and we can do that.
>
> (R. Heller, personal communication, February 8, 2012)

One example of this understanding was in the area of education reform supported by the William and Flora Hewlett Foundation and its funding of a new state-based nonprofit in California (The William and Flora Hewlett Foundation, n.d.-a). Foundation support for education reform is not unusual in the United States. American foundations have promoted education policy reform for decades and provide about $4 billion a year to transform K-12 education with programs centered on student performance, charter schools,[1] and teacher effectiveness (Barkan, 2011; Picciano & Spring, 2013). The Hewlett Foundation developed long-term detailed strategies aimed at improving public education and student skills particularly in disadvantaged districts. It funded research studies, webinars, tools, and assessment and implementation of its programs through hundreds of grants (The William and Flora Hewlett Foundation, n.d.-c). Its key education strategies centered on a deeper learning program developed for K-12 schools to deliver competencies such as "mastering rigorous academic content, learning how to think critically and solve problems, working collaboratively, communicating effectively, directing one's own learning, and developing an academic mindset – a belief in one's ability to grow" (The William and Flora Hewlett Foundation, n.d.-b). In 2016, $30 million was granted to 70 organizations in support of the program. The foundation granted an additional $10 million in 2016 to provide education-based learning, teaching, and research materials (The William and Flora Hewlett Foundation, n.d.-e).

The Hewlett Foundation was one of the inaugural funders of the Center for Investigative Reporting's state-focused news offshoot, *California Watch*. In 2009 and 2010, the Hewlett Foundation provided grants totaling more than $1.6 million to the center and, two years later granted it a further $400,000 in a special project gift. The foundation had no specific program for funding media. Rather, $1.6 million was donated under the Hewlett Foundation's education program in two batches. A donation of $1.2 million in 2009 was listed on the Hewlett Foundation's website as being for "multimedia reporting on California education and other policy issues" (The William and Flora Hewlett Foundation, n.d.-d). The grant would "build a team of experienced reporters" to cover the issues (The William and Flora Hewlett Foundation, 2009, para. 7). A $400,000 general operating grant in 2010 was specifically for the California schools report card project (The William and Flora Hewlett Foundation, n.d.-d).

The Hewlett Foundation's 2009 and 2010 funding of *California Watch* was part of a broader strategy of education reform and improvement. Hewlett's former communications officer, Jack Fischer, said that the foundation had invested heavily in reforming the state education system and was concerned that the issues it cared about were covered in the media. Grants for media typically came from the foundation's program directors wanting media coverage of an issue. In this case, the education program director "of course was pushing to do more education coverage" (J. Fischer, personal communication, February 3, 2012). *California Watch* published dozens of stories about charter schools particularly and education more broadly. Many of the stories were written by Louis Freedberg who became an education reporter after cofounding *California Watch* with Robert Rosenthal.

A guiding principle for journalists in Western democracies is to act independently and avoid conflicts of interest that can occur when faced with competing loyalties such as their organization's "economic needs as opposed to the information needs of the public" (Black, Steele, & Barney, 1993, p. 79). Hewlett was aware of the ethical sensitivities: its education program director did not want to "big foot" *California Watch* by insisting it had to cover particular items as everyone would have been uncomfortable with that, Fischer explained (personal communication, February 3, 2012). It was up to *California Watch* to decide how, when, and what stories it published. Nevertheless, the education program director was interested in the center's education coverage and had urged the center to do more. This was achieved in large measure as *California Watch* published multiple stories on state education. Many of its education stories did not disclose Hewlett's funding of *California Watch* or the foundation's interest in education reform.

One story in May 2011 was based on a study by the Rand Corporation and Policy Analysis for California Education (Freedberg, 2011). The story said that the study had been funded by three philanthropic organizations including the Hewlett Foundation but did not refer to Hewlett's funding of *California Watch*. Other education stories were more transparent and did refer to the foundation's underwriting of education reporting and funding *California Watch*. This is not to suggest that Freedberg's or other *California Watch* stories on education were influenced by anything other than normal journalistic standards, apart from an obvious editorial emphasis by the center on education issues. But for an investigative reporting organization to have an education reporter whose job was underwritten by a foundation that was campaigning to reform education and that funded studies and organizations that were then reported on by journalists at the center without declaring a potential conflict of interest lacked transparency. "The fact they are saying 'look at problems in particular types of education' may be not bad but at what level does it feed into a political campaign? That's when you start getting into issues that affect your credibility," media business expert Robert Picard commented (R. Picard, personal communication, July 10, 2014).

Freedberg responded to questions sent to him by email about Hewlett's funding of *California Watch* and the Center for Investigative Reporting. He said the Hewlett Foundation had no explicit reform agenda in 2009 when it provided its major grant and did not present a substantive conflict for reporting at the time (L. Freedberg, personal communication, September 18, 2012). Hewlett's goal in a general sense was to promote better education outcomes in California and eventually more school funding but it had no specific agenda.[2] Freedberg said that *California Watch*'s website listed Hewlett as a funder but citing it as a funding source in stories would be done on a case-by-case basis. It was not feasible or reasonable to expect *California Watch* to mention Hewlett's funding of organizations it reported on given that Hewlett supported multiple – in some cases hundreds – of organizations each year (L. Freedberg, personal communication, September 18, 2012).

Freedberg wrote that nonprofit reporters should disclose possible funding conflicts but that seemed a higher standard than applied for commercial media "which has almost no standards in this regard" (L. Freedberg, personal communication, September 18, 2012). For instance, a *San Francisco Chronicle* reporter was not expected to mention that Chevron provided advertising revenue while reporting a Chevron refinery fire. Yet, for-profit reporters arguably were more vulnerable to advertising pressures than nonprofits would be from a foundation. Advertisers could pull their advertising in response to a story but foundations more likely would not renew their grant when it expired rather than asking for their money back. "The relationship between a specific story or series of stories and how the funder felt about it would be much harder to pinpoint" (L. Freedberg, personal communication, September 18, 2012).

The issues associated with *California Watch*'s stories were not at the serious pole of ethical wrongdoing and could easily have been fixed with more disclosure of Hewlett's funding of education reporters and its agenda of education reform. The standards code developed by the Institute for Nonprofit News was adhered to because *California Watch*'s parent, the Center for Investigative Reporting, declared on its website that Hewlett was a funder (Institute for Nonprofit News, n.d.-b). But this did not adequately capture the nature of the relationship.

Funding by Corporate Sponsors

It was not just foundation grants that raised questions about the funding and independence of nonprofit journalism. In an analysis of the *Texas Tribune*'s sponsorship and donation income, former journalist James Moore found numerous examples where significant amounts were donated by corporations and lobbyists that also supported politicians and other office holders in order to influence legislation (Moore, 2014). Moore discovered that between 2011 and the first half of 2013, 50 individuals had donated $1 million to the *Texas Tribune* while also giving $18.8 million to candidates for the 208 elected offices that the *Texas Tribune* reported on.

The *Tribune* raised a further $1.4 million from corporate sponsors that donated $20.3 million to candidates in 2012. "… there is no conclusion to reach other than the *Texas Tribune* has to be considered corrupted by its sources of funding," Moore wrote (Moore, 2014, para. 9). Two-thirds of the *Texas Tribune*'s corporate sponsors were groups that lobbied the legislature or hired lobbyists, or were public relations firms hired to influence public opinion on legislation or government entities. One-third of all the money raised in 2011 and 2012 was donated by special interests, and one out of every five dollars raised by candidates in the 2012 state elections came from donors who also had sponsored the *Texas Tribune*. Moore argued that these donations transformed donors into partners with common goals, unlike advertisers and broadcasters in the mainstream media: "To assert ... that donors will somehow not act to have their money promote their interests in a similar manner is disingenuous in the extreme" (Moore, 2014, para. 18). He said the *Texas Tribune* did not reveal how much money came from its corporate sponsors and its stories often did not disclose that the people or interests being quoted were donors.

After Moore's story was published, the *Texas Tribune* decided that corporate sponsors would be listed by name and amount and that disclosures would be appended to each story (Batsell, 2015). Its web page of corporate sponsors now includes amounts given each year as well as multiyear totals under the categories of "digital revenue", "digital in kind", "events revenue", and "events in kind." In late 2017, there were 945 corporate sponsors that had provided $19.1 million in revenue since 2009 (Texas Tribune, 2017a). The *Tribune* also published a list of thousands of donors and members (Texas Tribune, 2017b).

The *Texas Tribune*'s editor used the firewall concept when defending the organization. "We have a wall – like any other independent newsroom in the world. Sponsors don't interact with reporting staff" (Robin, 2014, para. 7). The *Tribune*'s CEO and editor-in-chief Evan Smith predicted that the

> hand-wringing about native advertising will give way to hand-clapping at the prospect of someone paying for serious journalism. Yes, disclosure and transparency are the entire ballgame, but haven't they always been? There should be rules and regs and standards messaged from on high, and bad actors should be publicly stoned. Beyond that, the self-appointed integrity cops – you know who you are – need to take a chill pill.
>
> (Smith, 2013)

Funding and Claims of Bias

It is unsurprising that in the politically polarized United States, suspicion and conspiracy theories would encompass the funding of nonprofit media ventures. One target was the promarket Franklin Center for Government and Public Integrity that funds investigative organizations in several US states. Another was George Soros's Open Society Foundations that funds numerous nonprofit news sites that critics routinely describe as liberal or left leaning.

Funding by philanthropic organizations and wealthy individuals has been controversial because of the political advocacy and other funding of donors such as the Franklin Center, George Soros, Pierre Omidyar, and *ProPublica*'s founders, Herbert and Marion Sandler. However, evidence of interference in editorial processes – such as demands for particular slants or stories – by funders is hard to find. What appeared to be true and overlooked was that the Franklin Center-funded *Watchdog.org* organizations and those funded by Open Society Foundations and the Sandlers have provided valuable accountability journalism at a time when the for-profit model was struggling, especially at local and state levels.

The Franklin Center for Government and Public Integrity was created in 2009 with the aim of training and supporting investigative journalists to cover local governments and to "spotlight free-market, pro-liberty solutions to difficult public policy challenges" (Franklin Center for Government and Public Integrity, n.d., para. 1). The goal of its *Watchdog. org* project was to provide oversight of state governments, hold politicians and bureaucrats to account for their handling of taxpayers' dollars, and promote innovative solutions to public policy challenges (Watchdog. org, n.d.). The center's Form 990 return to the Internal Revenue Service shows the center had total revenues of $8.8 million in 2015 and had raised more than $45 million in gifts grants, contributions, and membership fees since 2011 (Franklin Center for Government and Public Integrity, 2017).

Jason Stverak, a former president of the center, was a senior executive of the Sam Adams Alliance and former executive director of the North Dakota Republican Party (Gibbons, 2010). Stverak refused to identify the center's sources of funding but the *Columbia Journalism Review* reported that 95 percent of it came from Donors Trust whose key contributors were the billionaire libertarian Koch brothers (Chavkin, 2013). Another funder was identified as the Sam Adams Alliance, an organization devoted to the promotion of free-market ideals (SourceWatch, 2012). A report by the Center for Public Integrity found that the Franklin Center had "numerous ties to Koch-connected Americans for Prosperity" and that recurring themes on its websites included union bosses, Marxian senators, and the perils of renewable energy (Abowd, 2013, para. 11). *PR Watch* said that numerous Franklin Center staff had ties to conservative activist groups and the Republican Party. It cited several stories written by Franklin-funded sites under the heading "Sloppy reporting, or manufacturing news?" (Jerving, 2011). Others said Franklin-funded stories were "thin and missing important context" which occasionally led to gross distortions (Wilce, 2013, para. 17). Even newspaper editors who reprinted Franklin Center-affiliated stories "speak warily of the group's ideological bent" (Strupp, 2012, para. 4).

The promarket mission of the Franklin Center is openly stated, but published evidence of overt manipulation of the journalism undertaken by its state-based *Watchdog.org* reporters was unpersuasive. A *Columbia Journalism Review* article said that the center's focus on government waste offered a "clear vision" and that there was a tendency to "occasionally blur reporting and opinion and to go beyond the facts of its findings" (Chavkin, 2013, paras. 20, 21). The implication in the use of the words "clear vision" was that government waste, and by extension questionable government spending, was an obvious target for libertarians and that the funders were promulgating this vision through their funded media. However, exposure of wasteful public programs is common in investigative reporting; a tendency to blur opinion and reporting would not be unique to *Watchdog.org* journalism.

The Franklin Center's vice president of journalism Steven Greenhut accused left-wing nonprofit enterprises of trying to portray the center as "right-wing-funded shills for the Republican agenda" without bothering to check its journalism (Greenhut, 2013, para. 3). Its stories had been published in mainstream outlets, and included stories taking aim at Republicans, corporate welfare, and promoting civil liberties and proposals to legalize marijuana. No one outside of the editorial board decided which stories would be covered or how they would be covered. Greenhut said a separation existed between the Franklin Center's conservative slant and the work of the news sites (Strupp, 2012). The critics of the Franklin's *Watchdog.org* reporting said little about the close ties the Sandlers and other supporters of nonprofit centers have with the Democratic side of politics. That was left to conservative critics.

Billionaire hedge fund operator George Soros is one of the most controversial public figures of the modern world: at various times admired and despised in the United States, Soviet Russia, Eastern Europe, and Lithuania (McLaughlin & Trilupaityte, 2012). It was reported in October 2017 that Soros had transferred $18 billion to Open Society Foundations, making it the third largest foundation in the world after the Bill and Melinda Gates Foundation and the Wellcome Trust (Weaver, 2017). Known in the United States as the renegade Democrat, he was the "kind of wealthy, culturally elite and socially liberal Democrat that populist and conservative Christian Republicans loved to hate" (McLaughlin & Trilupaityte, 2012, p. 435). *Fox News* hosts accused him of being part of a conspiracy with former President Barack Obama to ruin the American economy; they labeled him a sleazoid and suggested his philanthropy was funded by drug money (McLaughlin & Trilupaityte, 2012). Conservative commentators including politicians were particularly hostile to the funding of news organizations by foundations associated with Soros. Conservative bloggers accused Soros of manipulating the media to create a one-world socialist government and of being a communist felon (Commieblaster, 2014). They listed ties to more than 30 mainstream media organizations, as well as *ProPublica* – "almost laughably left-wing" – and the Center for Public Integrity – "mostly liberal" (Gainor, 2011, paras. 5, 19). A conservative contributor writing in *Forbes* reported that Soros had spent more than $48 million[3] funding media since 2003, often through foundations, which made outside accounting nearly impossible (Bell, 2013, para. 7). His Open Society Foundations had funded the Center for Public Integrity, the Investigative News Network, *Columbia Journalism Review*, the National Federation of Community Broadcasters, the National Association of Hispanic Journalists, the Committee to Protect Journalists, and the Organization of News Ombudsmen (Bell, 2013).

The Media Research Center, which views the national media as the propaganda arm of the Left, carried more than 330 articles mentioning Soros on its website in late 2017 (Media Research Center, n.d.). These were a fraction of the online attacks on Soros's funding of journalism and media sites. Open Society Foundations in turn was said to have donated $1 million to *Media Matters*, a liberal activist group that waged a rhetorical war on *Fox News* and others in the conservative press (Shear, 2010). A statement by Soros at the time accused *Fox News* hosts of incendiary rhetoric and stated that he hoped the money would be used to publicize the challenge *Fox News* posed to civil and informed discourse. Opponents noted that *Media Matters* was "deeply embedded within the Democrat establishment" (Nimmo, 2014, para. 3).

Despite these accusations, established nonprofit players like Brant Houston and Kevin Davis maintained that Open Society Foundations was one of the most hands-off foundations they had dealt with (K. Davis, personal communication, January 31, 2012; B. Houston, personal communication, November 19, 2010). *ProPublica*'s president Richard Tofel characterized the attacks on Soros as "dog-whistle anti-Semitism" (personal communication, April 24, 2018).

The volume and vehemence of the attacks demonstrated how the polarized political climate in the United States had extended to the philanthropic funding of nonprofit media. The political atmosphere had made Open Society's senior program officer wary of the "limits of what we can do" as opposed to what other foundations with a less polarizing impact might be able to fund (L. McGlinchey, personal communication, February 14, 2012).

The Sandler's support of Democratic Party-related groups such as Human Rights Watch, MoveOn.org, the Center for Responsive Politics, and Citizens for a Strong Senate also attracted sustained criticism of the family and *ProPublica* (Nocera, 2008; Shafer, 2009). *ProPublica* was accused of running left-wing hit pieces (Chumley, 2009, para. 1); being "as independent as a lapdog on a leash with allegiances sworn in advance to left-wing causes" (Arnold, n.d., para. 2) and was part of a financially and politically active elite (Browne, 2010, p. 894). *Slate*'s media commentator asked: "What do the Sandlers want for their millions? Perhaps to return us to the days of the partisan press" (Shafer, 2009, para. 6). A former mainstream editor noted the question mark over *ProPublica* due to Sandler's support of liberal causes (Cransberg, 2008).

The claims of bias were not borne out in a content analysis by the Pew Foundation that found *ProPublica* to be among the most mixed or balanced organizations in the focus of its coverage and the targets of its exposés (Holcomb et al., 2011). *ProPublica*'s stories proved to be one of the least ideological of all the nonprofit organizations examined by Pew. The survey found that the organization had made a substantial effort to be transparent about its operations, though one noticeable omission was detailed information about the Sandler Foundation (Holcomb et al., 2011, para. 39).

Some commentators believe that foundations with ideological agendas would increasingly fund investigative-style reporting ventures in the United States. "You'll have investigative reports which are not your Pulitzer-prize, neutral, omniscient, third-party narrated tones, but very much with a voice, sometimes with a polemical voice" (S. Coronel, personal communication, February 13, 2012). The future even may mirror a previous era when newspapers either were clearly Republican or Democrat, according to journalism professor Brant Houston (Gibbons, 2010, pp. 29–30). If this were to occur, it would mirror trends in the mainstream media where the *New York Times* and MSNBC were seen as liberal, and the *Wall Street Journal* and *Fox News* as conservative (Starr, 2010). It may be that partisan nonprofit sites would find it easier to raise funding due to networks of true believers (Steiger, 2015, para. 31).

Today, "what is partisan and what is factual reporting depends on who you ask" (S. Cross, personal communication, April 11, 2018). In such a contested political environment, the forces that countervail partisan journalism include both professional journalistic standards and authenticated facts (Starr, 2010, para. 23). Old fashioned as these concepts may appear in the world of digital media, they remain embedded in professional journalism practice. One ethics expert observed that "democracy needs passion, and partisanship provides it. Journalism needs passion, too, though the passion should be for the truth" (Starr, 2010).

Conclusion

The relationship between foundations and nonprofit journalism organizations potentially may be more ethically fraught than that between advertisers and legacy media, but it depends on the circumstances and the intentions and expectations of those involved. Dispensing funds is an exercise in power (Bogart, 1995, p. 103) and foundations, acting as the economic sector, hold the cards. They can help launch investigative reporting centers, fund specific programs, decline to renew existing grants, steer reporting toward a particular topic, and even financially paralyze and shut down a news operation.

Foundation program directors said in interviews that they supported accountability journalism as a bulwark for democracy, or words to that effect. Evidence suggests that beyond a handful of foundations that support journalism, many funders simply want coverage of the other areas they support, including their agendas for policy changes. This raises questions about how coterminous foundation grants are with the long-term sustainability and interests of independent journalism. Foundations that merely want media coverage of an issue are unlikely to be long-term funders of nonprofit journalism. The Hewlett Foundation's communications director made that clear. He said the foundation's grants to *California Watch* were a "content issue; it wasn't a concern about the specific function of journalism. And a whole series of consequences flow from that, in terms of how long your commitment is" (J. Fischer, personal communication, February 3, 2012).

To date, as far as it is known, direct interference by foundations and donors in editorial processes has not occurred despite the fears of academic critics and the power imbalance that exists between the sectors. Bigger donors have understood and respected the journalistic culture of independence and the sanctity of editorial processes. What remains unclear and untested is whether community and family foundations have the same understanding. Also unclear is whether emerging nonprofit news centers will have the same values as those former mainstream media journalists who moved to the nonprofit sector and rejected questionable funding proposals.

The nonprofit news sector differs from mainstream journalism and that difference ought to be acknowledged in the ethics that apply. What may seem questionable at a newspaper – such as advertisers suggesting story topics – may not be so at a nonprofit site because foundations do not have a commercial incentive. Foundation funding of health, environment, or criminal justice topics creates more quality journalism that is good for an informed citizenry as long as the funding is transparent and funders do not determine the content of the stories. That is a line that should never be crossed.

Notes

1 Foundations have funded nonprofit charter management organizations that operate and launch new schools, the management of which sometimes is given to for-profit companies. The number of charter schools increased from 1,651 in 2000–2001 to 5,712 in 2011–2012 and enrolled an estimated 1.9 million students, compared with the public school system with 59 million K-12 students (Levine & Levine, 2014).

2 Hewlett's website states that since 2002, its Education Program has "concentrated on improving the conditions for education policy reform in California" (The William and Flora Hewlett Foundation, n.d.-c).

3 Also reported as $52 million by same author in http://newsbusters.org/blogs/iris-somberg/2011/08/17/george-soros-media-mogul-executive-summary.

Bibliography

Abowd, P. (2013). Donors use charity to push free-market policies in states. Non-profit group lets donors fly "totally under the radar". Retrieved from Center for Public Integrity website: http://www.publicintegrity.org/2013/02/14/12181/donors-use-charity-push-free-market-policies-states

American Press Institute. (2017). Guidance on philanthropic funding of media and news. Retrieved from https://www.americanpressinstitute.org/publications/nonprofit-funding-guidance/single-page/

Arnold, R. (n.d.). ProPublica Inc. Retrieved from Ron Arnold's Left Tracking Library website: http://www.undueinfluence.com/pro_publica.htm

Barkan, J. (2011, Winter). Got dough? How billionaires rule our schools. *Dissent*. Retrieved from http://www.dissentmagazine.org/article/got-dough-how-billionaires-rule-our-schools

Batsell, J. (2015). Earning their keep: Revenue strategies from the Texas Tribune and other nonprofit news startups. Retrieved from John S. and James L. Knight Foundation website: http://features.knightfoundation.org/nonprofitnews-2015/pdfs/KF-NonprofitNews2015-Tribune.pdf

Bell, L. (2013). Billionaires battle over media influence: Koch Bros./Murdoch Vs. Soros/Buffett/GE. Retrieved from Forbes website: http://www.forbes.com/sites/larrybell/2013/05/05/billionaires-battle-over-media-influence-koch-bros-murdoch-vs-sorosbuffettge/

Black, J., Steele, B., & Barney, R. D. (1993). *Doing ethics in journalism: A handbook with case studies*. Greencastle, IN: Sigma Delta Chi Foundation and Society of Professional Journalists.

Bogart, L. (1995). *Commercial culture: The media system and the public interest*. New York, NY: Oxford University Press.

Browne, H. (2010). Foundation-funded journalism: Reasons to be wary of charitable support. *Journalism Studies, 11*(6), 889–903. doi:10.1080/14616 70X.2010.501147

Buzenberg, B. (2015). Thank you and farewell. Retrieved from Center for Public Integrity website: http://www.publicintegrity.org/2015/01/23/16655/thank-you-and-farewell

Chavkin, S. (2013, April). The Koch brothers' media investment. *Columbia Journalism Review*. Retrieved from http://www.cjr.org/united_states_project/the_koch_brothers_media_invest.php

Chumley, C. K. (2009). ProPublica: Investigative journalism or liberal spin? *Foundation Watch*. Retrieved from Capital Research Center website: http://capitalresearch.org/2009/05/propublica-investigative-journalism-or-liberal-spin/

Coddington, M. (2015). The wall becomes a curtain: Revisiting journalism's news–business boundary. In M. Carlson & S. C. Lewis (Eds.), *Boundaries of journalism: Professionalism, practices, and participation* (pp. 67–82). New York, NY: Routledge.

Commieblaster. (2014). George Soros is implementing a "one-world" socialist government. Retrieved September 20, 2014, from http://commieblaster.com/george-soros-fund/

Cotter, C. (2010). *News talk: Investigating the language of journalism*. New York, NY: Cambridge University Press.

Cransberg, G. (2008). New sources of funding, new sources of reporting. *Nieman Reports*, 62(1), 27–29. Retrieved from http://connection.ebscohost.com/c/articles/98722499/what-would-david-do

Cutbirth, J. (2016). Cash out: Philanthropy, sustainability, and ethics in non-profit news. In A. Davisson & P. Booth (Eds.), *Controversies in digital ethics* (pp. 186–201). New York, NY: Bloomsbury Academic & Professional.

Edmonds, R. (2002, March/April). Getting behind the media: What are the subtle tradeoffs of foundation support for journalism? *Philanthropy Magazine*. Retrieved from http://www.philanthropyroundtable.org/topic/excellence_in_philanthropy/getting_behind_the_media

Franklin Center for Government and Public Integrity. (2017). *Return of organization exempt from income tax*. Retrieved from http://990s.foundationcenter.org/990_pdf_archive/264/264066298/264066298_201512_990.pdf

Franklin Center for Government and Public Integrity. (n.d.). About: Why we're here. Retrieved May 8, 2016, from Franklin Center for Government and Public Integrity Reporting website: http://www.webcitation.org/6hM9ej87Q

Freedberg, L. (2011). Greater flexibility in spending hurts low-achieving students. Retrieved from California Watch website: http://californiawatch.org/dailyreport/greater-flexibility-spending-hurts-low-achieving-students-10455

Funt, D. (2015). Marshall Project stakes out high ground on journalism's slippery slope. *Columbia Journalism Review*. Retrieved from http://www.cjr.org/analysis/marshall_project_bill_keller.php

Gainor, D. (2011, May 11). Why don't we hear about Soros' ties to over 30 major news organizations? *Fox News*. Retrieved from http://www.foxnews.com/opinion/2011/05/11/dont-hear-george-soros-ties-30-major-news-organizations/

Gibbons, G. (2010). *Ants at the picnic: A status report on news coverage of state government* (Discussion Paper Series #D-59). Retrieved from the Shorenstein Center on Media, Politics and Public Policy website: http://www.hks.harvard.edu/presspol/publications/papers/discussion_papers/d59_gibbons.pdf

Greenhut, S. (2013). Elite publication readies another expose on Watchdog. *Watchdog*. Retrieved from Watchdog.org website: http://watchdog.org/75153/elite-publication-contacts-watchdog-parent-org-for-yet-another-expose/

Holcomb, J., Rosenstiel, T., Mitchell, A., Caldwell, K., Sartor, T., & Vogt, N. (2011). Non-profit news. Assessing a new landscape in journalism. Retrieved from Pew Research Center website: http://www.journalism.org/2011/07/18/profiles-types-sites-found-study/

Institute for Nonprofit News. (n.d.-a). Ethics and practices policies. Retrieved from https://inn.org/for-members/ethics/

Institute for Nonprofit News. (n.d.-b). Membership standards. Retrieved from Investigative News Network website: http://inn.org/for-members/membership-standards/

Jerving, S. (2011). Franklin Center: Right-wing funds state news source. Retrieved from PR Watch website: http://www.prwatch.org/news/2011/10/10971/franklin-center-right-wing-funds-state-news-source

Kaplan, A. D. (2008). *Investigating the investigators: Examining the attitudes, perceptions, and experiences of investigative journalists in the internet age* (Doctoral dissertation), University of Maryland, College Park, MD. Retrieved from http://hdl.handle.net/1903/8788

Kovach, B., & Rosenstiel, T. (2007). *The elements of journalism: What newspeople should know and the public should expect*. New York, NY: Three Rivers Press.

Lacy, S., & Simon, T. F. (1993). *The economics and regulation of United States newspapers*. Norwood, NJ: Ablex Publishing Corporation.

Levine, M., & Levine, A. (2014). Charters and foundations: Are we losing control of our public schools? *American Journal of Orthopsychiatry, 84*(1), 1–6. doi:10.1037/h0098942

MacArthur Foundation. (n.d.). About us. Retrieved from https://www.macfound.org/about/

McLaughlin, N., & Trilupaityte, S. (2012). The international circulation of attacks and the reputational consequences of local context: George Soros's difficult reputation in Russia, post-Soviet Lithuania and the United States. *Cultural Sociology, 7*(4), 431–446. doi:10.1177/1749975512457142

Media Research Center. (n.d.). MRC.org search. Retrieved October 10, 2017, from https://www.mrc.org/search/site/soros

Merritt, D. (2005). *Knightfall: Knight Ridder and how the erosion of newspaper journalism is putting democracy at risk*. New York, NY: Amazon.

Meyer, P. (2009). *The vanishing newspaper: Saving journalism in the information age* (2nd ed.). Columbia: University of Missouri Press.

Moore, J. (2014, February 18). The trouble with the Trib. *The Huffington Post*. Retrieved from http://www.huffingtonpost.com/jim-moore/the-trouble-with-the-trib_b_4806251.html

Nimmo, K. (2014). Media Matters boss admits Soros funded group works to destroy alternative media. Retrieved from InfoWars website: http://www.infowars.com/media-matters-boss-admit-soros-funded-group-works-to-destroy-alternative-media/

Nocera, J. (2008, March 9). Self-made philanthropists. *The New York Times*. Retrieved from http://www.nytimes.com/2008/03/09/magazine/09Sandlers-t.html?pagewanted=all&_r=0

Picard, R. (2005). Money, media, and the public interest. In G. Overholser & K. H. Jamieson (Eds.), *The press* (pp. 337–350). New York, NY: Oxford University Press.

Picciano, A. G., & Spring, J. (2013). *The great American education-industrial complex: Ideology, technology and profit*. New York, NY: Routledge.

Robin, M. (2014). The remarkable, surprising success of the *Texas Tribune*. Retrieved from Crikey website: http://www.crikey.com.au/2014/12/02/the-remarkable-surprising-success-of-the-texas-tribune/

Rosenstiel, T., Buzenberg, B., Connelly, M., & Loker, K. (2016). Charting new ground: The ethical terrain of nonprofit journalism. Retrieved from American Press Institute website: https://www.americanpressinstitute.org/publications/reports/nonprofit-news

Schilders, H. (2008). Non-profit journalism: Is philanthropy the answer? Retrieved from Pulitzer Center website: http://pulitzercenter.org/sites/default/files/helene%20article.pdf

Serrin, W. (Ed.) (2000). *The business of journalism: 10 leading reporters and editors on the perils and pitfalls of the press*. New York, NY: The New Press.

Shafer, J. (2009). Nonprofit journalism comes at a cost. Retrieved from Slate website: http://www.slate.com/articles/news_and_politics/press_box/2009/09/nonprofit_journalism_comes_at_a_cost.html

Shear, M. (2010, October 20). Soros donated $1 million to Media Matters. *The New York Times*. Retrieved from http://thecaucus.blogs.nytimes.com/2010/10/20/soros-donates-1-million-to-media-matters/?_php=true&_type=blogs&_r=0

Smith, E. (2013). Chill, self-appointed integrity cops. Retrieved from Nieman Lab website: http://www.niemanlab.org/2013/12/chill-self-appointed-integrity-cops/

SourceWatch. (2012). Franklin Center for Government and Public Integrity. Retrieved June 22, 2012, from http://www.sourcewatch.org/index.php?title=Franklin_Center_for_Government_and_Public_Integrity

Starr, P. (2010, January/February). Governing in the age of Fox News. *The Atlantic*. Retrieved from http://www.theatlantic.com/magazine/archive/2010/01/governing-in-the-age-of-fox-news/307845/?single_page=true

Steiger, P. (2015). Paul Steiger: Ten guiding principles for nonprofit investigative reporting teams. Retrieved from Netzwerk Recherche website: https://netzwerkrecherche.org/blog/paul-steiger-ten-guiding-principles-for-nonprofit-investigative-reporting-teams/

Strupp, J. (2012). How a right-wing group is infiltrating state news coverage. Retrieved from Media Matters for America website: http://mediamatters.org/blog/2012/07/11/how-a-right-wing-group-is-infiltrating-state-ne/187059

Texas Tribune. (2017a). Corporate sponsors. Retrieved October 10, 2017, from https://www.texastribune.org/support-us/corporate-sponors/

Texas Tribune. (2017b). Donors and members. Retrieved October 10, 2017, from http://www.texastribune.org/support-us/donors-and-members/

The William and Flora Hewlett Foundation. (2009). Education – Supporting journalism about public policy. Retrieved from http://www.hewlett.org/newsroom/press-release/educating-youth-oakland-africa

The William and Flora Hewlett Foundation. (n.d.-a). California education. Retrieved from https://hewlett.org/programs/education/

The William and Flora Hewlett Foundation. (n.d.-b). Deeper learning: Overview. Retrieved from https://www.hewlett.org/strategy/deeper-learning/

The William and Flora Hewlett Foundation. (n.d.-c). Education program. Retrieved from http://www.hewlett.org/programs/education-program

The William and Flora Hewlett Foundation. (n.d.-d). Grant record: Center for Investigative Reporting. Retrieved from http://www.hewlett.org/grants/search?order=field_date_of_award&sort=desc&keywords=%22center+for+investigative+reporting%22&year=&term_node_tid_depth_1=All&program_id=All

The William and Flora Hewlett Foundation. (n.d.-e). Open educational resources. Retrieved from https://www.hewlett.org/strategy/open-educational-resources/

Watchdog.org. (n.d.). About Watchdog.org. Retrieved from http://watchdog.org/about

Weaver, M. (2017, October 18). George Soros gives $18bn to his charitable foundation. *The Guardian*. Retrieved from https://amp.theguardian.com/business/2017/oct/18/george-soros-gives-18-billion-dollars-open-society-foundation

Wilce, R. (2013). Koch-funded Franklin Center "Watchdogs" infiltrate state capitols. Retrieved from PR Watch website: http://www.prwatch.org/news/2013/08/12161/koch-funded-franklin-center-watchdogs-infiltrate-state-capitols

10 Flash in the Pan or a Sustainable Business Model?

Is the philanthropically funded model of investigative and public interest journalism sustainable? It is a question that the most respected and experienced players in the sector do not know the answer to. "No-one has figured it out," a former executive director of the Center for Public Integrity said (B. Buzenberg, personal communication, February 8, 2012). Robert Rosenthal echoed the sentiment: "The challenges really for all of us in this sector is how to sustain it. No-one has figured out the business model" (MacArthur Foundation, 2012). Despite several successful examples of nonprofit organizations developing other sources of income, most remain reliant on foundation funding. It is not an ideal situation given the imbalance of power that exists between the two sectors. "Foundations are notoriously fickle. The question is to what extent will those birds fly off the wire and go somewhere else? Is this a flavor of the month? I don't know. Guess what, no-one knows," veteran nonprofit editor Charles Lewis said (C. Lewis, personal communication, November 8, 2010).

Lewis is right; no one knows. But the short-term trend is reassuring to those who care about quality journalism because developments in the nonprofit sector represent hope in a landscape where the news for journalism has been terrible for decades. Much has changed since the dire warnings about the future of journalism during the 2007–2009 financial crisis. The recession struck what many thought would be a death blow to an already ailing mainstream media. Thousands of journalists lost their jobs, newspapers closed, and the impact on US democracy worried those who recognized the Fourth Estate role of the media and cared about community, politics, accountability, freedom, and the public good.

In response, at least 102 nonprofit accountability news organizations were created between 2007 and 2017. At the time of writing, the Institute for Nonprofit News had more than 160 member organizations compared with fewer than 30 in 2009. Another 110 nonprofit news sites that are not members of the institute were producing accountability journalism. Hundreds of millions of dollars in foundation and private support were pumped into the sector. This is quite remarkable given that in earlier times the idea that philanthropists would donate scarce resources into media would have been downright offensive (Waldman, 2013, para. 5).

The nonprofit accountability news sector has moved from a rapid growth phase to now seeking long-term sustainability. Much will depend on whether institutional foundations continue to fund the sector and whether smaller community and family foundations recognize that local journalism is as much a public good as an art gallery, education, medical research, equality, civic and political participation, and the environment. Foundations to varying degrees and on an ongoing basis are integral to the business model:

> They aren't just launching us and then we do an IPO [Initial Public Offering] and turn into a business or we find a way to be sponsored by corporate advertisers. Those sources of funding just aren't available to us, it's not practical.
>
> (B. Keller, April 25, 2018)

Threats exist. One is that in the absence of a real or perceived danger to journalism or democracy, a key motivation for grant giving will be lost. That motivation was behind much of the support garnered since the financial crisis. Without a similar risk, foundations may look elsewhere. Second, many nonprofit centers have moved beyond a startup phase, which is when some foundations depart their grantees. After several years of support, foundations naturally expect that organizations will have developed other revenue sources. Many foundations do not want to be ongoing funders of day-to-day operations. A majority of nonprofit news organizations, however, rely heavily on foundation funding, even after five to seven years (Knight Foundation, 2015). A third challenge is that as the number of journalistic nonprofit centers increases, so too does the competition for foundation funding. In addition, some legacy outlets including the *New York Times* and the *Guardian* have established nonprofit arms to attract philanthropic funding in support of their journalism. Fourth, newsroom funding by about two dozen key foundations has concentrated on nonprofit organizations located on the East and West coasts, leaving "nonprofit media deserts" in many states and cities (Nisbet, Wihbey, Kristiansen, & Jajak, 2018, pp. 13–15). Many local and family foundations are yet to recognize journalism as an area of need and may never do so. The focus by nonprofits on elite audiences and policy makers has meant that funders were less likely to support reporting on issues relevant to minority and low-income communities or the media that report them (Nisbet et al., 2018, p. 17). Finally, the motivations and cultures of foundations and investigative journalists differ. Foundations might support democracy, but their understanding of what that might involve in practice differs from that of watchdog reporters: "offending their friends is not in their DNA," a former editor said of foundations (Rowe, 2011, p. 30). Foundations want coverage of the reforms and issues they support in other grants, while journalists value their independence and ability to report without paying deference to funders. Foundations that want media in their area of interest are less likely to be long-term funders of journalism.

Despite these threats, I believe foundation and donor support for non-profit investigative and public interest organizations will continue. First, there are thousands of private, family, and community foundations in the United States and many have programs for strengthening democracy, the accountability of government, and increasing knowledge of public issues. While foundations and major donors may not support a non-profit news organization indefinitely, some will continue their support for many years. Table 5.2, which showed the funding of 62 members of the Institute for Nonprofit News, demonstrated funding patterns between 2007 and 2015. During the years impacted by the financial crisis, 2009 and 2010, average funding was $1.8 million and $1.6 million. The average fell to $1.4 million in 2011, suggesting that funders believed the crisis was over. Nevertheless, average funding remained fairly constant over the next three years and increased to almost $1.8 million in 2015. Median funding followed a similar pattern.

This demonstrates that the crisis motivated giving but also that funders continued supporting nonprofit news centers in the years beyond. Such ongoing support in the absence of a crisis, perceived or real, is encouraging news for the sector. When I started researching the sector around the time of the financial crisis, the view among nonprofit editors and foundation officers was that in the following three to four years, foundations would move to other areas, expecting nonprofits to have achieved significant alternative sources of funding. That does not seem to be the case. In fact, 40 percent of the 94 nonprofits that responded to a survey in 2015 said they had more foundations supporting them than they did five years earlier (Rosenstiel, Buzenberg, Connelly, & Loker, 2016).

Second, the funding that was driven by concerns over US democracy and the legacy media's ability to monitor power attested to there being a self-righting mechanism in the United States that acts to restore public service institutions. The election of Donald Trump and his attacks on the media initiated thousands of individual donations to nonprofit news organizations. Prior to that, small donations had not figured highly as a source of income in the minds of most nonprofit media executives. An online platform, NewsMatch, established by the Knight Foundation in a partnership with the Democracy Fund, the MacArthur Foundation, the Gates Family Foundation, and the support of several other large foundations, made it easier for people to find and donate to nonprofit news organizations in their region. NewsMatch matched any donation up to $1,000 from individual donors. Other foundation supporters joined in to double-and triple-match public donations. In the final quarter of 2017, more than 202,000 donors had contributed $33 million to the program, which distributed the funds to members of the Institute for Nonprofit News. About 43,000 donors were first-time givers to nonprofit news (NewsMatch, 2018). If the trend for increased public donations continues, nonprofits will be less reliant on foundations and will have proof of their relevance to their communities.

Third, the United States' politics suggest that both liberal and conservative foundations will invest in nonprofit media because their ideological opponents do or because they want to counter perceived right-wing or liberal bias in the established media. Fourth, foundations with advocacy and reform agendas will continue to support reporting of the issues that matter to them. They know that nonprofit stories may also be published in prestigious media outlets, increasing the chances of political traction. They are aware also that niche-topic and local newsrooms produce stories that are read by legislators, senior officials, and policy advisers in their areas of concern.

Fifth, foundations are obliged to distribute a minimum 5 percent of their investment assets each year. Nonprofit founder Charles Lewis believed that requirement and the United States' "hyper-developed world of philanthropy" would ensure continued support for the sector (C. Lewis, personal communication, November 8, 2010). Sixth, large foundations such as Knight, MacArthur, McCormick, Ford, Open Society, Ethics and Excellence in Journalism, and the Omidyar Network have programs that specifically support accountability journalism.

Seventh, the recent past has shown that millionaires and billionaires in the United States are willing to support journalistic ventures. Some, such as Amazon founder Jeff Bezos with the *Washington Post* and business magnate Warren Buffett with local newspapers, invest in existing media while others, notably Pierre Omidyar, Neil Barsky, and Herbert and Marion Sandler, create new media organizations. New wealthy funders may emerge. Finally, companies such as Google, Amazon, and Facebook may support rather than just distribute journalism by directing their philanthropic giving to nonprofit reporting centers. They may look to nonprofit outlets to improve the quality of their content, especially on video platforms.

These are positive signs for the sector. We can make some cautious predictions about the future. More state- and city-based nonprofit organizations may merge or enter into mutually beneficial partnerships with public radio and television broadcasters, which have established revenue streams and better infrastructure. Mergers and other partnerships can be difficult due to institutional cultural practices and a lack of familiarity by journalists of different media platforms. But they seem a natural fit. Public broadcasters and accountability news organizations have similar audiences and a common public service mission. Public media have limited scope to produce the type of stories that investigative reporting organizations are expert at. Mergers provide nonprofit accountability organizations an immediate and substantially wider distribution of their stories. Common accommodation saves money and expands the number of journalists in newsrooms, creating more scope to cover breaking news. Such partnerships provide financial stability to nonprofit organizations and increased potential for fundraising through jointly hosted events and funding drives.

Several local and niche-topic organizations may be forced to close due to funders not renewing their grants and a lack of alternative support. A handful of nonprofit news organizations have been forced to shut in recent years for budgetary reasons. Small nonprofit organizations may become branch offices of bigger and more powerful nonprofit operations. The national nonprofits *ProPublica*, the Center for Public Integrity, and the Center for Investigative Reporting are likely to grow even larger as they continue to attract foundation support, build media partnerships, and extend their leadership roles in the sector.

This book has shown that many national and state newspapers retained or even increased their commitment to investigative reporting over the past decade. Some of the concern expressed about the future of investigative reporting at the time of the financial crisis was useful in drawing attention to newly created nonprofit organizations but was misleading. It failed to understand that investigative reporting is the "heart and soul" of journalism and that mainstream editors would protect it while cutting other staff. Of course, there are places where there is little or no media scrutiny of public officials and corporations. There are issues affecting minority and poor communities that appear on no news list. There are acts by enforcement and intelligence agencies that escape inquiry. There is corruption and bribery that are never reported. These are matters of intense interest to investigative journalists. But their numbers outside of the national news media and some state newspapers are few, and always have been. The expansion of the nonprofit news sector has added a much-needed layer of professional reporting to the thin ranks of legacy investigative journalists. It is hazardous to compare the amount of investigative reporting being done today with other eras, but a recent study suggests that newspapers are concentrating on it more than ever (Knobel, 2018, p. 8). Almost certainly, more people than in any other period are able to access investigative stories.

Other than government funding – problematic and probably impossible in the United States – there does not appear to be an alternative to foundation funding. A handful of nonprofits will build on their support from individual donors and corporate sponsors, but most organizations will continue to rely on foundation grants. Journalism practice has always been impacted by external forces: recessions, technology, subsidies, advertising, partisanship, corporatization, and social trends. In this case, those forces are the economic sector – foundations and wealthy donors – and government tax policies. Both have the power to shape what happens in the nonprofit accountability news sector. There is no indication that they will change their approach to nonprofit journalism, but editors remain anxious about the fragility of their base funding.

The longer-term financial sustainability of the nonprofit model is likely to be found in a combination of foundation support, mergers, increased donor support, and new revenue streams. Some nonprofit organizations may eventually convert into for-profit ventures. The investigative ecosystem in the United States will consist of a combination of for-profit online organizations, legacy media, public radio and television, and nonmarket specialist writers, with national and local nonprofit accountability organizations collaborating with all of them.

Bibliography

Knight Foundation. (2015). *Gaining ground: How nonprofit news ventures seek sustainability.* Retrieved from https://knightfoundation.org/reports/gaining-ground-how-nonprofit-news-ventures-seek-su

Knobel, B. (2018). *The watchdog still barks: How accountability reporting evolved for the digital age.* New York, NY: Fordham University Press.

MacArthur Foundation (Producer). (2012). *Center for Investigative Reporting, 2012 MacArthur Award for Creative & Effective Institutions* [Video file]. Retrieved from https://www.macfound.org/videos/88/

NewsMatch. (2018). *NewsMatch raises $4.8 million for nonprofit news.* Retrieved from Knight Foundation website: https://knightfoundation.org/press/releases/newsmatch-raises-4-8-million-for-nonprofit-news

Nisbet, M., Wihbey, J., Kristiansen, S., & Jajak, A. (2018). *Funding the news: Foundations and nonprofit media.* Cambridge, MA: Shorenstein Center on Media, Politics and Public Policy in collaboration with Northeastern University School of Journalism. Retrieved from https://shorensteincenter.org/funding-the-news-foundations-and-nonprofit-media/

Rosenstiel, T., Buzenberg, B., Connelly, M., & Loker, K. (2016). *Charting new ground: The ethical terrain of nonprofit journalism.* Retrieved from American Press Institute website: https://www.americanpressinstitute.org/publications/reports/nonprofit-news

Rowe, S. (2011, June). *Partners of necessity: The case for collaboration in local investigative reporting* (Discussion Paper Series #D-62). Retrieved from the Shorenstein Center on Media, Politics and Public Policy website: http://shorensteincenter.org/wp-content/uploads/2012/03/d62_rowe.pdf

Waldman, S. (2013). *The changing media landscape in a broadband age* [Blog post]. Retrieved from Knight Foundation website: http://knightfoundation.org/blogs/knightblog/2013/11/18/report-foundation-funding-media-ignites-crucial-discussion/

Index

Printed in the United States
by Baker & Taylor Publisher Services

Printed in the United States
by Baker & Taylor Publisher Services